Economic Policy and the Covid-19 Crisis

This book offers an assessment of the different monetary and fiscal policy responses that have been implemented by national governments in major European and Asian countries faced with the Covid-19 crisis since 2020; it also deals with the case of the US experience as a benchmarking example.

The book provides a comprehensive cross-country comparative study on health crisis management at the macroeconomic level. Its focus on monetary and fiscal policies across different countries in Asia, Europe and the US makes it unique. Divided into three parts following a general introduction that sets the context of the study, the book deals with the case of the US, EU, and European countries as well as with that of key Asian countries. Of specific relevance is the European Union and euro-area contexts that serve as a framework to the different EU national monetary and fiscal policy responses. Each chapter deals with a specific country, including Italy and the UK in Europe and Singapore and South Korea in Asia, and covers the following topics: the extent of the outbreak of the public health crisis and its macroeconomic impact; the comparative examination of fiscal and monetary policy responses to both crises; and an overall assessment of the effectiveness of these policies along with the public health policy to mitigate the economic impact.

Given the unprecedented nature of the Covid-19 crisis, anyone eager to know more about its macroeconomic impact and ensuing policies in a comparative framework will be keen to read this book. It will be essential reading to any researcher, policymaker and/or analyst working in the area of public policy and is also a unique contribution to the field of European studies, Asian studies, and Comparative Economic Studies.

Bernadette Andreosso-O'Callaghan is Jean Monnet Professor of Economics at the University of Limerick Ireland and International Research Fellow at the Ruhr Universität Bochum, Germany.

Woosik Moon is currently a professor of economics at the Graduate School of International Studies, Seoul National University (SNU) Seoul, Korea.

Wook Sohn is Professor and Associate Dean at the KDI school of Public Policy and Management Sejong, Korea.

Routledge Studies in the Modern World Economy

For more information about this series, please visit: www.routledge.com/
Routledge-Studies-in-the-Modern-World-Economy/book-series/SE0432

Economic Policy and the Covid-19 Crisis

The Macroeconomic Response in the US, Europe and East Asia

**Edited by
Bernadette Andreosso-O'Callaghan,
Woosik Moon and Wook Sohn**

LONDON AND NEW YORK

First published 2022
by Routledge
2 Park Square, Milton Park, Abingdon, Oxon OX14 4RN

and by Routledge
605 Third Avenue, New York, NY 10158

Routledge is an imprint of the Taylor & Francis Group, an informa business

British Library Cataloguing-in-Publication Data
A catalogue record for this book is available from the British Library

Library of Congress Cataloging-in-Publication Data
A catalog record has been requested for this book

ISBN: 978-0-367-72137-4 (hbk)
ISBN: 978-0-367-72139-8 (pbk)
ISBN: 978-1-003-15360-3 (ebk)

DOI: 10.4324/9781003153603

Typeset in Bembo
by Deanta Global Publishing Services, Chennai, India

Contents

Figures and graphs

Figures

Graph

Tables

Contributors

Bernadette Andreosso-O'Callaghan is Professor of Economic Integration at the University of Limerick (Ireland) and Visiting Professor of Economics at the Ruhr Universität Bochum (Germany). She has published in the areas of comparative economic integration (Europe–Asia) and of comparative economic growth models in Asian countries. She has done consultancy work for various international bodies including the International Trade Center (ITC) Geneva. She is co-editor of *The Changing Global Environment in Asia and HRM Strategies* (2020) Nova Science Publishers (with J. Jaussaud, R. Taylor and M. B. Zolin), and of *Sustainable Development and Energy Transition in Europe and Asia* (2020) ISTE Wiley Publishers (with S. Dzever, J. Jaussaud, and Robert Taylor).

Claudio Cozza is Assistant Professor in Economic Policy at the University of Naples "Parthenope", Italy. His research interests include the Economics of Science, Technology and Innovation, Regional Development, and Internationalization.

Hwee Kwan Chow is Professor of Economics and Statistics (Practice), Singapore Management University. She obtained her PhD at the London School of Economics, and is a past Lead Economist at the Monetary Authority of Singapore and Vice President at Overseas Union Bank. Her main research areas are Monetary Economics, International Finance and Economic Forecasting. Hwee Kwan is an Associate Editor of *Singapore Economic Review* and has served as a consultant to the Asian Development Bank, the Asian Development Bank Institute, to the ASEAN+3 Macroeconomics Research Office and to several central banks.

Alex De Ruyter is a Professor at Birmingham City University and serves as Director of its Centre for Brexit Studies. He brings a wealth of research experience and academic engagement in the areas of globalization, regional economic development, labor market, and social exclusion issues. He has published over 60 academic outputs in leading national and international economic journals and has been the recipient of research funding, including being the Principal Investigator on a supply chain mapping exercise of the automotive, aerospace, and rail sectors in the West Midlands, exploring resilience in the face of Brexit and Covid-19. Professor de Ruyter has undertaken numerous media interviews and is currently researching on the likely impact of Brexit on the UK automotive supply chain in addition to exploring working in the "gig economy". He also served as a Board member of the Regional Studies Association between 2017 and 2020.

David Hearne is a Researcher at Birmingham City University's Centre for Brexit Studies. His research interests include relative regional price differences, the drivers of spatial disparities in the UK and Europe, and the probable regional impact of disruptive events.

Kong Weng Ho is Associate Professor of Economics (Education) at the Singapore Management University. His research interests include meritocracy and inequality, relationship stocks and subjective wellbeing of youths, upward mobility and aspirations of workers, and economic–social issues related to the Singaporean society. He has been a member of research advisory panels of the Ministry of Social and Family Development, the Prime Minister's Office Strategy Group, and the Housing Development Board, and he has been working with the National Youth Council on several waves of the National Youth Surveys.

Seohyun Lee is an Economist at the International Monetary Fund (IMF) and the Bank of Korea. Her research focuses on uncertainty and other topics in empirical finance and macroeconomics. She also provides regional and country-specific macroeconomic policy advice at the Asia and Pacific Department of the IMF.

Woosik Moon is currently a professor of economics at the Graduate School of International Studies (GSIS), Seoul National University (SNU). He was a member of the Monetary Policy Board, Bank of Korea, from April 2012 to April 2016. His main area of expertise is monetary economics, international finance and monetary integration. His main recent publications are: "Inflation Targeting in Korea", with Frank Rövekamp et al. (eds.) *Monetary Policy Implementation in East Asia* (Springer 2020), *A Study on Monetary Policy* (In Korean 2018).

Leopoldo Nascia is Researcher of the Italian institute of statistics. He has been an Advisor to the Minister of Education and Research in the Italian government. He has published many articles and books in the field of innovation systems, industrial policy, and researchers' mobility.

Sophie Nivoix is Associate Professor of Finance at the University of Poitiers (France). She has published in the areas of stock market valuation, returns and volatility, in the European and the East Asian regions. She has published research papers in various academic reviews, for example she is the co-editor of *Economic Transition and International Business* (2020) Routledge, Taylor & Francis: New York (with E. Milliot), and co-author of *Management*

International (2017) Vuibert Publishing: Paris (with H. Beddi), and of *Finance d'entreprise* (2018) Vuibert Publishing: Paris (with C. Thibierge et al.).

Eiji Ogawa is Professor of International Finance at Faculty of Economics, Tokyo Keizai University (Japan). He has published many articles and books in the field of international finance. He is co-editor of *Who Will Provide the Next Financial Model? Asia's Financial Muscle and Europe's Financial Maturity*, Springer, 2013 (with Sahoko Kaji) and *Japan, the European Union and Global Governance*, Edward Elgar, 2021 (forthcoming) (with Jan Wouters and others).

Serge Rey is Professor of Economics at the University of Pau & Pays de l'Adour (France) and Dean of the Social Sciences and Humanities College. His research interests are in the areas of international macroeconomics, economic convergence, the economics of the exchange rate and applied econometrics. He has published on these issues in leading academic journals, with a focus on the following territories/countries: MENA countries, European Union, Pacific economies and in particular Japan and French Overseas territories.

Frank Rövekamp obtained his PhD from the University of Cologne and serves as Professor of Asian Studies and Director of the East Asia Institute at the Ludwigshafen University of Business and Society since 2009. Previously, he worked in industrial enterprises and held senior management positions in Germany, Japan and Hong Kong. His research interest covers regional integration, public finance and monetary policy.

Wook Sohn is Professor and Associate Dean at the KDI school of Public Policy and Management. He has published many articles in academic journals in the areas of financial intermediaries, financial markets, monetary policy, and international development. Sohn also participated in the collaborative research and consultation for the Korean, Hungarian, and Cambodian governments. He was Visiting Professor at the University of British Columbia's Sauder School of Business and Executive Director of Economic Research Institute of Bank of Korea.

Lifeng Su is Associate Professor of International Economy at the Shanghai University of International Business and Economics (P.R. China) and specially-invited researcher of the Shanghai Development Research Foundation. He has published in the areas of international economics and macro-finance of China. He is paper-reviewer for *Finance & Trade Economics*, which is sponsored by the National Academy of Economic Strategy, Chinese Academy of Social Sciences.

Acknowledgments

This study has been supported by KDI School of Public Policy and Management and by Seoul National University. We wish to extend our sincere gratitude to KDI School's Office of Development Research and International Cooperation for their assistance and coordination. This project benefitted greatly from many (virtual) meetings and discussions involving the different authors. We are especially grateful to the EU Center, Seoul National University, for organizing and supporting such meetings. This book could not have been completed without the participation and effort from the authors of each chapter for whose contribution we would like to express our deepest appreciation. Many thanks are due also to Frank O'Callaghan for his English editing work and to Su Gyoung PARK from SNU who helped to edit the book.

Finally, it will be appropriate for us to acknowledge that none of the individuals or entities quoted in this book are responsible for the content of the book, and we and the authors take full responsibility for any errors and omissions in this publication.

Abbreviations

3TS	Testing, Tracing, and Treatment
5G	Fifth Generation
ABSPP	Asset-Backed Securities Purchase Programme
AMLF	Asset-Backed Commercial Paper Money Market Mutual Fund Liquidity Facility
ANR	Agence Nationale de la Recherche (National Agency for Research)
APP	Asset Purchase Programme
BCE	Banca Centrale Europea (European Central Bank)
BOC	Bank of Canada
BOE	Bank of England
BOJ	Bank of Japan
BP	Basis Point
CARES ACT	Coronavirus Aid, Relief, and Economic Security Act
CBBLF	Corporate Bond-Backed Lending Facility
CBPP3	Third Covered Bond Purchase Programme
CDC	Community Development Council
CDO	Collateralized Debt Obligations
CDP	Cassa Depositi e Prestiti
CJRS	Coronavirus Job Retention Scheme
CMBS	Commercial Mortgage-Backed Securities
CNL	Centre National du Livre (National Book Center)
CODEFI	Comité Départemental d'Examen des Difficultés des Entreprises (Departmental Committee for the Examination of Business Financing Problems)
CP	Commercial Paper
CPC	Communist Party of China
CPER	Contrat de Plan État-Région (State-Regions Plan Contract)
CPF	Central Provident Fund
CPI	Consumer Price Index
CSPP	Corporate Sector Purchase Programme
DC	District of Columbia

DEF	Documento di Economia e Finanza (Economic and Financial Document)
DETR	Dotation d'Équipement des Territoires Ruraux (Equipment Allocation for Rural Areas)
DL	Decreto-Legge (Legislative Decree)
DORSCON	Disease Outbreak Response System Condition
DRAC	Direction Régionale des Affaires Culturelles (Regional Directorate of Cultural Affairs)
DSIL	Dotation de Soutien à l'Investissement Local (Local Investment Support Allocation)
EC	European Community
E-CARS	Electronic Cars
ECB	European Central Bank
EDG	Enterprise Development Grant
EFS	Enterprise Financing Scheme
EIB	European Investment Bank
EMU	Economic and Monetary Union
ER	Emergency
ERDF	European Regional Development Fund
ESCB	European System of Central Banks
ESF	European Social Fund
ESG	Enterprise Singapore
ESM	European Stability Mechanism
ETF	Exchange-Traded Fund
ETSP	Enhanced Training Support Package
EU	European Union
EUR	Euro
FDES	Fonds de Développement Économique et Social (Economic and Social Development Fund)
FIMA REPO	Facility Repo Facility for Foreign and International Monetary Authorities
FMSF	Finanzmarktstabilisierungsfonds (Financial Market Stabilization Fund)
FRB	Federal Reserve Board
FSA	Financial Services Agency
FSC	Financial Services Commission
FX	Foreign Exchange
FY	Fiscal Year
G-20	Group of Twenty
GDP	Gross Domestic Product
GFC	Global Financial Crisis
GFCF	Gross Fixed Capital Formation
GIC	Government of Singapore Investment Corporation
GST	Goods and Services Tax
GVA	Gross Value-Added

GVC	Global Value Chain
HBOS	Halifax Bank of Scotland
HDB	Housing and Development Board
HEROES ACT	Health and Economic Recovery Omnibus Emergency Solutions Act
HMRC	Her Majesty's Revenue and Customs
ICT	Information and Communication Technology
ICU	Intensive Care Unit
IFCIC	Institut pour le Financement du Cinéma et des Industries Culturelles (Institute for the Financing of Cinema and Cultural Industries)
ILSF	Intermediated Lending Support Facility
IMF	International Monetary Fund
IMU	Imposta Municipale Unica (Single Municipal Tax)
IRAP	Imposta Regionale sulle Attività Produttive (Regional Tax on Productive Activities)
ISTAT	Istituto Nazionale di Statistica
JGB	Japanese Government Bonds
JGI	Jobs Growth Incentive
J-REIT	Japan Real Estate Investment Trust
JSS	Jobs Support Scheme
KCDC	Korea Centers for Disease Control and Prevention
KFW	Kreditanstalt für Wiederaufbau (Credit Institution for Reconstruction)
KRW	Korean Won
LIBOR	London Interbank Offered Rate
LOLR	Lender of Last Resort
LPR	Lending Prime Rate
M&A	Mergers and Acquisitions
MAS	Monetary Authority of Singapore
MICE	Meetings, Incentives, Conference/Conventions and Exhibitions/Events
MISE	Ministero dello Sviluppo Economico (Ministry of Economic Development)
MLF	Medium-Term Lending Facility
MMIFF	Money Market Investor Funding Facility
MMLF	Money Market Mutual Fund Liquidity Facility
MSME	Micro-, Small- and Medium-Sized Enterprise
NACE	Nomenclature of Economic Activities
NCOV	Novel Coronavirus
NHS	National Health Service
NIRC	Net Investment Returns Contribution
NTUC	National Trade Union Congress
OECD	Organization for Economic Cooperation and Development

OFR	Official Foreign Reserves
OMO	Open Market Operations
PAYE	Pay As You Earn
PBOC	People's Bank of China
PCE	Personal Consumption Expenditures
PCR	Polymerase Chain Reaction
PELTRO	Pandemic Long-Term Refinancing Operations
PEPP	Pandemic Emergency Purchase Programme
PGE	Prêt Garanti par l'État (State Guaranteed Loan)
PHC	Private Hire Car
PIA	Programme d'Investissement d'Avenir
PLFR	Projet de Loi de Finances Rectificative (Remedial Legislative Proposal)
PNRR	Piano Nazionale di Resistenza e Resilienza (National Resilience Plan)
PPE	Personal Protective Equipment
PPP	Paycheck Protection Program
PPPF ACT	Paycheck Protection Program Flexibility Act
PPPLF	Paycheck Protection Program Liquidity Facility
PSG	Productivity Solutions Grant
PSPP	Public Sector Purchase Programme
PUP	Pandemic Unemployment Payments
QE	Quantitative Easing
QQE	Quantitative and Qualitative Monetary Easing
R&D	Research and Development
R&S	Ricerca e Sviluppo (Research and Development)
RBS	Royal Bank of Scotland
REACT-EU	Recovery Assistance for Cohesion and the Territories of Europe
REM	Reddito di Emergenza (Emergency Income)
RFF	Recovery and Resilience Facility
RMB	Ren Min Bi
RP	Repurchase Agreement
RRR	Required Reserve Ratio
RT	Transmission Rate
S PASS	Short-Term Employment Pass
S$NEER	Singapore Dollar Nominal Effective Exchange Rate
S&P 500	Standard and Poor's 500
SACE	Servizi Assicurativi del Commercio Estero (External Trade Insurance Agency)
SBA	Small Business Administration
SEM	Single European Market
SGD	Singapore Dollar
SIBOR	Singapore Interbank Offered Rate
SIRS	Self-Employed Person Income Relief Scheme

SME	Small and Medium-Sized Enterprise
SNB	Swiss National Bank
SPV	Special Purpose Vehicle
STEER	SG Together Enhancing Enterprise Resilience
TACS	Trade Associations and Chambers
T-BILL	Treasury Discount Bill
TBLP	Temporary Bridging Loan Programme
TLTRO III	Third Series of Targeted Longer-Term Refinancing Operations
TSLF	Term Securities Lending Facility
UK	United Kingdom
US	United States
UPB	Ufficio Parlamentare di Bilancio (Parliamentary Budget Office)
USD	United States Dollar
VAT	Value-Added Tax
VIX INDEX	Cboe Volatility Index
VSE	Very Small Enterprise
WCS	Wage Credit Scheme
WSF	Wirtschaftsstabilisierungsfonds (Economic Stabilization Fund)
WTO	World Trade Organization
WWII	Second World War

Introduction

Economic policy and the Covid-19 crisis: the macroeconomic response in the US, Europe, and East Asia

Woosik Moon and Wook Sohn

As of the time of the writing of this book, the coronavirus is continuing to rapidly spread throughout the world, having already infected more than 100 million people and causing more than 2 million deaths globally. Beyond its impact on public health, this pandemic has also led to serious economic and social damage. This means that countries have been obliged to implement not only public health policies to stem the spread of Covid-19, but also macroeconomic policies to mitigate the economic damage associated with the pandemic.

Governments around the world have indeed adopted the necessary pandemic public health policy measures, but they have had varied success in containing the pandemic based on many factors, such as the degree of public participation in social distancing, the state of each country's national health system, and the policy lessons drawn from prior outbreaks of similar infectious diseases. For instance, in contrast to East Asian countries, many European Union (EU) countries ended up enacting lockdown measures.

Along with public health policy, governments have also had to respond with unprecedented financial policies aiming to mitigate the economic damage caused by Covid-19. Various types of new and drastic monetary and fiscal policy responses were quickly introduced in attempts to assist economic recovery. However, the extent and effectiveness of these public health and financial/monetary policies differed substantially across regions and countries.

The main objective of this book is to offer an overview and an assessment of the different monetary and fiscal policy responses that were implemented by national governments in major EU and Asian countries, as well as the US in response to the Covid-19 crisis. To this end, this book tries to make two dimensional comparisons: first, it makes a longitudinal comparison of the monetary and fiscal policy responses taken by governments during the 2008 global financial crisis and the current crisis. This will help clarify the severity of the impact of the current Covid-19 crisis, as well as how different the policy measures required to deal with the pandemic will be. Second, it presents an analysis of the policy instruments used by EU and Asian countries along with the US, and it assesses their effectiveness and limitations while taking a cross-country comparative perspective. This cross-country comparison will be informative, given the contrasting severities of the Covid-19 crisis between EU countries

DOI: 10.4324/9781003153603-101

and the US, which all experienced either national or localized lockdowns, and the Asian countries which managed to avoid such drastic measures.

Each chapter will deal with a specific national/regional experience, and will cover the following topics: (1) the extent of the outbreak of Covid-19 and the associated public health crisis; (2) an assessment of the key public health policies and the macroeconomic policies implemented to mitigate the health and economic impact of Covid-19; (3) a comparative examination of the fiscal policy responses to the Covid-19 pandemic and the 2008 global financial crisis; (4) a comparative examination of the monetary policy responses to the Covid-19 pandemic and the 2008 global financial crisis; and (5) an overall assessment of the effectiveness of the fiscal and monetary policies implemented to mitigate the economic impact of Covid-19, along with the public health policy implemented to contain the pandemic.

Numerous studies covering the Covid-19 crisis have been published since the outbreak of the pandemic (for instance, see the e-books and papers under the label "COVID economics" on the portal site VoxEu), but very few studies have attempted a comprehensive comparative study. Our book will enable scholars and policymakers from the US as well as Europe and East Asia to learn from each other based on the varying responses to the Covid-19 crisis.

The rest of this book is divided into three parts. **Part I** deals with the experience of the US. In the US, the Covid-19 pandemic has severely affected not only the everyday lives of the population, but also the economy. As of the end of 2020, more than 20 million cases of Covid-19 have been confirmed in the US, with around 350 thousand deaths. The localized lockdowns and voluntary social distancing measures implemented to reduce the spread of the virus, have led to immediate financial distress and an unprecedented downturn in the real economy. Financial market sentiment began to deteriorate in mid-February, amid the backdrop of increasing uncertainty and in the expectation of a rapid economic fallout from the substantial disruption in economic activity. Localized lockdowns and social distancing have adversely affected the labor market and reduced its capacity to produce goods and services. The major restrictions on mobility have caused people to spend less in sectors associated with face-to-face interactions. Layoffs and income decline due to disruption in economic activity have also reduced consumption, resulting in a deeper recession.

Seohyun Lee examines the fiscal and monetary policy measures adopted by the US authorities to cope with the unprecedented shock of the Covid-19 pandemic. The US economy shrank by 3.5 percent in 2020, the worst annual negative growth rate since the Second World War. After increasing to 14.7 percent in April 2020, the unemployment rate in the US fell to 6.7 percent in December. The average unemployment rate rose quickly to 8.1 per cent in 2020 from a historically low 3.7 percent in 2019. In response to the Covid-19 crisis, US authorities acted swiftly. In March, the Fed lowered policy rates to a range of 0–0.25 percent and then promptly announced the restarting of large asset purchase programs. Furthermore, to help provide credit to businesses, households, and communities the Fed introduced several lending facilities as well. In particular, the Fed responded proactively by introducing new credit facilities, including *the Main Street Lending Program*, to support the most vulnerable sectors of the economy while maintaining the smooth functioning of financial markets. In addition, the US government passed four bills – the Coronavirus Preparedness and Response Supplement Appropriations Act, the Families First Coronavirus Response Act, the Coronavirus Aid Relief and Economic Security Act (CARES Act), and the Paycheck Protection Program Flexibility Act (PPPF Act) – to provide much needed fiscal support to individuals and businesses hit by the sudden reduction in economic activity.

Compared to the policy response of the US during the global financial crisis, these monetary and fiscal measures have been larger in scope and size. The Fed's asset purchase program in response to the pandemic is bigger, and the speed of the asset purchases has been even faster. Numerous credit facilities have been extended to support non-bank corporations, state and municipal governments, and nonprofit organizations. More importantly, the fiscal stimulus provided during the Covid-19 crisis is far more impressive, accounting for approximately 14 percent of GDP compared to 7 percent of GDP during the global financial crisis. Funding for small firms and the real sector also represent another important feature of the monetary and fiscal responses to the current pandemic.

While it is too early to fully assess the effectiveness of the policy measures taken during this pandemic, which is still ongoing, Seohyun Lee sees that swift and bold actions by the government and the Fed have played a pivotal role in addressing the Covid-19 pandemic and mitigating its economic and social damages. "Act fast and do whatever it takes", which has been the default universal crisis response since the global financial crisis, seems initially to be the appropriate response to the pandemic. However, the real economy is showing a more mixed picture, and the prospects for a quick recovery seem remote. Although real GDP has rebounded and labor market conditions have improved due to the partial lifting of localized lockdown measures, the US economy will clearly remain below its pre-crisis level, at least for the short term. This may require the US authorities to prepare for an extended period of a low-for-longer economic growth as well.

While the monetary and fiscal responses to Covid-19 have had some success in cushioning the adverse impact of the pandemic on the economy, they are accompanied by substantial costs as well. In particular, the risk of having an extended period of low interest rates and low economic growth may lead to a continuing increase in debt, particularly for non-financial corporations, leaving them vulnerable to future shocks. Furthermore, the costs of existing and additional future fiscal stimulus packages would increase the fiscal deficit and the debt level to unsustainable levels.

Part II focuses on the Covid-19 monetary and fiscal response in the euro-area and in the EU. Along with examining the policy actions of the EU, this section investigates how the European countries hit most seriously by the Covid-19 pandemic, that is, France, Germany, Italy, and the UK, have dealt with and responded to the Covid-19 crisis. Like in the US, the Covid-19 pandemic swept the EU. As of the end of 2020, the EU as a whole had more than 15 million confirmed cases and 370 thousand deaths. In particular, France, Italy, and the UK each had more than 2 million confirmed cases, while Germany had a little under 2 million cases. Thus, European countries were as heavily affected by the Covid-19 pandemic as the US.

First of all, **Bernadette Andreosso-O'Callaghan** addresses the EU and euro-area's monetary and economic policy response measures. Prior to the outbreak of the Covid-19 pandemic, EU countries had already been suffering lackluster economic growth as a whole. In 2020, the GDP of the 27 EU states is expected to have dropped by 7.4 percent with its annual average unemployment rate rising to 7.2 percent from 6.7 percent in 2019. Based on the previous lessons learned from the 2008 global financial crisis and the euro economic crisis, the EU institutions (the European Central Bank in particular) have responded relatively quickly to the Covid-19 crisis, through monetary policy easing measures and through the injection of additional liquidity to support credit to households and firms. In particular, the ECB launched a new series of pandemic emergency long-term refinancing operations (PELTROs) in support of the euro-area financial system, as well as the PEPP (Pandemic Emergency Purchase Programme), which was launched in March 2020 with an initial envelope of €600bn, increased to €1,350bn during the following summer. Subsequently, debt mutualization has been introduced with the €750bn Recovery Fund (or "Next Generation EU" Fund), which aims to provide macroeconomic assistance to member states in times of economic distress and to support national expenditure or investment, among other objectives. These monetary measures have two important implications. The first implication is associated with the fact that they have been financed through additional "assigned revenues" to the EU budget, which is expected to place a higher fiscal burden on EU households and firms, particularly SMEs, in the years to come, thus leading to issues with social cohesion. Secondly, these measures are likely to resuscitate ideas on industrial policies that can revive economic growth in the real economy. Already both the EU and the euro area have been highlighting the importance of Industry 4.0. However, the latter will not boost the labor market to the level required, since the fourth industrial revolution is particularly focused on saving a large portion of jobs in the manufacturing and services sectors. The EU needs to stimulate economic growth through policies that would revive the real economy with a boost to the labor market, and in particular through the building of a sovereign health *filière* – or a network rendering the EU a sovereign entity in this area and minimizing the impact of other health shocks in the future.

Sophie Nivoix and **Serge Rey** look into the economic, budgetary, and financial measures adopted by the French government in response to Covid-19. France, like its European neighbors, experienced severe pressure on its health care system that led to two successive national lockdowns, the first from

March to May 2020 and the second from October to December 2020. As a result, the French economy shrank by 9.8 percent. However, the unemployment rate, which was already very high before the arrival of Covid-19, changed little, remaining at around 8.3 percent. In order to deal with the economic crisis that followed, and to minimize business bankruptcies, the government has provided unprecedented amounts of financial support. An emergency plan costing 470 billion euros was followed by a recovery plan costing 100 billion euros, and in November 2020, new financial measures (PLFR4) were taken to address the second lockdown. The overall cost of the Covid-19 crisis for the 2020 public finances is estimated at €186 billion, due to revenue losses of €100 billion caused by a contraction in economic activity, and the emergency measures implemented had an impact amounting to around €86 billion on public finances in 2020. Consequently, French government debt rose from 98 percent of GDP in 2020 to about 120 percent in 2021. This crisis will therefore also weigh heavily on the 2021 budget, and on that of the following years, and it is necessary to rapidly improve the French economy in order to limit both the social impact of the crisis and its effects on France's already high national debt, which has been steadily deteriorating over the last few decades.

Frank Roevekamp examines the economic and budgetary pandemic response measures by the German government. German GDP contracted by 5 percent as the spread of the Covid-19 virus hit the economy. To cushion against the economic and social damage of the Covid-19 crisis, the German government reacted with an unprecedented set of measures. State aid, credits, and guarantees were provided to affected industries on a grand scale to compensate for losses. The German government directly supported enterprises deemed "too big to fail", and subsidies were given to fund short-time work, which was intended to reduce the labor costs of companies by up to 50 percent without the need to resort to layoffs. Due to this short-time work (*"kurzarbeit"*) system, the quite large output shock did not translate into an unemployment shock, with the annual average unemployment rate rising only slightly to 5.9 percent in 2020 from 5.0 percent in 2019. The total cost of these measures amounted to about €1,200 billion. Furthermore, an additional €130 billion fiscal spending program was devised containing a 3 percent cut in value added tax, further relief in other taxes, and large investments in digitalization infrastructure and technologies. Additionally, Germany committed to contribute to the €750 billion Recovery Fund at the European Union level.

The author emphasizes the unique nature of the current Covid-19 crisis. During the global financial crisis, quick action on a large scale helped to prevent the world from plunging into another Great Depression. While the global financial crisis was a demand shock, which necessitated unprecedented rescue measures, the current downturn is caused by a combined supply and demand shock. This means that similar quick and bold response measures cannot be fully effective as long as the pandemic goes on and social distancing measures continue to be necessary. Thus far, mass bankruptcies and large-scale unemployment have been avoided by the rescue measures. However, it is doubtful that a fiscal spending package to stimulate demand is particularly useful in a situation where demand needs to be continuously restricted to reduce social interactions. The VAT reduction measure is thus considered to be wasteful. Furthermore, there is a danger that the crisis measures hinder necessary structural changes, which might become even more urgent than they were before the pandemic. Therefore, although the recapitalization of companies by the German government has largely benefited the airline and travel industry, it is doubtful that this industry is of systemic importance, or that it will recover to pre-crisis levels in the near future. Given the comparatively healthy state of public finances in Germany in recent years, the current stimulus packages of the government do not seem unsustainable. However, that may change based on unforeseeable future obligations that may arise in the European context in the future. Relief measures should be tailored to the nature of the current crisis, instead of randomly spending large amounts of money without a clear focus.

Claudio Cozza and **Leopoldo Nascia** examine the economic and budgetary policy responses of the Italian government to Covid-19. Italy was officially the first European country hit hard by Covid-19. The pandemic outbreak shifted suddenly into a generalized lockdown, with the country running the risk of a collapse of its national health system together with a huge economic recession. Italian GDP in 2020 is expected to have fallen by around 10 percent with a partial recovery of around 4 percent forecasted in 2021. The unemployment rate continued to remain high at around 9.8 percent in 2020. The government tried to mitigate the economic and social damage inflicted by Covid-19 through a set of measures to sustain the national health system, to support the productive system and promote investment for rapid economic recovery, and to support the income of Italian households. An increase in public spending with the temporary suspension of the euro-area public budget constraints characterized the Italian government' policy response in the first half of 2020. For instance, the emergency spending implemented during the period from March to August 2020 has cost in excess of €100 billion. However, Claudio Cozza and Leopoldo Nascia point out that these measures have been insufficient, particularly regarding industrial policy. During the Covid-19 crisis, the Italian government allocated grants and subsidies to the business sector without any conditionality, unlike other European countries that imposed some conditions about employment and innovation to companies receiving support. The authors expect that the launch of the Next Generation EU fund, based on such conditionality, will provide the possibility of setting up a large-scale program to stimulate growth and to meet the requirements of sustainability. Nonetheless a new model of economic and industrial policy is a very urgent requirement to trigger economic growth, especially in view of the return of tight EU rules for public spending – with the Italian budget deficit among the largest in Europe.

Alex De Ruyter and **David Hearne** investigate the fiscal and monetary policy responses of the UK to the Covid-19 crisis, after outlining the UK's unique institutional framework and its missteps in public health policies.

Covid-19 has had a devastating impact on the UK. GDP is expected to have contracted by more than 10 percent in 2020. The unemployment rate rose to 5 percent, the highest level since early 2016. The magnitude of the economic shock that the fiscal and monetary policies are responding to is thus larger than elsewhere. The UK economy was particularly vulnerable to Covid-19 because of its underlying structural weaknesses, namely, a high share of employment in social consumption sectors, and a flexible labor market with a high incidence of precarious jobs without adequate sick pay provisions. In common with elsewhere in Europe, the UK government responded with many fiscal programs including the "Coronavirus Job Retention Scheme" for workers and the Coronavirus Business Interruption Loan Scheme and the Bounce Back Loan Scheme for small and medium-sized companies. These fiscal supports were introduced to mitigate the worst effects of the pandemic, by supporting industries which are particularly vulnerable to long-term damage from short-term shifts in demand. In addition, drawing on the knowledge gained during the 2008 global financial crisis, the Bank of England again undertook quantitative easing. The Bank relaunched the Term Funding Scheme for SME lending as well. Certain economic policy instruments have been used to good effect, although there are ongoing concerns around many, particularly around the value-for-money and the economic rationale of some schemes. However, concerns remain as to the impact of the UK government scaling back support as 2021 progresses. When coupled with the impact of a hard Brexit on the UK economy, the prognosis over the immediate coming years looks bleak.

Part III deals with the experiences of a few selected Asian countries. This part focuses on four Asian countries in which the economic impact of Covid-19 has been relatively limited compared to those in the European countries: China, Japan, Korea, and Singapore. There were more than 95 thousand cases and 4 thousand deaths reported in China, 23 thousand cases and 3 thousand deaths confirmed in Japan, around 60 thousand cases and 9 hundred deaths in Korea, and 58 thousand cases and 30 deaths confirmed in Singapore. Clearly the relative success of Asian countries in containing the spread of the Covid-19 virus suggests that their fiscal and monetary policy responses should not be the same as those in the US and Europe. These chapters will provide an informative contrast between the US and European and Asian countries in terms of their responses to the Covid-19 crisis.

Eiji Ogawa compares the monetary and fiscal policy responses of the Japanese authorities during the 2008 global financial crisis and the 2020 Covid-19 crisis. The Covid-19 crisis has had a tremendous impact on the domestic economy. The Japanese economy has been facing a depression equal to or worse than that of the global financial crisis. The rate of change in real GDP (annualized rate of changes from previous quarters) was recorded at minus 28.8 percent in the second quarter of 2020, representing a substantially larger reduction than the minus 17.8 percent recorded in the first quarter of 2009 during the global financial crisis. As a result, the Japanese economy shrank by 4.8 percent over the full year 2020. Nonetheless, the unemployment rate rose only slightly to 2.8 percent in 2020 from 2.4 percent in 2019. Unlike its Western counterparts, Japan is famous for its extremely low unemployment rate, which reflects a couple of structural factors such as the social aversion to layoffs and tight labor market conditions due to a shrinking and graying population. Clearly, the impact of Covid-19 on the labor market was better contained compared to other advanced economies. Furthermore, the pandemic has had unequal impacts, affecting more severely the services sectors and SMEs, compared with industrial sectors and large firms.

The Japanese government and the Bank of Japan (BOJ) have actively reacted to the Covid-19 crisis with both fiscal and monetary policy as well as effective public health policy measures. First of all, the government has implemented fiscal measures under the heading Emergency Economic Measures to Cope with Covid-19 in the first and second supplementary budgets in fiscal year 2020. In total, these budgets amounted to ¥67.4 trillion. These measures included emergency support for households and SMEs, measures intended to increase employment, and financial measures to support firms in terms of cash management and corporate financing. While the positive effects of these measures on the Japanese economy have not yet been apparent, these measures have increased the outstanding total of special deficit financing bonds of the Japanese government from 618 to 671 trillion yen. The ratio of total outstanding Japanese Government Bonds (JGBs) to GDP has also increased from 160.8 percent to 169.0 percent. The accumulation of outstanding JGBs is expected to have adverse effects on the Japanese economy, although the BOJ has been practicing an accommodative monetary policy against the accumulation of government bonds in order to keep the long-term interest rate at zero percent. Along with the government, the BOJ has continued its "Quantitative and Qualitative Monetary Easing (QQE) with Yield Curve Control" program. It extended its asset purchases to assets other than JGB purchases. Moreover, the BOJ has introduced new "Special Funds-Supplying Operations to Facilitate Financing in Response to Covid-19" to provide loans against corporate debt as collateral at zero interest rate, along with a New Fund-Provisioning Measure to Support Financing Mainly Small and Medium-Sized Firms. The BOJ has implemented a coordinated scheme to enhance the provision of US dollar liquidity via standing US dollar liquidity swap line arrangements with the central banks of other advanced countries. Currently, the BOJ's monetary policy measures have been contributing to keeping financial markets stable, as well as keeping long-term interest rates at lower levels in Japan. However, the corporate financing difficulties might become more severe in the coming years as well as in 2020, because Japanese firms, especially SMEs in Japan, would continue to face net cash outflows in circumstances where an ongoing Covid-19 crisis has extended adverse effects on their sales and profits.

Woosik Moon and **Wook Sohn** assess whether the fiscal and monetary policy responses taken by the Korean government and Bank of Korea after the outbreak of the Covid-19 pandemic are appropriate for the Korean economy. As in other major economies hit hard by Covdid-19, the Korean authorities reacted through speedy and massively accommodative policies, emphasizing that these would be preemptive actions as were those in respect of the 2008 global financial crisis. But Korea has had no lockdown. Although economic recovery has been delayed due to the minimum social distancing requirements, the impact of Covid-19 has remained rather limited to date. In 2020, the GDP in Korea contracted by only 1 percentage point and the unemployment rate increased very slightly to 4 percent from 3.8 percent in 2019. Like in Japan, the unemployment rate in Korea is more affected by social and structural factors than by business fluctuations. Woosik Moon and Wook Sohn emphasize that unlike in the case of the 2008 global financial crisis, the goal of economic policy in coping with the Covid-19 crisis should be put on curing economic malaise, not on directly stimulating the economy. This suggests that a more appropriate approach in dealing with Covid-19 in Korea may not be a speedy and large response but a smaller, more gradual response over a longer time frame, which should be taken in tandem with the evolution of Covid-19 to mitigate its economic impact. From this perspective, the current fiscal policy response of the Korean government seems particularly problematic in both its size and content. For example, the emergency disaster relief program targeting all Korean families, regardless of personal circumstances, should not have been an urgent policy requirement. The Korean government has been spending excessively, as the savior of first resort and not as the savior of last resort. As the Covid-19 pandemic has varying consequences on different groups and sectors, a more targeted fiscal policy response would have been desirable for the goal of alleviating the impact of the pandemic on the Korean economy. A gradual and targeted approach in place of a speedy and undiscriminating response might have been the right approach.

Lifeng Su looks at China's monetary and fiscal policies during Covid-19. The pandemic has had a substantial negative impact on China's real economic activities, particularly in the first quarter, due to the strict containment measures implemented, including the lockdowns of Wuhan city and Hubei province, where the outbreak of Covid-19 was first identified. In the first quarter of 2020, GDP fell by 6.8 percent. After April, the economy fully reopened and GDP in the second quarter returned to positive growth. As a consequence, the GDP growth rate dropped to 2.3 percent in 2020 from 6.1 percent in 2019. Although China is the only major economy that recorded a positive growth rate in 2020, the impact of the Covid-19 pandemic was substantial. Urban unemployment, which was at 5.2 percent in December 2019, went up to 6.2 percent in March 2020 and since then has gradually retreated to pre-pandemic levels. Given that the official urban unemployment rate does not include the approximately 150 million self-employed business owners and nearly 300 million migrant workers, the severity that Covid-19 had on the labor market cannot be easily dismissed.

The Chinese government and the People's Bank of China (PBOC) announced a series of fiscal and monetary policies in response to the pandemic. In terms of monetary policy, the benchmark interest rate was cut by

30 basis points; the PBOC provided relending and rediscount funds amounting to RMB 2.2 trillion to support the production of key medical supplies and daily necessities as well as supports for the reopening and development of the economy. Nonetheless, the total assets of the PBOC remained stable, which implies that China's monetary policy operations and fiscal assistance efforts are much more moderate due to the successful containment of the spread of Covid-19. Regarding fiscal policies, a series of tax and fee reduction policies for small-scale businesses were put in place from February. The Chinese government introduced a series of measures to increase the deficit-to-GDP ratio, issue special treasury bonds for Covid-19 containment, and implement further cuts in taxes and fees. The amount of direct fiscal assistance provided by the government thus far is around RMB 3.6 trillion, while the scale of the indirect reduction in taxes and fees in 2020 was around RMB 2.5 trillion. The sum of the two categories amounts to about 6 percent of GDP in 2019. These monetary and fiscal policies have stabilized market expectations, ensured basic production and employment, and increased household income. However, compared to the measures adopted during the 2008 global financial crisis, these measures are much more moderate, given the successful containment of Covid-19. China's monetary policy had returned to normal from the fourth quarter of 2020. It is also expected that by early 2021 there will be no further fiscal stimulus.

Hwee Kwan Chow and **Kong Weng Ho** examine the fiscal and monetary policy responses of Singapore to the spread of Covid-19. For the whole of 2020, the Singapore economy contracted by 5.4 percent, a reversal from the 1.3 percent growth recorded in 2019. Although the unemployment rate was little affected at around 4 percent, this contraction is assessed as more severe when compared to the contraction during the 2008 global financial crisis. The construction industry, sectors affected by international travel restrictions, and customer-facing retail trade and business services all shrank.

Singapore responded with an easing of its monetary policy stance, reinforcing financial stability, helping individuals to reduce debt obligations, easing business cashflow constraints, adjusting financial regulatory and supervisory protocols to cope with immediate challenges, and enabling the financial sectors to build long-term capabilities. Fiscal responses were unprecedented, with four consecutive special Covid-19 budgets and two ministerial statements incorporating further programs, initially focusing on immediate assistance in respect of jobs, businesses, households, and later refined to providing more sector-specific assistance as the pandemic evolved with more detailed information available and preparing for post-pandemic recovery and growth. Close to S$100 billion, or about 20 percent of Singapore's GDP, is committed to supporting Singaporeans, and the overall budget deficit for 2020 was S$74.2 billion; up to S$52 billion is planned to be drawn from national reserves. The public finance system in Singapore has three characteristics: fiscal responsibility, fiscal sustainability, and the accumulation of funds for future generations and long-term challenges. The Constitution requires the government to balance the budget by the end of each governmental term, and surpluses are accumulated as national reserves which are in turn invested. Funds are regularly topped up to prepare for key commitments in the future. Singapore's fiscal prudence over the years, together with its sustained economic growth, has contributed to its national reserves, which have been available for strategic access during the pandemic. Singapore seems to have managed the Covid-19 crisis well thus far. The monetary–fiscal policy mix of providing a stable yet accommodative monetary policy stance that allowed fiscal policy to play a more prominent role also helped mitigate the economic impact of the Covid-19 crisis. Nevertheless, the long-term effectiveness of the various policy responses in Singapore, which is a small and highly open economy, depends substantially on the global containment of the pandemic, the effectiveness and the pace of allocation of the vaccine, and the pace of recovery of the global economy.

The Covid-19 crisis is unprecedented, and as a result, scholars, policymakers, and the public at large are eager to know what lessons can be learned from the pandemic response measures undertaken. Against this backdrop, this book is timely and informative in that it provides the most up-to-date information and insights into government and central bank responses to the pandemic.

Part I

The experience of the USA

1 Monetary and fiscal policies in the United States

Seohyun Lee[1]

1.1 Introduction

In the US, the COVID-19 pandemic has taken a toll not only on human lives but also on the economy. The nationwide lockdowns and social distancing measures to prevent the spreading of the virus have led to immediate financial distress and an unprecedented downturn in the real economy. In response to the COVID-19 crisis, the US authorities have acted swiftly to cushion the adverse effects of the pandemic. The Federal Reserve Bank (Fed) lowered policy rates to a range of 0 to 0.25 percent in March and promptly announced a plan for a large asset purchase program. To help provide credit to businesses, households, and community services organizations (e.g. schools, hospitals, etc.), the Fed introduced several liquidity and lending facilities in March 2020 under Section 13(3) of the Federal Reserve Act. The four rounds of government responses to COVID—the Coronavirus Preparedness and Response Supplement Appropriations Act, the Families First Coronavirus Response Act, the Coronavirus Aid Relief and Economic Security Act (CARES Act), and the Paycheck Protection Program Flexibility Act (PPPF Act)—were approved early on in the pandemic to provide much needed supports to individuals and businesses heavily hit by the sudden disruption in economic activity.

Compared with the policy response during the global financial crisis (GFC), both the monetary and fiscal measures implemented during the COVID-19 crisis have been larger in scope and size. The Fed's asset purchase program was announced in a timely manner and the speed of asset purchases has been faster. Credit facilities have been extended to support non-bank corporations, states, municipal governments, and non-profit organizations. The fiscal stimulus during the COVID-19 crisis has been much larger—approximately 14 percent of GDP—than the 7 percent GDP stimulus packages during the GFC. Furthermore, funding for small firms suffering due to disruptions in face-to-face interactions has been a substantial component of the fiscal policy responses to the pandemic.

1 The views expressed in the chapter are those of the author and do not necessarily represent the views of the IMF, its Executive Board, IMF management, or the Bank of Korea.

DOI: 10.4324/9781003153603-1

While it is too early to fully assess the effectiveness of the policy measures, the swift and bold actions by the Fed have played a vital role in stabilizing financial markets and providing credit for otherwise sound borrowers who face a temporary period of decreased income. The real economy, partly reflecting the effect of the policy measures, shows a mixed picture and the outlook is largely dependent on the path of the pandemic. Fiscal policies supporting small and medium sized firms and moratoria on evictions and foreclosures have helped housing sector activities and prevented or delayed bankruptcies.

The remainder of the chapter proceeds as follows. Section 2 illustrates the evolution of the COVID-19 pandemic, the containment measures the US government has taken, and presents the financial market and macroeconomic impacts of the COVID-19 crisis. Section 3 provides details on the Federal Reserve's recent actions in response to the COVID-19 crisis, in comparison with those implemented during the GFC in 2008–09. Section 4 presents some details of the fiscal policy measures. Section 5 evaluates the overall effectiveness of the monetary and fiscal measures. Section 6 outlines the conclusions of this research.

1.2 Economic impacts of the COVID-19 crisis

1.2.1 Developments of the COVID-19 pandemic and containment measures

The COVID-19 pandemic in the US has created not only a public health crisis but also an economic crisis. The pandemic has taken lives and slowed down economic activities as the government had to impose stringent lockdown measures to prevent the rapid spread of the virus. Social distancing in response to a rapid increase in COVID-19 cases has also contributed to economic contractions (IMF, 2020b). As of December 4, there have been over 14.1 million confirmed cases of COVID-19 and more than 276,000 deaths in the US (Figure 1.1). Following a gradually expanding outbreak in March 2020, broad-based lockdown and stay-at-home restrictions were imposed, and the number of new cases declined thereafter. Nevertheless, a second wave of the coronavirus occurred during the summer as economic activity and traveling resumed. In response to a surge in cases, the government slowed the reopening of the economy and reinstated partial lockdowns. Although the infection curve temporarily flattened during September due to the stringent government response, the US once again confronted renewed steep upticks in infections as the winter season approached.

An important factor that contributes to the COVID-19 recession is the degree of lockdown measures. While effective in containing the spread of the virus, strict lockdown measures imposed by governments involve short-term economic costs. Due to the severity of the pandemic in the US, the reopening of the economy has stalled and the degree of stringency of government responses, as measured by the Stringency Index (Hale et al., 2020),

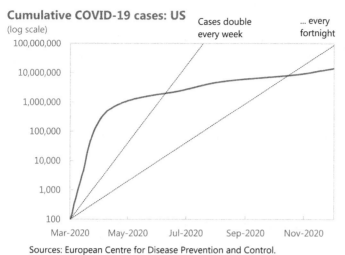

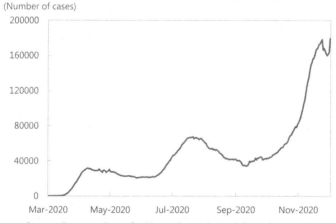

Sources: European Centre for Disease Prevention and Control.

Figure 1.1 COVID-19 cases in the US

has been substantially higher than the global average since May 2020 (Figure 1.2).[2] Another substantial determinant of economic contraction is behavioral changes—e.g. voluntary reductions in social interactions to avoid contracting

2 The Stringency Index, provided by the University of Oxford's COVID-19 Government Response Tracker, is an index that averages several sub-indicators including school closures, workplace closures, cancellations of public events, restrictions on gatherings, public transport closures, stay at home requirements, restrictions on internal movement, international travel controls, and the existence of public information campaigns on COVID-19.

Stringency Index
(Index, ranges from 0 to 100)

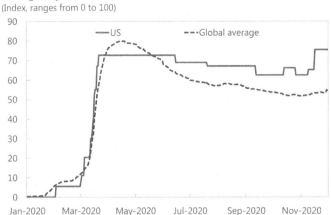

Sources: Blavatnik School, University of Oxford.

Figure 1.2 Stringency Index

or spreading the virus (IMF, 2020c). If the recession were mostly driven by the adoption of lockdown measures, economic activities would recover quickly when such measures are lifted. However, as voluntary social distancing and associated behavioral changes may also play important roles in the recession, economic activity could remain subdued for an extended period even after the government measures are removed.

1.2.2 Financial market impacts of the COVID-19 crisis

The deterioration in economic activity due to the COVID-19 pandemic immediately affected financial markets (Figure 1.3). Financial market sentiment deteriorated from mid-February with the increase in uncertainty and the expectation of a sudden economic fallout from the disruptions in economic activities. As of March 23, the US equity market index (S&P 500) was down 31 percent from the start of 2020. Option-implied stock market volatility, as measured by the VIX Index, recorded a peak of 83 on March 16, reaching the same peak level as during the 2008–09 GFC. The yields on 10-year Treasury securities decreased below 1 percent in May and remained low with negative term premiums.

The flight to safe assets and to liquidity raised borrowing costs and limited credit access, amplifying the negative effects on the economy. Credit spreads sharply increased in March to 10.6 percentage points; however, the increase is smaller than what was experienced during the GFC. The dollar has depreciated against Euro and Yen since the initial spreading of the pandemic.

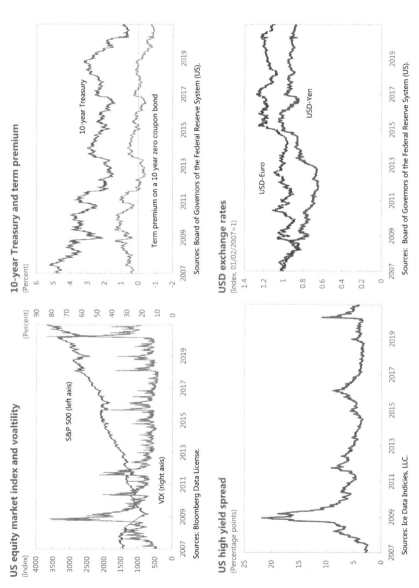

Figure 1.3 Financial market developments

1.2.3 Macroeconomic impacts of the COVID-19 crisis

Lockdowns and social distancing negatively affect labor markets and reduce capacity to produce goods and services (Brinca, Duarte and Faria-e-Castro, 2020; Gupta et al., 2020). Reduced mobility due to stay-at-home restrictions and social distancing lead people to spend less in sectors associated with face-to-face interactions (Alexander and Karger, 2020). Layoffs and income decline due to disruptions in economic activity hamper consumption, resulting in further recession. The COVID-19 shock contracted the US economy at an annualized rate of 31.7 percent in the second quarter and the unemployment rate rose sharply to 14.7 percent in April. The initial downturn triggered by the pandemic has been deeper than the GFC recession (Figure 1.4). Real GDP growth in private goods and services and government sectors dropped sharply, recording declines of over 30 percent in 2020Q2 (Figure 1.5). The recent recession is different from that during the GFC. In the previous crisis, service sectors suffered less severely than manufacturing. In the current pandemic-led downturn, most economic activities have been disrupted substantially and service sectors reliant on face-to-face interactions—e.g. wholesale and retail trade, hospitality—have been the most seriously affected.

The pandemic hit both households and businesses substantially at the onset of the outbreak (Figure 1.6). Real personal consumption expenditure plummeted sharply by −16.5 percent (y/y) in April, which was much larger than the drop during the GFC. Real business equipment investment dropped by −14.9 percent (y/y) in 2020Q2. However, the decline in investment during the current crisis was not as drastic as the collapse in investment during the previous crisis in 2008–09. The manufacturing capacity utilization rate was 60.5 percent in April, 17.7 percentage points below its long-run average.

Deeper contraction than 2007-09 global financial crisis

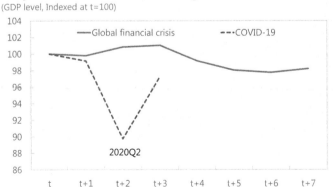

Notes: The basis period (t) is the peaks of NBER's US business cycle reference dates, 2007Q4 (global financial crisis), 2019Q4 (COVID-19 crisis).
Sources: U.S. Bureau of Economic Analysis.

Figure 1.4 Nominal GDP level: global financial crisis vs. COVID-19 crisis

Real GDP by industry: Global Financial Crisis

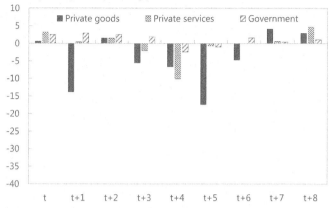

Sources: U.S. Bureau of Economic Analysis.

Real GDP by industry: COVID-19 crisis

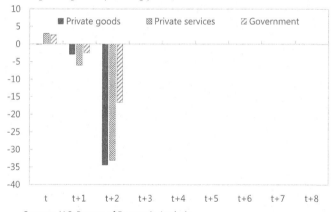

Sources: U.S. Bureau of Economic Analysis.

Figure 1.5 Real GDP by industry: global financial crisis vs. COVID-19 crisis

The much-reduced economic activity due to the shutdown and social distancing caused the unemployment rate to surge (Figure 1.7). The unemployment rate rose from 3.5 percent in February to 14.7 percent in April, the highest level since 1948. The labor force participation rate fell from 63.4 percent in February to 60.2 percent in April. The sharp increase in the unemployment rate was mainly driven by a large increase in temporary layoffs. The share of job losers on temporary layoffs rose from 29.4 percent in February to 87.6 percent in April. Permanent layoffs jumped by 721 thousand to 2 million in April and

Disposable income and consumption

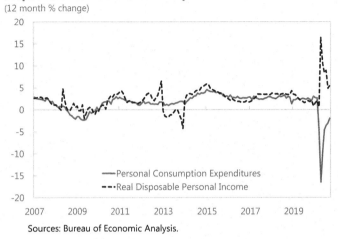

Sources: Bureau of Economic Analysis.

Equipment investment and capacity utilization

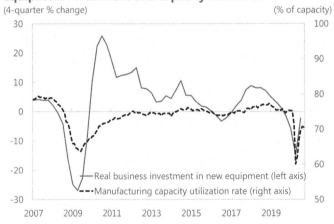

Sources: Bureau of Economic Analysis and Federal Reserve Board.

Figure 1.6 Households and business sector indicators

continued to rise to 3.7 million in October. Job losses have had disproportionate effects especially on those who have insufficient buffers to cope with a profound shock in the current pandemic. In April, the unemployment rate rose more sharply for women (16.1 percent), those without college education (18.7 percent), African Americans (16.7 percent), and Hispanics (18.9 percent).[3]

---

3 See the U.S. Bureau of Labor Statistics for time series data of unemployment rate by sex, educational attainment or race: www.bls.gov/web/empsit.supp.toc.htm.

Labor market indicators

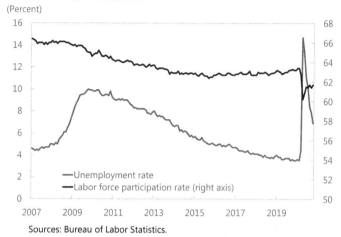

Sources: Bureau of Labor Statistics.

Permanent and temporary layoffs

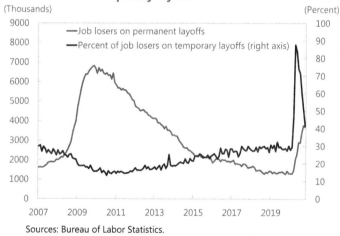

Sources: Bureau of Labor Statistics.

Figure 1.7 Labor market indicators

Personal Consumption Expenditure (PCE) price inflation fell from 1.8 percent in February to below 0.5 percent in April, reflecting downward pressure on wages due to high levels of unemployment and weak global commodity prices (Figure 1.8). Core CPI inflation also fell from 2.4 percent in February to 1.4 percent in April and further dropped to 1.2 percent in May–June. However, the three-year future inflation expectations have remained at around 2.6 percent on average since February.

PCE deflator

(12 month percent change)

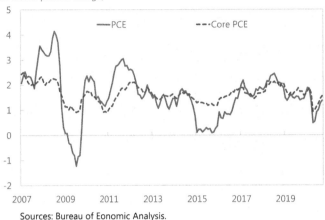

Sources: Bureau of Eonomic Analysis.

Core CPI inflation and 3-year ahead inflation expectations

(Percent)

Sources: Bureau of Labor Statistics and Survey of Consumer Expectations.

Figure 1.8 Inflation

Housing sector activities are depressed due to the adverse effects from the COVID-19 pandemic. Housing starts fell sharply by 26.3 percent (y/y) in April 2020 with limitations in construction activity during the lockdown period. Existing home sales also showed a significant decline, recording a 24.8 percent yearly decrease in May.

The duration of the shock remains uncertain and relates to factors inherently difficult to predict, including the path of the pandemic and related government stringency measures, the adjustment costs it imposes on the economy, the effectiveness of the economic policy response, and the evolution of financial sentiment.

1.3 Monetary policy responses to the COVID-19 crisis

1.3.1 Conventional monetary policies

In terms of monetary policy, the Fed has acted swiftly and aggressively to ensure the financial market continued functioning smoothly in response to the crisis. The Fed lowered its policy rates to a range of 0 to 0.25 percent from a range of 1.50 to 1.75 percent in March (Figure 1.9). As forward guidance, it announced that the rates will remain low until it is confident that the economy

Effective Fed Funds Rates

(Percent)

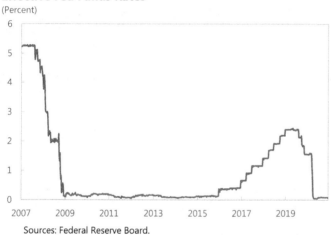

Sources: Federal Reserve Board.

Total assets of the Federal Reserve

(In billion USD)

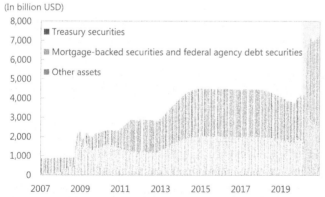

Notes: Other assests include swaps, repos, loans, and liquidity and credit facility LLCs.
Sources: Federal Reserve Board.

Figure 1.9 Monetary policy measures

has weathered recent events and is on track to achieve its maximum employment and price stability goals.

On August 27, the Fed switched to a new average inflation targeting framework, pushing back the timing of an eventual lift-off until inflation runs moderately above 2 percent for some time and joblessness falls to the Fed's long-term unemployment targets.[4] The amended policy framework will allow the Fed to remain accommodative for an even longer period of time to promote economic recovery.

In addition, the Fed undertook large-scale overnight and term repo operations(term repurchase operations); lowered the cost of discount window lending; reduced the existing cost of swap lines with major central banks (Bank of Canada, Bank of England, Bank of Japan, ECB, and Swiss National Bank) and extended the maturity of FX(foreign exchange) operations. It also broadened US dollar swap lines to central banks of nine countries—Australia, Brazil, Denmark, Mexico, New Zealand, Norway, Singapore, South Korea, and Sweden—and offered temporary repo facilities for foreign and international monetary authorities (FIMA Repo Facility) with accounts at the Federal Reserve Bank of New York.

1.3.2 *Unconventional monetary policy: asset purchase and credit facilities*

The Fed has increased its assets by expanding asset purchase programs to support the smooth functioning of fixed income markets (Figure 1.9). In March, the Fed announced that it would increase its holdings of Treasury securities by at least US$500 billion and its holdings of agency mortgage-backed securities by at least US$200 billion. Since then, the Fed's total assets have risen by around US$2.9 trillion—including an increase in Treasury securities of US$2.1 trillion—to US$7.2 trillion. Such purchases keep markets working when assets are otherwise difficult to sell, inject cash into the economy, and convey that the Fed stands ready to backstop important parts of the financial system.

To help provide credit to businesses, households, and community service organizations, the Fed introduced several liquidity and lending facilities in March under the Federal Reserve Act. Section 13(3) of the Act permits the Fed to provide liquidity to the financial system by discounting the liabilities of individuals, partnerships, and corporations in unusual and exigent circumstances. Under the CARES Act, funding of US$454 billion was appropriated to the Treasury to backstop the facilities and to absorb potential credit losses.

The credit facilities introduced during the COVID-19 crisis can be broadly classified into five groups—credit to financial institutions, non-bank corporations, households, states and municipal governments, and non-profit

---

4 See the FOMC press release for additional information: www.federalreserve.gov/newsevents/pressr eleases/monetary20200827a.htm.

Table 1.1 Monetary policies during the global financial crisis and the COVID-19 crisis

GFC	COVID-19
Credit to financial institutions	
• Primary Dealer Credit Facility	• Primary Dealer Credit Facility
• Money Market Mutual Fund Liquidity Facility	• Money Market Mutual Fund Liquidity Facility, including a wider range of securities, municipal
• AMLF, MMIFF, TSLF (expired)	variable rate demand notes and bank certificates of deposit.
Credit to non-bank corporations	
• Commercial Paper Funding Facility	• Commercial Paper Funding Facility
	• Primary Market Corporate Credit Facility
	• Secondary Market Corporate Credit Facility
	• Main Street Lending Program
	• Paycheck Protection Program Liquidity Facility
Credit to households	
• Term Asset-Backed Securities Loan Facility	• Term Asset-Backed Securities Loan Facility ($100 billion): Eligible collateral includes the triple-A rated tranches of both outstanding CMBS and newly issued CDO.
Credit to states and municipal governments	
• N/A	• Municipal Liquidity Facility ($500 billion): Purchases of short-term notes directly from U.S. states and eligible counties and cities.
Credit to non-profit organizations	
• N/A	• Non-profit Organization New Loan Facility
	• Non-profit Organization Expanded Loan Facility

organizations (Table 1.1). First, the Fed reactivated or expanded the standing facilities to provide loans to financial institutions that were used during the GFC.[5] The *Primary Dealer Credit Facility* provides up to 90 days financing to the Fed's 24 primary dealers, collateralized by a wide range of investment grade securities, including Treasury and agency debt, investment grade corporate debt, international agency securities, commercial paper, municipal bonds, mortgage and asset-backed securities, and equities. The *Money Market Mutual Fund Liquidity Facility* (MMLF) provides loans up to 12 months to depository institutions, collateralized by assets that are purchased from prime money market funds. The MMLF extended eligible assets to a wider range of securities, municipal variable rate demand notes, and bank certificates of deposit.

---

5 Some of the credit facilities which operated during the 2008-09 GFC had expired. These include the *Asset-Backed Commercial Paper Money Market Mutual Fund Liquidity Facility* (AMLF), *Money Market Investor Funding Facility* (MMIFF), and *Term Securities Lending Facility* (TSLF).

Second, the Fed reactivated several existing facilities and introduced new facilities to support non-bank corporations. The *Commercial Paper Funding Facility* was reactivated to facilitate the issuance of commercial paper by companies and municipal issuers. The *Primary Market Corporate Credit Facility* allows the Fed to lend to corporations by buying new bond issuances and providing loans. Under the *Secondary Market Corporate Credit Facility*, the Fed can purchase existing corporate bonds as well as exchange-traded funds investing in investment-grade corporate bonds. These facilities backstop up to US$750 billion of corporate debt. The *Main Street Lending Program* allows the Fed to set up a special purpose vehicle (SPV) to purchase new or expanded loans to small and medium-sized businesses with maturities up to five years, with deferral of principal payments for two years, and deferral of interest payments for one year.[6] Banks providing the loans retain a 5 percent share in the loan and firms are subject to certain conditions—e.g. they must make reasonable efforts to retain workers, not use the loans for early repayment of other debts, and comply with the limits on executive compensation, stock buybacks, and payment of dividends. The *Paycheck Protection Program Liquidity Facility* (PPPLF) provides liquidity (term financing) to financial institutions that provide loans under the Small Business Administration's Paycheck Protection Program (PPP). PPP loans incentivize small businesses to keep their workers on the payroll.

Third, to support households and small businesses, the Fed reactivated the *Term Asset-Backed Securities Loan Facility* which lends to holders of asset-backed securities collateralized by new loans. Eligible collateral includes student loans, auto loans, credit-card loans, and loans guaranteed by the Small Business Administration. The Fed expanded the eligible collateral to the triple-A rated tranches of both outstanding commercial mortgage-backed securities (CMBS) and newly issued collateralized debt obligations (CDO).

Fourth, the Fed introduced the *Municipal Liquidity Facility* that offers loans to US states, eligible counties, and cities. The loans, up to US$500 billion, are to government entities in exchange for notes tied to future tax revenues with maturities of less than three years. Lastly, in July 2020, the Fed expanded the *Main Street Lending Program to Non-profit Organizations*, including hospitals, schools, and social services organizations.

The credit facilities are established around three different structures. First, for the *Primary Dealer Credit Facility*, the *Money Market Mutual Fund Liquidity Facility*, and the *Paycheck Protection Program Liquidity Facility*, the Fed operates the facilities by providing liquidity to financial institutions in exchange for a certain range of collateral.[7] Second, for the *Commercial Paper Funding Facility*, the *Primary/Secondary Market Corporate Credit Facility*, the *Term Asset-Backed*

---

6 Eligible firms are those with fewer than 15,000 workers or annual revenues of less than US$5 billion.

7 The operating counterparties for each facility are as follows. The Primary Dealer Credit Facility: 24 primary dealers; the Money Market Mutual Fund Liquidity Facility: depository institutions and bank holding companies; the Paycheck Protection Program Liquidity Facility: eligible PPP lenders, both depository and non-depository institutions.

Table 1.2 Amount of lending facilities

Federal Reserve 13(3) Facilities (in USD billion)

	Loans outstanding (as of Aug 31, A)	Loans outstanding (as of Nov 30, B)	A–B
Primary Dealer Credit Facility	0.2	0.2	0.0
Money Market Mutual Fund Liquidity Facility	9.7	5.1	−4.6
Commercial Paper Funding Facility	0.0	0.0	0.0
Primary Market Corporate Credit Facility	0.0	0.0	0.0
Secondary Market Corporate Credit Facility	12.5	13.7	1.2
Main Street Lending Facility	1.1	6.0	4.9
Paycheck Protection Program Liquidity Facility	68.2	55.4	−12.8
Term Asset-Backed Securities Loan Facility	2.6	3.6	1.0
Municipal Liquidity Facility	1.7	1.7	0.0
Total	96.0	85.7	−10.3

Source: Reports to Congress Pursuant to Section 13(3) of the Federal Reserve Act in response to COVID-19, available at: www.federalreserve.gov/publications/reports-to-congress-in-response-to-covid-19.htm.

Securities Loan Facility, and *Municipal Liquidity Facility*, the Fed provides funding to a special purpose vehicle (SPV) which, in turn, provides collateralized loans to financial institutions or purchases bonds and loans outright. Third, under *the Main Street Lending Program*, the Fed established a SPV that directly purchases participations in loans originated by eligible lenders.

As of November 30, the amount of outstanding loans of credit facilities fell to US$85.7 billion from US$96.0 billion in August (Table 1.2). The outstanding loan amount for the *Paycheck Protection Program Liquidity Facility* is the largest, at US$55.4 billion, followed by the *Secondary Market Corporate Credit Facility*, amounting to US$13.7 billion. The outstanding loans under the *Main Street Lending Program* increased by US$4.9 billion in August to US$6.0 billion as of the end of November. As concerns about the liquidity of financial institutions mitigated, the outstanding loans under the *MMFL* declined by US$4.6 billion to US$5.1 billion in November. Compared to the August data, the total outstanding amount of all advances under the *PPPLF* fell by US$12.8 billion to US$55.4 billion.[8]

1.4 Fiscal policy responses to the COVID-19 crisis

To cushion the unprecedented economic fallout during the pandemic, the US government swiftly announced large-scale fiscal measures amounting to US$3

8 Under the CARES Act, the amount of PPP loans available is up to US$659 billion and, as of August, 80 percent of the funding was already exhausted (https://home.treasury.gov/policy-issues/cares/assistance-for-small-businesses).

Table 1.3 Fiscal measures during the global financial crisis and the COVID-19 crisis

	Global financial crisis	COVID-19 crisis
Total amounts	US$1.0 trillion (7% of GDP)	US$3.0 trillion (14% of GDP)
Programs	The Economic Stimulus Act of 2008 (US$170 billion): $600 tax rebates to households	The Coronavirus Preparedness and Response Supplemental Appropriations Act (US$8.3 billion)
	The American Recovery and Reinvestment Act of 2009 (US$840 billion)	The Families First Coronavirus Response Act (US$192 billion)
		The Coronavirus Aid, Relief and Economy Security Act (CARES Act, est. US$2.3 trillion): tax rebates US$1,200 for each adult, US$500 for each child
		The Paycheck Protection Program and Health Care Enhancement Act (US$483 billion)

trillion, accounting for around 14 percent of GDP (Table 1.3). The overall size of the stimulus packages during the current crisis is much larger than those provided during the GFC which amounted to 7 percent of GDP.

As fiscal responses to COVID-19, there were four rounds of legislation in March and April 2020. The first two focused on emergency health care, food assistance, and paid sick and family leave related to COVID-19, providing funds amounting to 1 percent of GDP. *The Coronavirus Preparedness and Response Supplemental Appropriations Act* (March 6) provided funding of US$8.3 billion, including funding to the Public Health and Social Services Emergency Fund (US$ 3 billion), and to the Centers for Disease Control and Prevention (US$2 billion), for epidemiology, infection control and mitigation, and the development of vaccines and therapies. The *Families First Coronavirus Response Act* (March 18) with funding of US$192 billion entails support to employees including two weeks paid sick leave and up to three months emergency leave for those infected; food assistance to low-income women and children (US$1 billion); and transfers of funds to states for extended unemployment benefits through December 2020.

On March 21, the third and by far the largest piece of legislation, the *Coronavirus Aid, Relief, and Economic Security Act* (CARES Act), was passed by Congress with estimated funding of US$2.3 trillion (Table 1.4). It includes US$293 billion tax rebates to individuals ($1,200 for each adult, $500 for each child); US$268 billion for the expansion of unemployment benefits;[9] US$349

9 The CARES Act provides unemployment benefits through December 31, 2020, to people who are unemployed, partially unemployed, or otherwise unable to work because of the coronavirus, but who

Table 1.4 CARES Act

- US$293 billion to provide one-time tax rebates to individuals
- US$268 billion to expand unemployment benefits
- US$25 billion to provide a food safety net for the most vulnerable
- US$510 billion to prevent corporate bankruptcy by providing loans, guarantees, and backstopping the Federal Reserve 13(3) program
- US$349 billion in forgivable Small Business Administration loans and guarantees to help small businesses that retain workers
- US$100 billion for hospitals
- US$150 billion in transfers to state and local governments
- US$49.9 billion for international assistance (including SDR28 billion for the IMF's New Arrangement to Borrow)

Source: IMF Policy Tracker: Economic Responses to COVID-19 by 196 countries, available at: http://IMF.org/COVID19policytracker.

billion in forgivable Small Business Administration (SBA) loans and guarantees to help small businesses that retain workers;[10] US$127 billion for medical care and research related to the pandemic;[11] US$150 billion to provide grants to states and local governments for spending related to the pandemic. It also includes US$510 billion to prevent corporate bankruptcy by providing loans, guarantees, and backstopping Federal Reserve 13(3) programs.

The fourth piece of legislation, the *Paycheck Protection Program and Health Care Enhancement Act* (April 24), provides funding of US$483 billion. It includes an additional US$321 billion for forgivable Small Business Administration loans (PPP loans) and guarantees; US$75 billion in reimbursements to health care providers for expenses or lost revenues that are attributed to the pandemic; US$25 billion to develop, purchase and administer COVID-19 tests; US$62 billion for the *Economic Injury Disaster Loan Program*, including US$50 billion to cover the subsidy costs of loans and US$10 billion for grants; US$60 billion for loan guarantees through community financial institutions, smaller depository institutions, and credit unions.

On August 8, President Trump issued executive orders mainly to extend the expiration dates of certain reliefs provided by previous legislations. These

---

would not otherwise have been eligible for the benefits; those people include self-employed workers, independent contractors, and people without enough work history. It increases the weekly benefit by US$600 through July 31, 2020 and the number of weeks benefit eligibility through December 31, 2020.

10 It funds loan guarantees for loans to small businesses through the PPP to cover payroll and other costs for eight weeks. It also provides debt relief by modifying loans to small businesses made through September 27, 2020, and by expanding eligibility for certain SBA loan programs.

11 It provides US$100 billion to reimburse health care providers, such as hospitals, for expenses or lost revenues that are attributable to the pandemic; US$27 billion, including US$16 billion for the Strategic National Stockpile, for the development and purchase of vaccines, therapeutic treatments and drugs, and medical supplies.

include extending unemployment benefits at a reduced rate of US$300 per week;[12] continuing student loan relief; deferring collections of employee social security payroll taxes; identifying options to help renters and homeowners to avoid evictions and foreclosures respectively.[13]

A potential US$3 trillion stimulus package, the *Health and Economic Recovery Omnibus Emergency Solutions Act* (HEROES Act), was proposed by the House of Representatives Democrats and passed in May and an updated bill with reduced allocations amounting to around US$2.2 trillion was also passed by the House in October, and was sent to the Senate for consideration.[14] The updated bill includes over US$300 billion support for households ($1,200 for each adult, $500 for each child); US$600 per week federal unemployment benefits through January 2021; over US$300 billion for PPP loans for businesses; US$436 billion for state and local government aid; US$225 billion for health responses including funds for testing and tracing, vaccine production and distribution, support for hospitals and health care workers, and US$225 billion funding for education.

Overall, the fiscal measures from the four rounds of legislation are estimated to provide support equaling 3.7 percent of GDP to households, 5.4 percent to businesses, 1.5 percent to the health system, and 2.3 percent for backstopping the Fed's emergency lending program (IMF, 2020a).

1.5 Evaluation of policy measures during the COVID-19 crisis

1.5.1 Comparative assessment of policy measures: the global financial crisis vs. the COVID-19 crisis

The monetary policy responses during the COVID-19 pandemic have been implemented swiftly and with an unprecedented scope and magnitude compared to the measures adopted by the Fed in response to the GFC (Table 1.1). The Fed lowered its policy rates from 5.25 percent in September 2007 to a range of 0 to 0.25 percent in December 2008. While the rate reduction to the lower bound during the GFC took over a year, the Fed moved quickly by reducing the rate by 1.50 percentage points in March when the pandemic started to worsen in the US.

---

12 US$44 billion from Disaster Relief Fund is used to fund the extra unemployment benefits.
13 See Presidential Memoranda for details. www.whitehouse.gov/presidential-actions/memorandum
   -authorizing-needs-assistance-program-major-disaster-declarations-related-coronavirus-disease-2
   019/; www.whitehouse.gov/presidential-actions/memorandum-continued-student-loan-paymen
   t-relief-covid-19-pandemic/; www.whitehouse.gov/presidential-actions/memorandum-deferring
   -payroll-tax-obligations-light-ongoing-covid-19-disaster/; www.whitehouse.gov/presidential-act
   ions/executive-order-fighting-spread-covid-19-providing-assistance-renters-homeowners/.
14 See press release from House Committee on Appropriations for details. https://appropriations.ho
   use.gov/news/press-releases/house-passes-heroes-act; https://appropriations.house.gov/news/press
   -releases/house-passes-updated-heroes-act.

The Fed's assets purchase program, which also helped push down long-term rates, was announced early on in the pandemic and the speed of asset purchases has been faster during the current crisis compared with the GFC. Since the Fed first announced its asset purchase programs in September 2008, its total assets have increased by US$3.5 trillion to US$4.5 trillion in September 2014 when the normalization plan was announced. In response to COVID-19, it took about nine months, from March 2020, for the Fed's total assets to grow by around $2.9 trillion to US$7.2 trillion. Since the epicenter of the GFC was the housing market, the asset purchase programs aimed at reducing the cost of credit for home purchases. Therefore, the initial responses focused on purchasing US Agency mortgage-backed securities and the debt securities of housing related US government agencies (Fannie Mae, Freddie Mac, and the Federal Home Loan banks). The Fed's holdings of mortgage-backed securities and federal agency debt securities increased to US$1.2 trillion in November 2010. Later in March 2009, the Fed announced a program to purchase longer-term Treasury securities and since then the Fed's holdings of Treasury securities have increased by US$1.2 trillion to nearly US$1.7 trillion at the end of 2012. For the COVID-19 crisis, the Fed responded differently by increasing Treasury securities purchases (US$2.1 trillion) compared to mortgage-backed securities and federal agency debt securities (US$0.6 trillion), as the main purpose of the asset purchase program is to lower public and private borrowing rates in general.

In response to the pandemic, the credit facilities used during the GFC have been reinstituted, including the *Primary Dealer Credit Facility*, the *MMLF*, the *Commercial Paper Funding Facility*, and the *Term Asset-backed Securities Loan Facility*. Some of the expired credit facilities that provided liquidity to financial institutions to foster the functioning of financial markets during the GFC were not reintroduced during the current crisis. These include the *Asset-Backed Commercial Paper Money Market Mutual Fund Liquidity Facility* (AMLF), the *Money Market Investor Funding Facility* (MMIFF), and the *Term Securities Lending Facility* (TSLF).[15]

Since March 2020, several new credit facilities to support non-bank corporations, states, and municipal governments or non-profit organizations have been introduced by the Fed. While the *Primary Market Corporate Credit Facility* and *Secondary Market Corporate Credit Facility* were introduced to support larger companies that can issue corporate bonds, the *Main Street Lending Program* aims at providing funding for small and medium sized firms that have been hit hardest during the pandemic. The PPPLF is designed to provide liquidity to financial institutions participating in the PPP and is expected to improve the

---

15 The AMLF was a lending facility used to finance purchases of high-quality asset-backed commercial paper from money market mutual funds. The MMIFF, complementing the AMLF, provides liquidity to US money market investors to facilitate an industry-supported private sector initiative. The TSLF has offered Treasury securities held by the System Open Market Account (SOMA) for loan over a one-month term against other eligible collaterals.

effectiveness of policy measures by linking the monetary and fiscal policies. For the credit facilities supporting states and municipalities, the Fed resisted the idea of backstopping the state and municipal borrowings during the GFC, seeing that as the responsibility of the Administration and Congress. However, the Fed has adopted a new stance to help states and local government better manage cash flow pressures as the pandemic has increased the demand for state and municipal level spending.

The fiscal stimulus provided during the COVID-19 crisis has been much larger (approximately 14 percent of GDP) than the stimulus packages provided during the GFC (Table 1.3). Fiscal policy measures during the GFC amounted to US$1 trillion, around 7 percent of GDP. There were two rounds of legislation in respect of the GFC stimulus programs. First, the *Economic Stimulus Act of 2008*, provided a US$170 billion stimulus, including tax rebates of US$600 to individual taxpayers who were below the income cap of US$75,000 (US$1,200 for married taxpayers filing joint returns less than US$150,000) and additional rebates of US$300 for each child.[16] In early 2009, Congress passed the US$787 billion *American Recovery and Reinvestment Act* to further stimulate the economy.[17] It included US$288 billion in tax cuts and benefits and more than US$150 billion for education, energy, and infrastructure.

In response to stringent government directives heavily restricting economic activity, the US government supports households through large-scale income tax rebates and enhanced unemployment benefits under the CARES Act compared to the programs implemented during the GFC. In respect of fiscal support to business sectors, funding for small firms suffering due to disruptions in face-to-face interactions has been substantial. Large health spending on the testing and tracing of the virus and pandemic-related research is also an important feature of COVID-related spending, which is markedly different from the stimulus packages provided during the GFC.

1.5.2 Assessment of the effectiveness of the policy measures during the COVID-19 crisis

Swift and bold responses by the Fed have played a vital role in boosting financial market sentiment and preventing further amplification of the shocks through the financial system. Financial conditions continued to ease from June, having positive spillover effects on global financial markets. The S&P 500 index exceeded the level it was at the start of the year by 11.2 percent as of the end of November 2020. The equity market performance was boosted largely by the top five S&P tech firms—Apple, Amazon, Microsoft, Google, and Facebook—as the pandemic had highlighted the benefits to such tech giants from societal changes, such as working from home and consumption

16 See further details of the Act available at: www.congress.gov/bill/110th-congress/house-bill/5140.
17 See further details of the Act available at: www.congress.gov/bill/111th-congress/house-bill/1/text.

behavior changes encouraging spending on new technologies. The VIX index fell sharply in May to a level around 20–30, but rose again to 40 right before the presidential election in November, before it dropped to 20 as of end November. The yields on ten-year Treasury securities are broadly unchanged since June and corporate spreads have dropped further benefitting from the Fed's lending facilities. The expansion of swap lines with other central banks and a temporary FIMA Repo Facility have helped to mitigate stress in global dollar funding markets.

The Fed's credit facilities under the Federal Reserve Act 13(3) have played a significant role in stabilizing financial markets and providing credit for otherwise sound borrowers who face a temporary period of low income. Such programs served to boost liquidity in credit markets immediately after their announcement. Direct purchase of non-financial firms' debt administered through the *Main Street Lending Program* is expected to be highly effective during the current crisis, where production is facing significant cash flow shortages (Sims and Wu, 2020).

Although financial markets have been stabilized, the real economy which partly reflects the effectiveness of the policy measures has shown a mixed picture, and the outlook is largely dependent on the path of the pandemic. Real GDP surged at a 33.1 percent annual rate in 2020Q3, partly driven by the lifting of government lockdown measures, but remained below the pre-crisis level (Figure 1.4). The nationwide increase in COVID-19 cases and its impact on economic activities have weighed on growth prospects. Personal saving rates sharply increased to 33.7 percent in April, then fell to 13.6 percent in October, but are still up from around 8 percent prior to the pandemic. The large boost in household income due to government transfers (income tax rebates and unemployment benefits) and compressed consumption has contributed to a spike in personal savings. While the medium-term consumption response to government transfers is difficult to examine at this time, research suggests that the consumption response to the CARES Act will depend on the persistence of the pandemic (Carroll et al., 2020). If the pandemic is short-lived, the combination of unemployment benefits and stimulus payments will be sufficient for a consumption recovery to pre-crisis level. However, if the pandemic persists longer, enhanced unemployment benefits are expected to support consumption especially for the unemployed.

Labor market conditions have improved although most indicators continued to be well below pre-crisis level (Figure 1.7). In October, the unemployment rate fell to 6.9 percent and the labor force participation rate rose to 61.7 percent. Using various traditional and non-traditional high frequency data, Bartik et al. (2020) find that states that received more PPP loans to support small businesses and states with more generous unemployment insurance benefits had milder economic declines and faster recoveries.

Policy measures in response to the pandemic have helped housing-sector activities and prevented or delayed bankruptcies. Home sales activity advanced in 2020Q3, reflecting historically low mortgage rates, continued recovery in jobs, and increased demand due to working from home. The total number of bankruptcy filings by consumers and businesses declined by 40 percent (y/y) in 2020Q2. The *Paycheck Protection Program* and *the Federal Reserve's Main Street Lending Program* together with forbearance policies and moratoria on evictions and foreclosures have helped to reduce financial distress for businesses and consumers alike.

1.6 Conclusions

Given the severity of the COVID crisis, the monetary and fiscal response policies have been implemented swiftly and on an unprecedently large scale. However, this massive monetary and fiscal support came at a substantial cost while cushioning the impact of the pandemic on the macroeconomy. The risk around extended periods of low-for-longer economic activity will lead to a continued increase in debt, especially of non-financial corporations, leaving the economy vulnerable to a potential tightening of financial conditions. The four rounds of existing fiscal stimulus packages along with an additional package under the HEROES Act will increase fiscal deficit and debt levels to an unsustainable level. The federal government's primary deficit rose from around 3 percent of GDP in 2019 to 15 percent of GDP in 2020 and is expected to decrease to 10 percent in 2021 (CBO, 2020; CBO, 2021). The federal debt stood at 100 percent of GDP at the end of fiscal year 2020 and is projected to reach 102 percent of GDP in 2021, decrease slightly for a few years before rising further (CBO, 2021). Moreover, the fiscal stimulus could further widen trade deficits and increase the current account imbalances with trading partners, potentially further escalating trade tensions.

Despite the potential risks, the stimulus packages and the Fed's extraordinary measures provided much-needed support and will help post-pandemic recovery. By providing income tax rebates, enhanced unemployment benefits, and moratoria on evictions and foreclosures, the fiscal measures have helped lessen the lasting scarring effects from the decrease in economic activity. The Fed has responded proactively by introducing new credit facilities including the *Main Street Lending Program* to support the most vulnerable sectors while maintaining the smooth functioning of financial markets.

References

Alexander, D. and Karger, E. 2020. *Do stay-at-home orders cause people to stay at home? Effects of stay-at-home orders on consumer behavior.* (June 22, 2020). FRB of Chicago Working Paper No. 2020-12, Available at SSRN: https://ssrn.com/abstract=3583625 or http://dx.doi.org/10.2139/ssrn.3583625.

Bartik, A.W., Bertrand, M., Lin, F., Rothstein, J. and Unrath, M., 2020. *Measuring the labor market at the onset of the COVID-19 crisis* (No. w27613). Cambridge, MA, USA: National Bureau of Economic Research.

Brinca, P., Duarte, J.B. and Faria-e-Castro, M., 2020. *Measuring sectoral supply and demand shocks during COVID-19.* FRB St. Louis Working Paper, (2020–011).

Carroll, C.D., Crawley, E., Slacalek, J. and White, M.N., 2020. *Modeling the consumption response to the CARES Act*. (No. w27876). National Bureau of Economic Research.

Congressional Budget Office (CBO), 2021. The Budget and Economic Outlook: 2021 to 2031, February 2021. Available at: www.cbo.gov/publication/56970.

Congressional Budget Office (CBO), 2020. The Budgetary Effects of Laws Enacted in Response to the 2020 Coronavirus Pandemic, March and April 2020, June 2020. Available at: www.cbo.gov/publication/56403.

Gupta, S., Montenovo, L., Nguyen, T.D., Rojas, F.L., Schmutte, I.M., Simon, K.I., Weinberg, B.A. and Wing, C., 2020. *Effects of social distancing policy on labor market outcomes* (No. w27280). National Bureau of Economic Research.

Hale, T., Petherick, A., Phillips, T. and Webster, S., 2020. *Variation in government responses to COVID-19*. Blavatnik school of government working paper, 31.

International Monetary Fund (IMF), 2020a. *Staff Report for the 2020 Article IV Consultation, IMF Country Report 2020/241*. Washington, DC: International Monetary Fund.

International Monetary Fund (IMF), 2020b, *World Economic Outlook: The Great Lockdown*. Washington, DC: International Monetary Fund, April.

International Monetary Fund (IMF), 2020c, *World Economic Outlook: A Long and Difficult Ascent*. Washington, DC: International Monetary Fund, October.

Sims, E.R. and Wu, J.C., 2020. *Wall street vs. Main street QE* (No. w27295). National Bureau of Economic Research.

Part II

Monetary and fiscal policies in the euro-area and the EU

2 The Covid-19 Monetary and Fiscal Response in the Euro-Area and the EU

Bernadette Andreosso-O'Callaghan

2.1 Introduction

The long-term growth trajectory of the European Union (EU) and, particularly, of the euro-area therein since 1999, has been marked by: (i) an unimpressive performance in relative terms and, (ii) a number of shocks or sudden structural breaks in real GDP data points, which when persisting beyond two or more quarters developed into recessions and crises. By analyzing the case of the monetary and fiscal response to shocks in the EU and euro-area, this chapter shows that the policy responses to the 2008 global financial crisis (GFC) served as a useful template for the subsequent fine-tuning of the project of economic and monetary union (EMU).

The SARS nCov 2019 virus responsible for the Covid-19 disease, which diffused from Wuhan province, China, and which allegedly took the form of a "pandemic" (according to the World Health Organization, despite relatively low mortality rates) has led to a new sudden structural break. This new shock, referred to as the "Covid-19 crisis" hereafter is an exogenous shock, given its alleged origin outside of the EU, but it is worth recalling that this shock has been largely amplified by inadequate health policies in the EU arising from the Single European Market (SEM). As discussed by Hermann (2010), several rulings by the European Court of Justice, based on European Commission proposals, have led to services – including health services – being gradually considered as an economic activity that needs to comply with the principles of the SEM in terms of free movement of goods, persons, capital, and services. As a result, rules in terms of public procurement – in outsourcing key medical equipment for example – and state aids (state funding) apply also in principle to health care services, and the gradual withdrawal of the state from the public sector can be compensated for by the entry of private investors (see for example Barlow et al., 2010 and also Torchia et al., 2015). The obvious consequence of this "marketization" trend of health care provision in the EU has been the decline in public sector funding across EU countries and in hospital beds, so as to abide by the Maastricht principle of avoiding excessive budgetary deficits and of promoting efficiency in the health sector. It can therefore be argued that the Covid-19 shock can also been considered as being an *endogenous* shock in

DOI: 10.4324/9781003153603-2

the case of the EU, given that those countries that have performed better in dealing with the crisis are also those that have a higher ratio of intensive care unit beds (or acute care beds) per head of the population (such as Germany and Austria) and/or who have been able to respond with a great deal of flexibility in terms of redeploying resources across hospitals (such as Sweden).

The Covid-19 crisis has manifested itself into both a supply and demand shock; on the supply-side, because large sections of the EU economy have been closed down for a number of months (such as retail trade, catering and hotels, transport and entertainment); on the demand-side, because domestic consumption has been heavily suppressed. The central question dealt with in this chapter will be to look at the pertinence of the EU and euro-area monetary and fiscal response to this unprecedented health shock. One aspect which will emerge is the differentiated impact of the shock, in particular across industries and sectors and also across EU countries. Section 2 will look at the macroeconomic indicators before and after the Covid-19 outbreak for the EU as a whole and will briefly discuss the differentiated economic impact of the shock. Section 3 will critically appraise the monetary and fiscal policy measures as a response to the crisis. Section 4 will highlight a number of critical issues that ought to be dealt with, to comply with the aim of economic policy being driven by sustainable and shared economic growth in the EU and in the euro-area. Finally, the main findings will be summarized in the conclusion section.

2.2 Macroeconomic indicators before and since the Covid-19 outbreak

Slow macroeconomic growth has characterized the growth trajectory of the euro-area and of the EU-28 both in the recent past and historically, particularly since the advent of stage 3 of the EMU in 1999. Long-term real GDP growth data do not support the view that the fixing of exchange rates between the currencies of a pool of EU countries since 1999 has invigorated growth among this select group of euro countries above and beyond that of the EU as a whole; understandably, this EU generalization conceals notable differences across EU countries, as will be discussed later.[1] According to EU Commission data (2020a), GDP growth fell by −3.3 percent in 2020Q1 globally, and this corresponds to the sharpest contraction since World War 2 (WWII). For the year 2020 as a whole, the contraction of GDP is forecast to be −4.3 percent at the world level, versus a GDP slump of −7.4 percent for the EU-27 (and −7.8 for the euro-area), with the euro-area performing yet again less well than the EU-27. A strong rebound of growth was perceptible during the third quarter of 2020, but this was halted by the introduction of a second

---

1 At the time of writing, the euro-area comprises 19 member countries (see the list in the Appendix). This chapter will relate to the European Union of 27 countries unless otherwise specified; data and information on the UK will be added for comparative purposes.

round of confinement measures from the end of 2020Q3; all such measures impinging once again mostly on some particular sectors of activity, such as transport, catering and hotels, retail trade, the arts, and entertainment. A comparative analysis with previous recessions, and/or crises (such as the 1974 oil shock) in what is known today as the euro-area, shows that the return to pre-recession levels of economic activity is expected to take longer, until 2024Q4 (EU Commission, 2020b). The only exception is the economic recession of 2008, which started in the first quarter of that year, and which subsequently developed into a global financial/economic crisis; with the 2008 GFC, a full return to the pre-recession real GDP level in the euro-area happened indeed after several years. This compares with a little more than a one-year recovery period in the case of the 1974 oil shock and seven quarters in the case of the 1992 currency speculation shock.

During a typical recession, private domestic consumption falls less than the other components of GDP, and it tends to be less sensitive to a recovery when compared with foreign consumption (exports) and investment (Gross Fixed Capital Formation or GFCF); this is in line with the permanent income hypothesis. The severe containment measures implemented to combat the spread of the SARS nCov-2019 virus, combined with much uncertainty, have led to extremely limited consumption opportunities and, not surprisingly, to private domestic consumption falling more than GDP during the first two quarters of 2020. With the closure of many retail outlets, restaurants, and cultural goods venues such as cinemas, consumption opportunities shrank, leading to a noteworthy change of consumption patterns with for example the share of non-durable goods increasing and that of services and durable goods falling. Investment, which is normally a much more volatile component of GDP during times of uncertainty, declined by more than 18 percent in the EU as a whole during the January–July 2020 period. The fall of net trade (exports – imports) is less important whereas disrupted consumption patterns and disrupted supply value added chains led to a positive increase in stocks (European Commission (2020a).

Economic uncertainty explains the postponing of investment decisions by firms. A myriad of emergency measures (see section 3) have kept firms solvent and have helped protect jobs and incomes in the short and medium term. These measures have enabled the easing of favorable financing conditions, allowing firms to build cash buffers, at least in the case of some firms and some industries (Banerjee et al., 2020). Protecting jobs has meant that in Ireland for example – a euro-area country that was able to embark upon a strong growth momentum in 2015 – the Covid-19 adjusted unemployment rate was close to 30 percent in May 2020, up from 4.8 percent in January 2020 (CSO, 2020).

As hinted at above, a striking feature of the Covid-19 crisis is its differentiated impact, at several levels of analysis. First and in terms of real GDP growth, the crisis has hit primarily countries such as Spain (–12.4 percent in 2020), Italy (–9.9 percent), Portugal (–9.3 percent), France (–9.4 percent), Belgium (–8.4 percent), and Slovakia (–7.5 percent), all euro-area member countries.

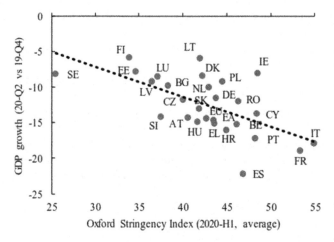

Figure 2.1 Oxford stringency index and GDP growth in EU countries (Q2 of 2020 versus Q4 of 2019). Source: EU Economic Forecast, Autumn 2020, Brussels (p. 15).

By contrast, countries such as Lithuania (–2.2 percent), Sweden (–3.4 percent), and Poland (–3.6 percent), the latter two EU countries not being members of the euro-area, have managed to minimize the adverse economic impact of the Covid-19 crisis (European Commission, 2020b). A notable exception is the case of Ireland, an euro-area economy that experienced a positive growth rate of 3 percent in 2020 (as confirmed subsequently by the European Commission's Winter 2020 Economic Forecast) (Burke Kennedy (2020); European Commission (2020b)).

Interestingly, Sweden is one of the rare countries in the EU, and also in the western world, that has not imposed any containment measures. The question arises as to the pertinence of halting large sections of economic activity in times of a "mild" pandemic, and in particular after the summer months.[2] An answer is provided by the *Oxford Stringency Index* which is a composite index of eight containment measures and of one health component.[3] The index shown in Figure 2.1 relates to the measures implemented during March and April 2020, when they reached the highest level.[4]

---

2 "Mild" in relation to influenza and to other viral diseases. According to Ioannidis (in press), the infection fatality rates of the Covid-19 disease, based on 61 studies (74 estimates), ranged from 0.00 percent to 1.63 percent and the median rate was found to be 0.27 percent; this suggests huge variations in reported case-fatality rates, a normal feature for viral diseases and this is in line with other comparable viral illnesses (Gøtzsche, 2020).

3 The containment measures to limit the spread of the virus are: the closure of schools, of the workplace; the cancellation of public events; restrictions on gathering size; the closure of public transport; stay-at-home requirements; and restrictions on internal and international movements.

4 Note that the situation eased somewhat during the summer 2020 and tightened again in September 2020 with several Member States imposing restrictions again in response to the resurgence of "cases", albeit with much lower mortality rates than during the spring of 2020.

Figure 2.1 shows a clear connection between the level of stringency during the first months of the health crisis and the overall level of economic disruption in terms of negative GDP growth. It shows that countries with the lowest levels of stringency (Sweden, Estonia, Finland, Latvia, and Luxembourg) suffered least in terms of GDP contraction over the 2019Q4–2020Q2 period. Conversely, countries with the highest stringency levels (Italy, France, Portugal, Cyprus, and Spain) had the sharpest GDP contractions over the same period. A notable exception is Ireland, where a relative resilience to the Covid-19 shock is due to the productive structure and specialization of the economy, with a differentiated impact across two distinctive groups of sectors (Andreosso-O'Callaghan, 2020; Fitzgerald, 2020). Ireland is indeed relatively specialized in two industries that have been able to withstand the Covid-19 debacle: the pharmaceutical industry in the manufacturing sector, and financial services in the services sector.[5] Given the country's still tight economic links with the UK, Ireland is however subject to two different shocks, namely Covid-19 and Brexit; when crossing the impact of both shocks, it is found that the hospitality and construction sectors have been the most severely affected sectors by the health crisis, but that they have also been rather sheltered from the Brexit shock. A reverse scenario applies to the case of the financial and insurance sector (Daly and Lawless, 2020).

Another differentiated impact across the euro-area and EU countries is in terms of the unemployment performance. Clearly, the Covid-19 crisis amplifies the disequilibrium existing in the countries' labor markets; the countries with unemployment rates which were "sticky" at a high level before the Covid-19 crisis (such as Greece, Spain, and Italy) experienced an increase in unemployment. The differentiated impact can further be explained by the productive structure and industrial specialization of the different countries. Again, whereas tradable goods, retail, transport, and hospitality (including entertainment/arts) have been the most affected industries and sectors, others such as packaging, pharmaceutical, and financial services have been the least affected. Consequently, EU countries with large tourism sectors (Greece, Cyprus, Malta, Italy, Spain, and also France) have been particularly hit.

The differentiated impact can also be seen across regions in the same country, increasing the urban/rural divide in certain cases, and also across different income groups. At the world level, there is a reversal of global poverty trends although poverty reduction was slowing before the Covid-19 crisis at the world level. Worldwide, the policy response to the Covid-19 crisis has been hitting already-poor and vulnerable people, while also creating millions of "new poor"; the World Bank (2020) estimates that an additional 88 million

---

5 Ranking well before the food, chemical products, and computers industries, the pharmaceutical industry is indeed the largest manufacturing industry in Ireland in terms of net selling value (NSV). In 2018, this industry represented about 40 percent of the total manufacturing NSV (or half of that of the "big four"), compared with only 3.5 percent for the EU as a whole (CSO, 2020).

to 115 million people will fall into the extreme poverty group in 2020, with a total that could rise to as many as 150 million by 2021. About 82 percent of the people falling into the extreme poverty category will be in middle-income countries. At the EU level, figures by Eurostat (2020) show that the low-income earners present higher risks for both being on layoff schemes and losing their job all together in most EU countries. These workers, who are below the risk of poverty threshold (i.e. 60 percent of the national median disposable income), face a higher probability of suffering from the policies implemented in response to the Covid-19 crisis. This implies that, generally, the labor market shocks caused by the health crisis have a stronger impact on the disadvantaged group of workers. Again, the impact differs across EU countries with countries such as Spain, Italy, and Cyprus being more affected. As reported by *Le Monde* (2020), the 2020 health crisis has been responsible for an extra 1 million people falling into poverty in the case of France; this adds to the already high level of 9.3 million people living below the poverty threshold before the crisis in that country.[6]

2.3 Monetary and budgetary policy measures as a response to the Covid-19 crisis

This section will highlight the main types of policy response at EU and euro-area levels to the Covid-19 crisis, and the focus of this section is on the 19 euro-area countries, given the constraint represented by fixed exchange rates therein and the perceived necessity to safeguard the architecture of monetary union. A brief reminder of the measures taken in the aftermath of the 2008 global financial crisis will help understand the platform upon which the specific Covid-19 centered measures were devised.

A first strand of immediate measures taken in March 2020 saw an extension of pre-existing key programs involving the mobilization of EU budget resources or of EU budget-linked resources: (i) by revising the multiannual financial framework, and (ii) by devising an emergency European Recovery Instrument, a temporary instrument aimed at raising additional financing on the financial markets (see below). Additional resources at the EU level were therefore immediately made available for budgetary commitment from the existing Structural Funds (ERDF, ESF, and Cohesion Fund)[7] under the "investment for growth and jobs goal" for the period 2020/22 (EU Commission, 2020c). This shows a great deal of flexibility in the implementation of the programs supported by the ERDF and ESF. Other EU-based funding vehicles such as

---

6 This critical threshold is calculated at 1,063 euros per month and by unit of consumption, and it concerned some 14.8 percent of all French households in 2018.

7 European Regional Development Fund (ERDF) and European Social Fund (ESF) which are part of the EU budget. Note that the reference to the Funds is complemented or replaced by a reference to the "REACT-EU" project (Recovery Assistance for Cohesion and the Territories of Europe).

the European Investment Bank (EIB) loans, and the European Investment Fund in support of SME need also to be mentioned.

A second group of measures falls within the ambit of monetary policy proper (Section 2.3.1), whereas the last type of measures are monetary and fiscal policy measures (Section 2.3.2).

2.3.1 Monetary measures at the euro-area and EU levels

With the 2008 global financial crisis, and after much "muddling through" behavior by the EU Commission and the ECB at the time, the ECB eventually switched to "new monetary policy" tools – i.e. to non-standard measures – in 2012. Consequently, the ECB's Asset Purchase Program (APP) was initiated in mid-2014 to support the monetary policy transmission mechanism in the euro-area, as part of measures including targeted long-term refinancing operations. The APP consists of the corporate sector purchase program (CSPP), the public sector purchase program (PSPP), the asset-backed securities purchase program (ABSPP) and the third covered bond purchase program (CBPP3). Monthly net purchases under the ECB's APP were €20 billion from November 2019.[8] With the Covid-19 pandemic starting in February 2020 in the EU, this new monetary policy tool was expanded with the ECB Governing Council adding on 12 March 2020 an envelope of additional net asset monthly purchases of €120 billion until the end of 2020. The ECB Governing Council expects these purchases to be temporary and therefore to end with the end of the 2020 pandemic, before it starts raising the key ECB interest rates. Table A in the Appendix depicts the different tranches of the APP by type of sub-program between 2015 and December 2020. The predominance of the PSPP in the total APP, when compared for example to the CSPP, is striking (Figure 2.2). The 2020 ECB measures in respect to the Covid-19 outbreak are therefore a continuation and amplification of measures taken since the mid-2010s by the ECB. As a result of the APP cumulative net purchases program, the stock of eurosystem APP bonds amounted to €2,999 billion at the end of October 2020. Figure 2.2 illustrates the cumulative APP net purchases by category as stipulated above.

The temporary envelope of additional net asset purchases created in March 2020, known as the Pandemic Emergency Purchase Programme (PEPP), is supposedly aimed at minimizing and neutralizing the risks posed by the Covid-19 outbreak to the euro-area economy. The envelope of the PEPP increased from €750 billion in March 2020 to €1,350 billion at the end of October 2020,

---

8 Note that the monthly purchase pace averaged €60 billion from March 2015 to March 2016; €80 billion from April 2016 to March 2017; €60 billion from April 2017 to December 2017; €30 billion from January 2018 to September 2018; €15 billion from October 2018 to December 2018 (Source: ECB – Eurosystem – Monetary Policy, available at: www.ecb.europa.eu/mopo/implement/omt/htm l/index.en.html, accessed on 3 November 2020).

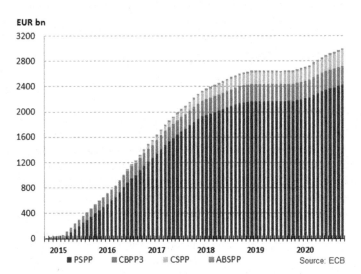

Figure 2.2 Cumulative APP net purchases by program category (January 2015–December 2020; in € bn). Source: European Central Bank – Eurosystem – Monetary Policy; available at: www.ecb.europa.eu/mopo/implement/omt/html/index.en.html

based on several ECB Governing Council decisions. In December 2020, the PEEP program was extended further by another €500bn, reaching thus a new total of €1,850 billion. It is interesting to note that the Governing Council declared in December 2020 that it will terminate net asset purchases under the PEPP once "it *judges* that the COVID-19 crisis phase is over, but in any case not before the end of March 2022" (sic!).[9] In the case of the public sector securities under this scheme, the allocation across euro-area central banks follows a *capital key* of the various central banks. As a result, the allocation of cumulative net purchases of public sector securities under the PEPP at the end of September 2020 was the largest for the German Bundesbank, followed by the Banca d'Italia, which received some 12 percent more than the Banque de France. With the different extensions of the asset purchase program and the inability of the EU and EU governments to bring an adequate response, it follows that the *temporary* nature of this asset purchase program of private and public sector securities is open to debate.

Other monetary policy easing measures decided and implemented by the ECB Governing Council include the pandemic long-term refinancing operations (PELTROs), still in support of the euro-area financial system. This comes

9 It should be noted that all asset categories eligible under the existing APP become also eligible under the new PEEP. Also, the maturing principal payments from securities purchased under the PEPP will be reinvested until at least the end of 2023. For more in this, the interested reader can refer to: www.ecb.europa.eu/mopo/implement/pepp/html/index.en.html accessed on 25 January 2021.

in addition to the third series of targeted longer-term refinancing operations (TLTRO III) which supports bank lending to firms and to households. Finally, the "new" monetary policy tools such as zero, near-zero, and negative interest rates have been re-conducted. Interest rates on the main refinancing operations, on the marginal lending facility and on deposit facilities will remain unchanged at 0.00 percent, 0.25 percent and −0.50 percent respectively. The Governing Council of the ECB expects the key ECB interest rates to remain at their present low levels until the inflation rates converge to a level sufficiently close to, but below, the 2 percent mark (ECB, 2020). Also, the temporary loosening of bank's capital requirements, in order to boost banks' lending, ought to be mentioned (Botta et al., 2020).

The table in the main Appendix of this book shows how the main policy measures of the ECB, as a response to the Covid-19 crisis, compare with policies by the US Federal Reserve and by the central banks of other major economies not studied in this book, such as Canada, Russia, and Australia.

2.3.2 Other monetary and fiscal policy measures for 2021 and beyond

The twin issue of debt mutualization and of solidarity has re-surfaced quite prominently in EU debates during the GFC and even more so since the outbreak of the Covid-19 crisis. Crises revive the debate on the necessity of supranational borrowing in Europe, a debate that goes back to the 1975 Community Loan Mechanism which was set up as a response to the impact of the oil shocks on the then European Community (EC); the EC Commission was then empowered to issue bonds in favor of crisis-hit countries and these bonds were guaranteed by the Community budget (Horn et al., 2020). During the discussions following the outbreak of the 2008 GFC, proposals were mooted to pool pre-existing national debt, and to create a permanent treasury-like body, proposals that did not come to fruition. With the recent Covid-19 outbreak, the view finally prevailed that a temporary mechanism to mutualize the costs of the crisis should be introduced and that this would take the form of a one-off joint or supranational bond issuance. Debt mutualization implies again that the EU budget would act both as a guarantee and as the vehicle for disbursement (Eisl and Tomay, 2020).

It is in this evolving context that the Recovery Fund (or "Next Generation EU" Fund) of €750bn was finally agreed on 23 July 2020, the fruit of a compromise between the lukewarm countries such as Germany and other northern EU countries on the one hand, and the Southern EU countries on the other. On 23 April 2020, the European Council had been endorsing the "Roadmap for Recovery" which contains a strong investment component and it had mandated the EU Commission to "analyze the needs so that the resources would be targeted towards the sectors and geographical parts of the Union most affected, while clarifying also the link with the Multiannual Financial Framework for 2021–27" (EU Commission, 2020c: 9). Conceived therefore in addition to the multiannual financial framework 2021/27 of €1.07 trillion, the Recovery Fund comprises some €390bn in grants and the rest (€360bn) in loans. The allocation of bonds by country, issued in the name of the EU, will be overseen by the EU Commission. The attractiveness of the mechanism is clear for highly indebted countries which can still refinance themselves on the international financial markets (attracting AAA ratings).

These crisis-response mechanisms devised at the EU level set the framework within which the different individual EU country members can design specific measures in order, for example, to support their industrial sectors most affected by the Covid-2019 crisis. For example, in September 2020, the EU Commission approved a €6bn aid package by the German government to the German airline company Deutsche Lufthansa AG in order to recapitalize the company. This measure falls under the ambit of the State Aid Temporary Framework adopted by the EU Commission on 19 March 2020 (EU Commission, 2020), bearing in mind that state aids are prohibited under EU competition law but that they can be *temporarily* re-introduced in cases of major economic shocks. Other companies in this industry have recently benefited from state aids, such as SAS (Scandinavian Airlines), Finnair, TAP Air Portugal, Air France as well as KLM.[10] Many countries, such as Ireland for example, have been able to disburse pandemic unemployment payments (PUP) since the very beginning of the Covid-19 crisis in order to minimize the adverse effect on their economy and society. Other schemes include also differed tax payments in some countries, all measures with a direct impact on the public finances of the euro-area and EU countries, an issue to which that needs to be further investigated.

From the above, it can be inferred that many of the described monetary and budgetary policy measures imply that sovereign debt levels will continue to soar, an issue to which we now turn.

2.4 New monetary policy: implications and the issue of sustainability

As a direct consequence of the expansion of the ECB quantitative easing (QE) program, stock markets have recovered since April 2020 and have become less volatile. Moreover, the euro has been able sustain its parity (or has appreciated) vis-à-vis other major currencies such as the US$, the Japanese Yen, the Yuan, and the Polish zloty outside the euro-area bloc. The QE program has been well received by international investors with for example the ten-year German bund yields oscillating between −0.3 and −0.6 percent in 2020Q2 (*The Financial Times*, 8 December). In the medium to long-term, a number of questions and issues arise, first and foremost the issue of increasing sovereign debts.

10 Note that, at the time of writing, these decisions have being challenged by the CEO of the low cost carrier Ryanair, on the basis that these decisions undermine the principle of fair competition in the SEM.

2.4.1 The question of the sovereign debt

The most obvious impact of the monetary policy response to Covid-19 is in terms of the swelling of the ECB balance sheet, and also of other euro-area and EU central banks' balance sheets. The balance sheet of the ECB increased by 21.02 percent in the first months of 2020 (up to 5 June) and reached the unprecedented amount of €5.66 trillion. This increase compares with +71.76 percent for the FED (up to 10 June), +30.41 percent for the Bank of England (up to 10 June), and +10.26 percent for the Bank of Japan (ECB, 2020). The impact of the ECB asset purchase programs on the money base needs to be scrutinized. Recent figures released by the ECB (2020) show a sudden upward surge of the money base in the euro-area (M1, M2, and M3) since the spring of 2020 (see Graph 2.A1 in the Appendix and Figure 2.3). In particular, by assessing the recent evolution of M3, which is the sum of M2, repurchase agreements, money market fund shares/units, and debt securities with a maturity of up to two years, it can be seen that its different allocations since the Covid-2019 crisis has favored credit to general governments as opposed to the private sector (Figure 2.3).

As a result, and not surprisingly, a related issue is the impact that the ECB asset repurchase programs is having on the sovereign debt of the different euro-area and EU countries. Since only part of the public debt in the EU is mutualized, with a common issuing of bonds at the EU level, and owing to the

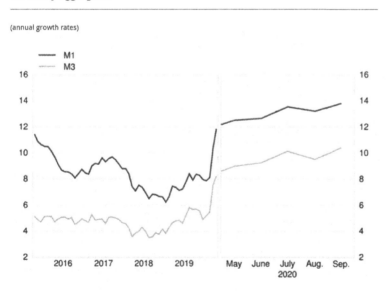

Graph 2.A1 – Evolution of Monetary Aggregates – euro-area (2016 – September 2020). Source: ECB, European Central Bank, Directorate General Communications, Press Release, Monetary Developments in the euro area: September 2020, 27 October 2020.

Contribution of the M3 counterparts to the annual growth rate of M3

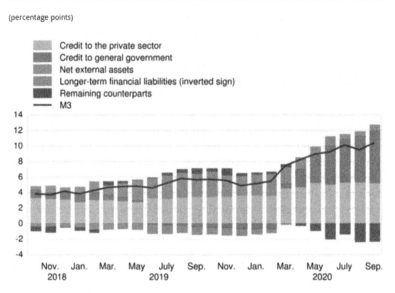

Figure 2.3 Contributions of the M3 counterparts to the annual growth of M3. Source: ECB, European Central Bank, Directorate General Communications, Press Release, Monetary Developments in the euro area: September 2020, 27 Oct 2020.

allocation per country, the different euro-area and EU countries are saddled with an increasing sovereign debt burden, in contradiction with the stringent Maastricht rules which are temporarily suspended during times of crises (Table 2.1). In the case of Ireland, a country that performs relatively well in terms of debt/GDP data, the issuance of Irish Government bonds by 30 June 2020 was already 4.3 times that for the entire year of 2019 (Department of Finance, 2020). The debt/GDP ratio of euro-area countries such as Greece (187.4 percent), Italy (149.4 percent), Belgium (115.3 percent), France (114.1 percent), and Spain (110.1 percent) at the end of the summer of 2020, are worthy of specific consideration. In the case of Italy alone, the government debt is expected to rise to almost 160 percent of GDP in 2021. Also, and relatedly, many countries are running budget deficits above 10 percent of GDP, including Italy, France, and Spain.

Another long-term question arising from the ECB monetary policy response to recent crises and in particular to the Covid-19 shock, is the question of whether the sovereign debt is being monetized, that is, of whether the ECB creates money *ex nihilo* as a counterpart of the debt. Although price stability is still the over-riding objective of the ECB, with an inflation rate expected to converge to a level sufficiently close to, but below, the 2 percent mark, its monetary policy has been focusing on the objectives of low interest rates and

Table 2.1 Debt/GDP levels (EU countries and euro-area countries, 2008–2020Q2)

Summarized data	Currency	2008	2015	2019	2020 (Q2 latest data)
Euro-area – 19 countries (from 2015)	–	69.6	90.9	84	95.1
Euro-area – 18 countries (2014)	–	69.8	91.1	84.2	-
EU (27 countries – from 2020)	–	64.9	84.8	77.6	-
EU (28 countries)	–	61.3	84.9	79.2	87.8
EU (27 countries – 2007–2013)	–	61.4	84.9	79.2	-

Euro-Area Member Countries	**Currency**	**2008**	**2015**	**2019**	**2020 (Q2 latest data)**
Austria	EUR	68.7	84.9	70.5	82.6
Belgium	EUR	93.2	105.2	98.1	115.3
Cyprus	EUR	45.5	107.2	94	113.2
Estonia	EUR	4.5	10	8.4	18.5
Finland	EUR	32.6	63.6	59.3	68.7
France	EUR	68.8	95.6	98.1	114.1
Germany	EUR	65.5	72.3	59.6	67.4
Greece	EUR	109.4	177	180.5	187.4
Ireland	EUR	42.4	76.7	57.4	62.7
Italy	EUR	106.2	135.3	134.7	149.4
Latvia	EUR	18.6	37.1	36.9	42.9
Lithuania	EUR	14.6	42.5	35.9	41.4
Luxembourg	EUR	15.4	22	22	23.8
Malta	EUR	61.8	55.9	42.6	51.1
Netherlands	EUR	54.7	64.7	48.7	55.2
Portugal	EUR	75.6	131.2	117.2	126.1
Slovakia	EUR	28.6	51.9	48.5	60.2
Slovenia	EUR	21.8	82.6	65.6	78.2
Spain	EUR	39.7	99.3	95.5	110.1

Non Euro-Area Member Countries	**Currency**	**2008**	**2015**	**2019**	**2020 (Q2 latest data)**
Bulgaria	BGN	13	26	20.2	21.3
Croatia	HRK	39.3	84.3	72.8	85.3
Czech Republic	CZK	28.1	39.7	30.2	39.9
Denmark	DKK	33.3	39.8	33.3	41.4
Hungary	HUF	71.8	75.8	65.4	70.3
Poland	PLN	46.7	51.3	45.7	55.1
Romania	RON	12.3	37.8	35.3	41.1
Sweden	SEK	37.5	43.7	35.1	37.1
United Kingdom	GBP	49.3	86.7	85.4	96.6

Source: EUROSTAT https://ec.europa.eu/eurostat/tgm/table.do?tab=table&init=1&language=en &pcode=teina225&plugin=1 (Accessed on 15 September 2020).

of resorting to the so-called "helicopter money" strategy as emphasized with the new 2020 health crisis. With respect to the inflation rate, the low inflation rate observed since the outbreak of the Covid-19 crisis (rather than deflation) can be explained by the parallel increase of the demand for (mostly by the public sector) and supply of money; the deflationary trends generated by firm closures, job destruction, and purchases of gold have all been more than compensated for by the quantitative easing strategy of the ECB.[11] Artus (2020) argues that there is no pure money creation in the case of the ECB; assets are stockpiled into the central banks of the euro-system and, through a monetary policy centered on interest rates, liquidity to the financial system is being made available. As a result, there is no monetization of debt, but rather a simple swap between reserves and assets, as in the case of the FED. According to this author, the real problem is therefore not so much the excess of government debt per se, but rather the consequences of the monetary financing of public deficits (and in particular the problem of inflated assets and, by extension, of another substantial leap into the "financialization" of the euro-area and EU economies).

Another related problem is the time frame implied by the issuance of bonds, with all liabilities to be repaid by the end of 2058 in the case of the Recovery Fund. Even if done centrally and in the name of the European Institutions, borrowing on international financial markets will place a heavy burden on the Multiannual Financial Framework of the EU for several decades and thereafter on generations to come.[12] The related question that arises at this juncture is whether the EU (and the euro-area therein) can afford a Japanese-style sovereign debt level, given the lack of both a social and cultural cohesion and solidarity in the EU, by contrast to the Japanese case (see the Chapter on Japan in this volume).

It is therefore clear that the conversion of the ECB to the tenets of new monetary policy thinking brings the key question of sustainability to the fore. A number of solutions to these issues have been proffered.

2.4.2 Solutions to the EU and euro-area sovereign debt problem

The different solutions that can respond to the mounting debt problem are as follows: economic growth and inflation; structural change; debt cancellation; EU Institutions and their credibility; other solutions.

---

11 Note that the situation is reminiscent of a *liquidity trap*, where increases in money supply are fully absorbed by excess demand for money (liquidity); because of the near-to-zero interest rates, investors and households hoard the increased money available instead of spending it because the opportunity cost of holding cash is zero.

12 The name "Next Generation EU" could ironically suggest that the time frame for repayment will be extended over the next generation. This begs the question as to the sustainability of the EU funding mechanism, since sustainability implies precisely minimizing the impact of today's policies on the next generation.

1. Economic growth and/or inflation

Theoretically, inflation would gradually erode government debt but this solution is limited by the key objective of the ECB, which is price stability within a certain target in terms of inflation. After the 2008 GFC, very few countries in the euro-area and in the EU have been able to embark upon a path of sustained growth so as to allow a decline in their debt/GDP ratio; these few countries are Ireland (thanks to its tight economic connections with the US economy), the Netherlands and to some extent, Luxembourg. One way for growth to resume is to allow a country to go through a period of structural change.

2. Structural change

Structural change refers to a major change in the productive structure, normally thanks to technological change leading to substantial total productivity gains. The work of Wallerstein (1979) based on Kondratiev's cycle theory describes how the capitalist process follows long cycles which are themselves determined by major technological breakthroughs (or radical innovations as opposed to incremental innovations). The 1929 Great Depression ended in the USA first in the early 1940s with notable structural change epitomized by the new era of computerization. By contrast, the 2008 GFC did not lead to structural change; it proceeded in parallel with rather low growth rates generally, combined with unemployment rates sustained at high levels, with a few exception in the euro-area and in the EU as discussed above. It is extremely doubtful whether the much awaited "Industry 4.0" cum 5G industrial "revolution", as the next major structural change in sight, will solve the problem of unemployment and growth, although it might lead to substantial productivity gains.

3. Debt cancellation

The idea of debt cancellation, which goes a priori against the spirit of the EU Treaty, is nevertheless curiously very much in vogue in certain EU global circles and among senior Italian officials who suggest that the ECB could forgive debt bought through its asset purchase program or else it could swap it for perpetual bonds, which will never be repaid (*The Financial Times*, 9 December 2020). In particular, Micossi (2020) suggests that a substantial share of the debt purchased by the European System of Central Banks (ESCB), corresponding to 20 percent of euro-area GDP, could gradually be transferred to the European Stability Mechanism (ESM). These assets would be rolled over and would become equivalent to irredeemable bonds; this means that the ESM would issue its own assets in international financial markets with the ECB and central banks of the system acting as guarantors. The idea of (partial) debt cancellation is far from convincing all parties involved in monetary policy, for the risk in terms of destabilizing consequences and trust in the EU institutions needs to be noted, an issue to which we now turn.

4. The credibility of the EU institutions

It can be seen that a lot of the debt question revolves around the issue of credibility of the EU-based issuing institutions, institutions that need to be perceived by investors as a guarantor of the bond. In this vein, other assets can be pooled and can play the role of guarantee or collateral. For example, the assets of households and firms in a country, including banks deposits – which have been increasing formidably since the advent of Covid-19 –, are ultimately the guarantee of last resort of the sovereign debt. A rather extreme view needs to be mentioned here: already in 2017, the French Think Tank *France Stratégie*, advisor of the French Prime Minister at the time, had mooted the idea of nationalizing residential land to compensate for the mounting sovereign debt. This extreme view would pool de facto all French, and further afield all EU residential land assets into a Leninist China-type market, something that goes radically against the spirit of national Constitutional Law in several EU countries, and that would undoubtedly stir further major social unrest.[13]

5. Other probable solutions

The EU has nevertheless been stirring up the idea to let the debt servicing costs be picked up by the EU multiannual financial framework. This implies that other sources of funding for the €750bn Recovery Fund and for other safeguard initiatives need to be found. To that effect, new environmental levies and digital taxes are being mooted in EU circles so as to beef up the "own" resources of the EU budget. This is in line with the EU Commission insistence on promoting initiatives in the area of a "green" and "digital" economy. Obviously, this ultimate solution, which is the most likely in the medium term given the inability of the euro-area *in toto* to grow, seems to be the preferred option. The downside of this solution is that it will, yet again, increase the fiscal burden of EU households and that it will reignite the social cohesion issue, which comes back as a central issue that needs to be tackled.

2.4.3 The question of sustainability

To conclude this section, one ought to highlight the limits of the new monetary policy implemented by the ECB since the 2008 GFC and expanded dramatically with the new Covid-19 crisis. Although some euro-area and EU

---

13 For example, in Ireland and in Italy, private property is a fundamental natural right enshrined in these countries' respective Constitutions (Article 42 for Italy and article 43 for Ireland). The transfer of private property to the State can be done only under the motive of general interest with a monetary indemnity.

banks are better capitalized than in 2008 – in part through the accumulation of forced and/or precautionary savings since the Covid-19 crisis erupted – and although these banks seem to be more resilient to shocks, the prolonged closure of businesses during what has been termed the "second wave" of the epidemic and during the *expected* "third wave" in 2021 (sic!) could provoke another major macroeconomic shock and financial crisis. In several countries, such as France, Italy, and Belgium, the liquidity problems of firms could turn into insolvency problems in the medium term, with the usual cohort of bankruptcies and redundancies.[14] The consequence is the building up of a hidden leverage on the banks' balance sheets in the form of derivatives, swaps etc. Finally, the printing of money, even though backed by assets, combined with very low or near-zero interest rates, tends to prop up asset prices, a phenomenon that has been observed on stock markets during 2020. These inflated assets can be interpreted as the prelude of another financial crisis with, yet again, another blow to the confidence in the euro-area financial system. When added to the need of finding new own resources through higher taxation, in some already highly taxed jurisdictions such as France, the policies to combat the health crisis seem therefore to be bringing to the fore the crucial issue of sustainability.

2.5 Conclusion

This chapter has shown that, owing to the cold shower represented by the 2008 GFC, the euro-area (and EU) have been relatively responsive to the Covid-19 crisis by implementing monetary policy easing measures, in particular by injecting additional liquidity to support credit to households and firms, resorting like the FED, to non-conventional tools of monetary policy. In particular, the ECB launched new series of PELTROs in support of the euro-area financial system as well as the PEPP launched in March 2020 with an initial envelope of €600bn and increased to €1,350bn during the following summer. Subsequently, partial debt mutualization has proceeded with the €750 Recovery Fund (or "Next Generation EU" Fund) which functions as a means to provide macroeconomic assistance to member states in times of economic distress and to support national expenditure or investment among its main objectives. The Recovery Fund and other REACT-EU initiatives imply additional budgetary commitments for the years 2020 and beyond, which will be "financed from external assigned revenues" (EU Commission, 2020c: 5).

The implications of this new monetary policy implemented by the ECB are multifold. First, the size of both the public deficit and sovereign debt has soared in all EU countries under review, opening the question of their sustainability and a number of solutions and ways forward have been suggested in terms of

---

14 Note that in his debt-deflation theory of Great Depressions, Fisher (1933) argued that over-indebtedness can lead to deflation and subsequently to the liquidation of collateralized debt.

debt cancellation for example. Second, the financing of these costly measures through additional "assigned revenues" to the EU budget implies a higher fiscal burden placed on EU households and firms particularly SMEs in the years to come, aggravating the problem of social cohesion. Third, ideas in terms of industrial policies on how to revive economic growth in the real economy of both the euro-area and the EU as a whole have been kept in the background, apart from the pre-Covid-19 discussion surrounding Industry 4.0 cum G5 (or "fourth industrial revolution"); the latter is far from boosting the labor market as required since the fourth industrial revolution is precisely aimed at saving a large portion of jobs in the manufacturing and services sectors.

In particular, too little emphasis has been placed on the key issue at stake in this health crisis which is to address the weakness of the EU health *filière*. The health *filière* includes sub-sets of the chemicals and pharmaceutical sectors as well as the health service sector (Andreosso-O'Callaghan, 2020). Owing to its manufacturing specialization in the pharmaceutical industry (Nace Code 21) which accounts for about 40 percent of its total manufacturing sales, Ireland, a small open economy at the very edge of Europe, is specifically well positioned in the manufacturing part of this *filière*, implying that every EU country can optimally be embedded in this *filière* making the EU a sovereign entity in this area. What needs to be changed are the EU policies. Given that in the future viral epidemics of the SARS type could be the normal course of events – as has actually been the case in the past – building such a strong *filière* at the EU level should be a top priority of EU policy. Constructing a sovereign health *filière* would reverse dramatically the EU policy of "marketization" of health care provision in the EU, which has led, for example, to the disappearance of intensive care unit (ICU) beds all along since the 2000s due to the exigencies of the EU Treaty principles such as avoidance of excessive budgetary deficits and promotion of efficiency in the sector. In spite of these obvious lines of action, there is very little evidence, at the time of writing, that such is the willingness of EU policymakers, starting with the EU Commission; the latter blindly follows its deterministic approach of favoring a "green" and "digital" EU economy. As a result, the sustainability of the euro-area as a monetary union, and of the EU as an entire economic project, are at stake, and the social cohesion issue is bound to gain paramount importance in the future.

References

Andreosso-O'Callaghan, B. (2020), "Industrial policy response to the Covid19 crisis in Ireland – a filière approach", *Symphonya – Emerging Issues in Management*, Special issue on The New European Industrial Strategy: Companies and Territories, (2), 80–88. DOI: http://dx.doi.org/10.4468/2020.2.09andreosso

Artus Patrick (2020), "Une mauvaise compréhension assez générale de quelques mécanismes budgétaires ou monétaires importants", *Melchior.fr*.

Banerjee, R., E. Kharroubi and U. Lewrick (2020), "Bankruptcies, unemployment and reallocation from Covid-19". *BIS Bulletin 31*, October.

Barlow James, J. K. Roehrich and S. Wright (2010), "De facto privatization or a renewed role for the EU? Paying for Europe's healthcare infrastructure in a recession", *Journal of the Royal Society of Medicine*, February 1, 103(2), 51–55.

Botta, A., E. Caverzasi and A.Russo (2020), "Fighting the Covid-19 crisis: Debt monetisation and EU recovery bonds", *Intereconomics*, 55(4), 239–244.

Burke-Kennedy Eoin (2020), "Ireland on course to be the fastest growing economy in world in 2020", *The Irish Times*, 4th December, Dublin.

CSO (2020), Industrial production by sector. Accessed on 30 September at: https://www .cso.ie/en/releasesandpublications/er/iips/irishindustrialproductionbysector2018/.

Daly, L. and M. Lawless (2020), *"Examination of the Sectoral Overlap of COVID19 and Brexit Shocks"*, Economic and Social Research Institute, Dublin, Working Paper No. 677. September.

Department of Finance (2020), *Fiscal Monitor – Incorporating the Exchequer Statement*, Department of Finance, Dublin.

ECB (2020), *Monetary Developments in the Euro Area: September 2020*, European Central Bank, Directorate General Communications, Press Release, 27 October 2020, Frankfurt.

Eisl, A., and M. Tomay (2020), *"European debt Mutualisation, Finding a Legitimate Balance between Solidarity and Responsibility Mechanism"*, Jacques Delors Institute Policy Paper, No. 255, July 2020.

European Commission (2020a), *European Economic Forecast*, Summer 2020 (Interim), Institutional Paper 132, July, Brussels.

European Commission (2020b), *European Economic Forecast*, Autumn 2020, Institutional Paper 136, November, Brussels.

EU Commission (2020a), *"Proposal for a Regulation of the EP and the Council"*, COM(2020) 451 final, Brussels, 28 May 2020.

EU Commission (2020b), "Communication from the Commission" on a Temporary Framework for State aid measures to support the economy in the current COVID-19 outbreak", (2020/C 91 I/01, Brussels).

Eurostat (2020), "COVID-19 labour effects across the income distribution", October, https ://ec.europa.eu/eurostat/statistics-explained/index.php?title=COVID-19_labour_ef fects_across_the_income_distribution&oldid=503441, Accessed on 15 November 2020.

Fisher Irving (1933), The debt-deflation theory of great depressions, *Econometrica*, 1(4), October, 337–357.

Fitzgerald, John (2020), "Understanding recent trends in the Irish economy". Economic and Social Research Institute, Dublin; ESRI Special Article, June.

Gøtzsche Peter C. (2020), "Rapid response to: Infection fatality risk for SARS-CoV-2 in community dwelling population of Spain: Nationwide seroepidemiological study", *British Medical Journal*, 371, m4509. doi: https://doi.org/10.1136/bmj.m4509

Hermann Christoph (2010), "The marketisation of health care in Europe", *Socialist Register*, Available at: www.academia.edu/812430/The_marketisation_of_health_car e_in_Europe

Horn Sebastian, Josefin Meyer and Christoph Trebesch (2020), "Coronabonds – The forgotten history of European Community debt," *Vox CEPR Policy Portal*, 15 April.

Ioannidis, John, P. A. (in press), "Infection fatality rate of COVID-19 inferred from seroprevalence data", *Bulletin of the World Health Organization*, Available at: www.who .int/bulletin/online_first/BLT.20.265892.pdf. Accessed on 17 December 2020.

Le Monde (2020), "Covid-19: la crise sanitaire a fait basculer un million de Françaises et de Français dans la pauvreté" (article by I. Rey-Lefebvre, R. Schittly, G. Rof, Ph. Gagnebet, B. Keltz and J. Pouille, 6 October, Paris).

Micossi Stefano (2020), "Sovereign debt management in the euro-area as a common action problem", CEPS, 13th December, Available at: www.ceps.eu/ceps-publications/sover eign-debt-management-in-the-euro-area-as-a-common-action-problem/

Torchia Mariateresa, Andrea Calabrò and Michèle Morner (2015), "Public-private partnerships in the health care sector: A systematic review of the literature", *Public Management Review*, 17(2), 236–261.

Wallerstein Immanuel (1979), *The Capitalist World-Economy*. New York and London: Cambridge University Press.

World Bank (2020), "COVID-19 to add as many as 150 Million extreme poor by 2021", Press Release 7 October 2020. Available at: www.worldbank.org/en/news/press-rel ease/2020/10/07/covid-19-to-add-as-many-as-150-million-extreme-poor-by-2021

Appendix

List of euro-area countries:

Belgium, Germany, Ireland, Spain, France, Italy, Luxembourg, the Netherlands, Austria, Portugal, Finland, Greece, Slovenia, Cyprus, Malta, Slovakia, Estonia, Latvia, and Lithuania.

Note that **M1** is the sum of currency in circulation and overnight deposits; **M2** is the sum of M1, deposits with an agreed maturity of up to two years, and deposits redeemable at notice of up to three months; and **M3** is the sum of M2, repurchase agreements, money market fund shares/units, and debt securities with a maturity of up to two years.

3 The case of France

Sophie Nivoix and Serge Rey

3.1 Introduction

Until 2020, the subprime crisis was usually presented as the most serious economic and social crisis, outside wartime, since 1929. However, with the Covid-19 crisis we have a totally new situation. It is not the difficulties of companies (high leverage) or banks (default risk) that are the triggering factor, but an epidemic linked to a new virus that has forced France, like most countries in the world, to totally halt part of its economic activity. Unlike other crises, healthy companies experienced difficulties because they were suddenly unable to continue their business. If there is no specificity of the health crisis that has similarly affected most continents, there is on the other hand a specificity of the responses. The behavior of populations in Asia, China, Japan, and South Korea has been repeatedly highlighted, as they have responded effectively by limiting the spread of the epidemic and consequently the negative impact on their economies. In Europe, population lockdown, and therefore the activity stop, has been the norm. France is no exception and the debate has focused on the organization of this lockdown.

During the year 2020 on two occasions, from March 17 to May 11, and from October 30 (see Figure 3.1), the French authorities decided lockdown measures for the population and the temporary stoppage of some activities, particularly services considered as "non-essential" for the economy. On November 24, 2020, president Macron announced that the lockdown would continue until December 15 and that it would be followed by a curfew, while a further step could take place to lift restrictions (such as, eventually, the reopening of universities and restaurants) at the end of January 2021 (Figure 3.1).

Facing what could appear to be an economic disaster, the authorities have implemented policies to support the economy and revive activity on an unprecedented scale. Some would argue that the French government has arbitrated between reducing short-term economic and social risk and a longer-term financial risk linked to public deficits and public debt that could rise from 98 percent of GDP at the end of 2019 to 120 percent of GDP in 2021. It should be noted that by the end of 2020, less than 1 percent of companies have filed for bankruptcy, which will not, however, prevent the unemployment

DOI: 10.4324/9781003153603-3

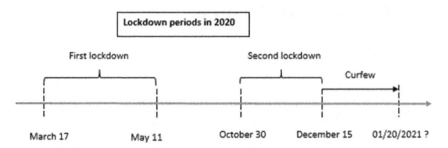

Figure 3.1 Lockdown periods in France during the year 2020

rate from rising from 8 percent at the end of 2019 to 9 percent at the end of 2020.

The purpose of this chapter is to present the economic, budgetary, and monetary policy measures adopted by the French authorities. In order to emphasize the unprecedented nature of this crisis in a modern economy, we will first (in Section 2) make a comparison with the subprime crisis, while Sections 3 and 4 will present the main measures of the short-run support plan and of the recovery plan. These budgetary measures will be accompanied by monetary measures, the main features of which are recalled in Section 5, while Section 6 concludes the chapter.

3.2 Covid-19 versus subprime crises

In order to document the importance of the current crisis, we will make a brief comparison of some macroeconomic indicators with the subprime crisis.

3.2.1 Real economy

The impact of both the subprime and Covid-19 crises on the real economy is considerable. In Figures 3.2 and 3.3 we can see that while GDP fell during four successive quarters following the bankruptcy of Lehman Brothers on September 15, 2008, these declines appear very limited compared to −5.9 percent and −13.8 percent in mid-2020. While the reduction in consumption[1] has contributed to these declines in GDP, it is the fall in investment (gross fixed capital formation) that is the main factor. In the end, the drop in GDP will have been −2.9 percent in 2009, while a 10 percent drop is expected in 2020.

However, unlike previous crises, the productive system being for the most part intact, the economic recovery should be just as spectacular if the epidemic becomes under control. This was observed in Q3 of the year 2020, but the

---

1 Facing the uncertainties related to the crisis, the Banque de France estimates the additional (precautionary) savings made by households in 2020 compared to previous years at 100 billion EUR. The consequence has been a drop in consumption.

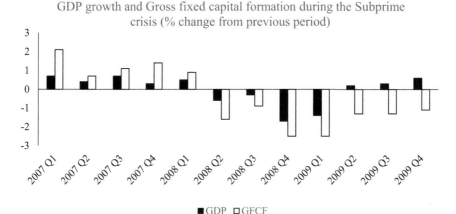

Figure 3.2 GDP growth and gross fixed capital formation during the subprime crisis. Source: INSEE, various economic activity notes

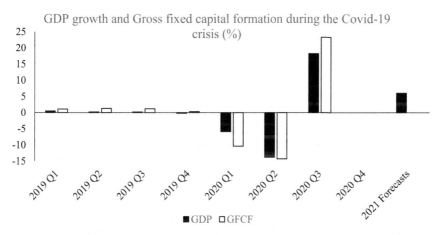

Figure 3.3 GDP growth and gross fixed capital formation during the Covid-19 crisis. Source: INSEE, various economic activity notes (before the second lockdown, the 2021 GDP growth rate forecast was 8%)

second lockdown will severely slow down this recovery. The most unfavorable scenario would be several successive lockdowns that would eventually lead to a chain of bankruptcies.

Figure 3.3 GDP growth and gross fixed capital formation during the Covid-19 crisis.

3.2.2 The financial consequences

Ambitious recovery plans have been implemented after both crises. But the GDP fall in 2020 will impact more heavily on the public deficit ratio than in

2009 and it will have huge consequences on the debt ratio (Figures 3.4 and 3.5). It is also possible that this ratio will be even higher in 2021, since the plans were implemented before the second lockdown was decided. The economy is thus moving always further away from the limits set under the Maastricht Treaty (3 percent for the deficit and 60 percent for the debt in terms of GDP).

While in the short term this policy seems judicious, in the longer term it raises the problem of debt sustainability. Indeed, today the French Treasury can issue negative-rate loans; the 10-year maturity loans fetch a rate of −0.307 percent (as of November 13, 2020), and 30-year maturity loans attract an interest rate of 0.373 percent at the same date (see Banque de France). However, the rise in interest rates over the next few years or decades could

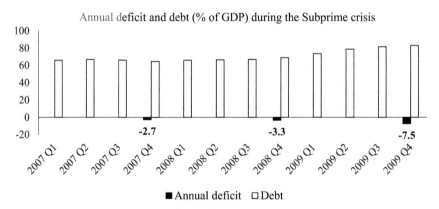

Figure 3.4 Annual deficit and debt of the general government according to the Maastricht definition during the subprime crisis (in % of GDP) Source: INSEE, various economic activity notes

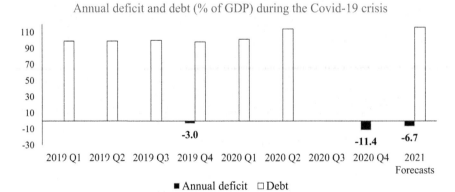

Figure 3.5 Annual deficit and debt if the general government according to the Maastricht definition during the subprime crisis (in % of GDP) Source: INSEE, various economic activity notes

place a very heavy burden on future generations by increasing the cost of refinancing the debt. This situation would be all the more sensitive since in Q3 of 2020 51.3 percent of the French government's negotiable debt is held by non-residents.[2]

3.3 Short-term support plan

Launched in March, following the first lockdown, this emergency plan aims to fight both a crisis in terms of supply (shut down in the activity of many companies) and in terms of demand (drop in household purchasing power and investment reduction).

By the end of July 2020, some 470 billion EUR will have been used to support businesses, particularly very small and small business, and to protect employees. Without making an exhaustive presentation of all the measures in the plan, we will mention the main decisions in the following paragraphs. They concern the commerce (3.1), the industry (3.2), and the tourism sectors (3.3). It should be noted, however, that among these 470 billion EUR, only 64 billion will be new spending, the remaining being financed by redeployment of appropriations.

3.3.1 Plan for local commerce, crafts, and the self-employed

The plan in favor of local commerce, crafts, and the self-employed[3] aims to support professionals during the sensitive recovery phase, after the period of confinement. This support plan also reinforces the national strategy for crafts and local commerce launched in October 2019.

The main support measures for local shops, artisans, and the self-employed during the health crisis are as follows:

- Partial[4] activity: more than 4 million employees working in companies with less than 20 employees were the subject of a partial activity request,

---

2 See Bulletin Mensuel, Agence France Trésor, n°367, décembre 2020. www.aft.gouv.fr/files/medias-aft /7_Publications/7.2_BM/367_Bulletin%20mensuel%20d%C3%A9cembre%202020.pdf

3 www.economie.gouv.fr/covid19-soutien-entreprises/plan-commerce-proximite-artisanat-independants#

4 The company may apply for a partial activity allowance for one or more employees unable to work, if it falls into one of the following cases:

- it is affected by the decrees providing for a closure,
- it faced a drop in activity and/or supply difficulties,
- it is impossible for it to implement the preventive measures necessary for the protection of employee health (teleworking, social distancing, etc.) for all its employees.

The employee receives a partial activity allowance from his employer, in replacement of his salary. This indemnity corresponds to 70 percent of his gross salary with a minimum of 8.03 EUR per hour. Employees whose remuneration was lower than the SMIC (minimum wage) benefit from an

or 31 percent of the total requests, of which almost half in the retail sector. This system has made it possible to save jobs on a massive scale.

- Solidarity fund: as of June 25, 2020, 1.6 million very small businesses have benefited from the solidarity fund, for a total aid amount of 4.8 billion EUR, including 740 million for trade.
- State-guaranteed loans (PGE): as of June 19, 2020, some 458,000 very small enterprises (VSEs) were able to obtain a PGE, for a total granted amounting to 42.3 billion EUR, or 41 percent of the amounts granted. The retail sector is the first beneficiary of the system (25 percent of amounts) and the one with the highest intensity of demand for these loans (amount/value added).
- Deferral of tax and social charges: on June 11, 2020, nearly 7,000 requests for deferral of tax charges had been submitted by very small businesses.
- During the period of gradual resumption of activity following the confinement, the government will continue its support through targeted short-term measures, but also through structural transformation actions in the sector.

3.3.2 Plan for the industry

3.3.2.1 Book and publishing industry

Since the beginning of the state of health emergency, more than 230 million EUR have been mobilized by the State in favor of the book and publishing industry in 2020.[5]

- A support fund of 25 million EUR has been set up at the level of the national book center (CNL), in conjunction with the regional directorates of cultural affairs (DRAC), to enable independent bookstores to deal with their financial difficulties.
- A support fund amounting of 5 million EUR has been set up at the CNL, in connection with the DRACs, to financially support publishing houses with a turnover between 100,000 and 10 million EUR. Local authorities and professional partners were invited to participate financially in this fund.
- The State used an amount of 12 million EUR, spread over 2020 and 2021 to help bookstores modernize their equipment. The objective is to enable bookstores, via a fund managed by the CNL, to accelerate investments in modernization.

---

indemnity equal to their previous remuneration. Then, the company benefits from an allowance paid by the State corresponding to 85 percent of the amount of the employee's partial activity allowance, up to a maximum of 4.5 SMIC (minimum wage). This mechanism is reinforced with the payment of 100 percent of the indemnities until the end of 2020 for companies in the tourism, hotel, catering, sports, culture, events, and air transport sectors.

5 www.economie.gouv.fr/covid19-soutien-entreprises/soutien-filiere-livre

- More than 100 million EUR have been mobilized by the State from the Institute for the Financing of Cinema and Cultural Industries (IFCIC) in the form of loans, in particular with support from the Banque des Territoires. Within this envelope, an amount of 40 million EUR will be available to book and publishing firms according to their needs.

This fund is being extended to a greater number of companies, namely those employing up to 20 employees and having a turnover of up to 2 million EUR. The aid paid under the second part of the fund may reach 10,000 EUR. This component was accessible without condition of refusal of a bank loan.

With reference to the partial activity measures, bookstores and publishing houses have submitted requests for 8.2 million hours since the system was put in place and have received compensation payments of 17 million EUR for the months of March and April 2020. Publishing houses will be able to continue to benefit from a partial activity allowance for hours not worked in the coming months. For those who experience a loss of at least 80 percent of their turnover, a support of 100 percent of the wages paid to the employees is planned.

At the end of May 2020, 729 bookstores and 298 publishing houses benefited from a state-guaranteed loans (PGE) for a total outstanding amount of almost 115 million EUR. Meanwhile, the CNL released initial emergency aid amounting to 5 million EUR for authors, bookstores and publishing houses.

During the lockdown, there has been an automatic exemption from social contributions: small publishing houses with fewer than 250 employees, whose turnover has fallen by more than 80 percent benefited from an automatic exemption from social contributions for the months of March to June 2020. The same applies to authors who benefited from a flat-rate exemption over this period. Bookstores with 1 to 10 employees benefited from nearly 10 million EUR of automatic exemption from social contributions, for the months of March, April, and May 2020, during which they were forced to remain closed.

3.3.2.2 *Construction industry*

Construction is one of the sectors that saw its activity the most sharply reduced: −88 percent at the beginning of April, i.e. the same drop as the hotel and catering industry, even though it was not the subject of an administrative closure from mid-March.

From March 2020 on, the construction industry benefited from public support mechanisms. Given its weight in the economy and its importance in terms of activity across the various regions (*territoires*) (construction represents 2 million jobs and 11 percent of GDP), the government has been working since March on the resumption of activity in the construction industry, in conjunction with local authorities and professional federations. It was also a question of making it possible to respond to real estate or renovation projects of individuals.

The construction industry has benefited greatly from different public support mechanisms such as: a solidarity fund (360,000 companies for 510 million EUR); loans guaranteed by the State (60,000 loans for 8.2 billion EUR); and partial activity (requests deposited for 1.4 million employees and 1.3 billion EUR already paid during March and April 2020).[6]

The sector has also been the subject of specific initiatives to support its resumption with specific measures not to slow down the authorization or implementation of projects, the mobilization of prefectural authorities to encourage and support the rapid resumption of work sites. This enabled a strong acceleration in the resumption of activity since mid-May, thanks to the commitment of companies and their employees: only 1 percent of public works sites and less than 15 percent of building sites were still in progress in July 2020.

New measures are being taken to help construction companies offset the additional costs and speed up the recovery. In order to help local authorities to finance part of these additional costs, the prefectural authorities can use their power of derogation to mobilize State allocations: local investment support allocation (DSIL) and equipment allocation for rural areas (DETR).

Under the Third Amending Finance Law[7] (PLFR 3), companies with fewer than 50 employees who have suffered significant losses in terms of turnover will be able to benefit from social security contributions discounts of up to 50 percent on their due dates from March to May. All companies will be able to request a plan to clear their social charges, postponed since March, for a period of up to 36 months. Regarding support for the recovery, 1 billion EUR has been added by the State in its PLFR 3 financial law to the local investment support endowment (DSIL), bringing its envelope from 0.6 to 1.6 billion EUR. It aims to support the structuring of investment of communities relating to health, environmental transition, in particular with respect to the thermal renovation of public buildings, and the renovation of heritage. Taking into account the leverage effect on local authority funding, this allocation should make it possible to increase local investments by 4.8 billion EUR. Thus, the state will pay local communities in 2020 nearly 10 billion EUR in investment grants. Under the PLFR 3 financial law, the state credit insurance guarantee system is strongly reinforced in PLFR 3 to allow companies to keep their coverage. This measure is very important for construction companies whose cash flow depends a lot on inter-company credit. The measure will be implemented immediately by decree for SMEs and medium-sized companies.

Within the framework of the PLFR 3, and in order to support the cash flow of companies, the companies subject to corporation tax will be able to request, from 2020, the immediate repayment of their carried back debts, as well as

---

6 www.economie.gouv.fr/covid19-soutien-entreprises/soutien-batiment-travaux-publics
7 The Covid-19 crisis has led the French authorities to review the orientation of economic and budgetary policy. Since the beginning of the year, four amending finance laws ("*Projet de Loi de Finance Rectificative*, PLFR") have been adopted by the Parliament: PLFR 1 (March 23, 2020), PLFR 2 (April 25, 2020), PLFR 3 (July 30, 2020), PLFR 4 (November 30, 2020).

receivables that would come to be recognized in 2020 due to losses caused by the health crisis.

In order to maintain a certain level of skills within companies and in order to boost their renewal, the government has announced the creation of assistance for the recruitment of apprentices, from 5,000 EUR to 8,000 EUR per contract with a view of preparing for a diploma up to a professional degree. This aid will be paid to companies with fewer than 250 employees without conditions, and to companies with more than 250 employees on the condition that they commit to achieving the objective, set by law, of 5% work–study students in 2021. This should represent more than 130 million EUR for the sector.

3.3.2.3 Aeronautics

The aeronautics sector, which had previously been growing overall, has, with the outburst of the health crisis, faced financial difficulties and a loss of turnover that could jeopardize its very survival.

Beyond this crisis, the aeronautics industry faces the unavoidable challenge of environmental transition. The two main objectives of the plan are stated as follows.

- Support for demand with the renewal of a greener fleet. This will be possible thanks to three measures. 1) Increase Bpifrance[8] assurance export's support for the sector's exports, with public credit insurance playing the role of a crisis damper. 2) Establishment of a moratorium on principal repayments of export credits granted to airlines for 12 months from the end of March 2020. In return for obtaining the moratorium, the beneficiary companies undertake, until the full repayment of the deferred portion of the credit, not to pay dividends or other amounts to their shareholders and not to implement any share buyback programs. Otherwise, beneficiaries are obliged to immediately repay the amounts of credit carried over. 3) A temporary relaxation of the reimbursement terms for purchases of new aircraft. 4) Help to the military, civil security, and gendarmerie forces. The sector's load plan will be fueled by advance orders for planes, helicopters, and military drones, thus providing concrete and immediate support for the preservation of employment, in particular in SMEs and mid-cap-companies (employing between 500 and 5,000 people). The total amount of these advance orders will be 832 million EUR.[9]

8 Bpifrance is a public investment bank, created in December 2012, whose purpose is to finance business development. Bpifrance finances companies with credit, guarantees, and equity. It is an essential cog in the wheel for the implementation of the policy undertaken by the state. It is Bpifrance that will provide the public guarantee on the cash loans granted to companies. Eventually, it may also be used as a vehicle in the event of a public equity investment.

9 www.economie.gouv.fr/covid19-soutien-entreprises/plan-soutien-filiere-aeronautique

- Support for supply by consolidating the sector and strengthening its investments to improve its competitiveness. France must preserve and develop its share in the development and manufacture of the next generations of air carriers and devices. Very significant financial resources will thus be concentrated on R&D for future carbon-free planes as well as on the modernization of production chains, on industry 4.0 (embracing robotization, digitalization, and/or environmental innovation). First, the government created an aeronautics investment fund, an equity support tool to preserve critical know-how and improve the competitiveness of SMEs and mid-caps. The objective is to deploy a total amount over time of 1 billion EUR (in debt and equity) for the benefit of the aeronautical sector through this instrument, with a first fundraising of 500 million EUR in capital, available from July 2020. Second, the government created a public support fund for the diversification, modernization, and environmental transformation of processes. The amount of state funding will be 300 million EUR over three years. Third, there will be an intensification of support for R&D efforts to make France one of the most advanced countries in "green" aircraft technology. The roadmap that the State sets with French manufacturers, in a partnership approach, is structured around 20 major themes, which cover all the major areas of excellence of the national sector.

3.3.2.4 Tech firms

In order to support French technology companies develop the technologies of the future and help them better finance themselves, the government is launching an investment fund managed by Bpifrance. More precisely, the benefit of this envelope concerns companies operating on the national territory and developing sovereign technologies of the future whose investment risk is high (quantum, health, cybersecurity, artificial intelligence, etc.), and start-ups at any stage of development. This fund has an initial envelope of 150 million EUR to support these companies.[10] Depending on needs, the size of this fund may be increased in 2021 to reach more than 500 million EUR.

3.2.5 Automotive industry

The French automotive industry was hit hard by the health crisis. Plants have stopped and dealerships have remained closed during the lockdown period. In April 2020, the sector experienced an average drop in activity of more than 80 percent The fall is of the same order for automobile sales. Current forecasts for the automotive market point to a decline in 2020 of at least 20 percent worldwide and 30 percent in Europe. The government has therefore decided to support the French automotive industry, which must also be accompanied

---

10 www.economie.gouv.fr/covid19-soutien-entreprises/plan-soutien-entreprises-technologiques

in order to succeed in the two most important technological revolutions since the invention of the combustion engine: that of the electric vehicle and the autonomous vehicle.

In order to remain a major automotive nation and to produce in France the clean vehicles of tomorrow, three directions have been chosen for this support plan.[11]

First, renewing the French vehicle fleet in favor of clean vehicles. The subsidy for the purchase of an electric vehicle increases from 6,000 to 7,000 EUR for individuals, for the purchase of a vehicle valued at less than 45,000 EUR. The subsidy for the purchase of an electric vehicle for company fleets increases to 5,000 EUR, for the purchase of a private vehicle or light commercial vehicle worth less than 45,000 EUR. Moreover, there will be a new subsidy of 2,000 EUR for the purchase of plug-in hybrid vehicles for vehicles worth less than or equal to 50,000 EUR. The conversion subsidy increases to 3,000 EUR for low income households for the purchase of a combustion engine vehicle and to 5,000 EUR for the purchase of an electric or plug-in hybrid vehicle. The eligibility criteria for vehicle scrappage by including Crit'air 3 for "very low income" households and Crit'air 4 for others were relaxed. Public sector purchasers, including within the State, will accelerate the renewal of their vehicle fleets. In the coming weeks, the government will adopt a circular on vehicle fleets imposing a 50 percent target of electric, hybrid or hydrogen vehicles for public purchasers, while accelerating the deployment of electric charging stations.

Second, invest and innovate to produce the vehicles of tomorrow. The government created the Automotive Future Fund, endowed with 1 billion EUR, intended for the modernization and digitization of production chains, for the environmental transformation of the automotive industry and for innovation. Some 600 million EUR of equity investments are intended for the consolidation of the sector, 200 million EUR for the modernization and decarbonization of the productive tool and 150 million EUR in aid for R&D and innovation in the sector.

The third direction is in relation to support measures for companies in difficulty so as to protect employees. The will be a deployment of a massive skills development plan. Given the prospects of a very difficult start to the work–study program (apprenticeship and professional training contracts), an emergency plan will be implemented to significantly reduce the cost of a young work–study program and allow the sector to aim for a stabilization of the work–study level.

3.3.3 Plan for the tourism sector

Tourism companies will be able to continue to use the partial activity measures under the same conditions as those set up during the lockdown until the end of

---

11 www.economie.gouv.fr/covid19-soutien-entreprises/mesures-plan-soutien-automobile

2020. Beyond that, the partial activity will remain open to them under conditions that will be reviewed if necessary.

- The solidarity fund will remain open for companies in the tourism, events, sports, and culture sector until the end of 2020. Its access will be extended to larger companies, those with up to 20 employees and up to 2 million EUR in revenue. The aid to which it may give entitlement will be increased up to 10,000[12] EUR.
- An exemption from social security contributions applies to both very small enterprises (VSEs) and to small and medium-sized enterprises (SMEs) in the tourism, cultural, and sports events sector, during either the period of closure or of very low activity, at least from March to June 2020, for an estimated amount of 2.2 billion EUR. The exemption will automatically apply to all these companies, whether or not they have already paid their contributions.
- In addition to the exemption from employer contributions, a contribution credit equal to 20 percent of wages paid since February 2020 will be added. This credit contribution will be chargeable on all contributions due by the company and will support the resumption of activity. Exemptions from employer contributions may be extended as long as the mandatory closure of the establishment lasts. Moreover, a seasonal state-guaranteed loan (PGE) has been implemented: its conditions are more favorable than the classic PGE with a higher ceiling (currently the loan is capped at 25 percent of the 2019 turnover; the ceiling of the seasonal PGE season will be raised to the best three months of the year 2019 – which for seasonal businesses makes a big difference. Rents and fees for occupying the public domain due to national lessors (State and operators) have been cancelled for VSEs and SMEs in the tourism and sports events sector for the period of administrative closure.

Moreover, 3 billion EUR in investments will accompany the recovery and transformation of the sector as follows. The tourism loan offered by Bpifrance will be increased to 1 billion EUR. Around 600 million EUR of resources from the Caisse des Dépôts et Consignations Group (Bpifrance, Banque des Territoires, La Banque Postale) will be mobilized to offer short- and long-term loans. Finally, more than 1.3 billion EUR will be invested in equity by the Caisse des Dépôts et Consignations and Bpifrance in the tourism sector, for an expected investment impact of 6.7 billion EUR.

Nearly 1,500 companies and their managers will benefit from specific support from Bpifrance through consulting, training, and acceleration programs, while support for the regions (*territoires*) will be amplified by the Banque des Territoires with, in particular, a reinforcement of the capacity of France Tourisme Ingénierie for 29.5 million EUR for the whole.

12 www.economie.gouv.fr/covid19-soutien-entreprises/plan-soutien-secteur-tourisme

As of 2020, the Social Tourism Investment Fund will be tripled with an increase in its investment up to 225 million EUR and with more flexible eligibility criteria.

3.4 The recovery plan during and after Covid-19 in France

While it was necessary to take significant emergency measures following the first lockdown, the recovery plan launched in September 2020 is part of a longer-term perspective. On September 3, the government launched "France Relance", the 100 billion EUR plan, of which 40 billion EUR comes from financing from the European Union. This 100 billion EUR recovery plan should be implemented over the next 24 months and is divided into several major orientations. The main goals are the creation of new jobs as well as the transformation of the French economy thanks to investments in growing sectors. Consequently, the country should be able to experience after two years its pre-Covid economic level. The three priorities of the plan are the environment (30 billion EUR), competitiveness (34 billion EUR), the regions (*territoires*), and social cohesion (36 billion EUR). They should reinforce the effects of the first 470 billion EUR emergency.

3.4.1 The environment

The environment is at the heart of the recovery plan. The objective is to accelerate the environmental conversion of the French economy so that it is more sustainable and thriftier with the natural resources and may achieve carbon neutrality by 2050. This strategic orientation is reflected in the recovery plan through the following measures.

- First, energy renewal will be funded up to 706 million EUR, in order to help the thermal renovation of public buildings, to make the energy renovation and major rehabilitation of social housing (500 million EUR), to finance energy renovation of small and medium enterprises (200 million EUR), and foster energy renovation of private housing.
- Second, the biodiversity maintenance and struggle against the artificialization of soils will be shared between the rehabilitation of wastelands and aid to mayors for the densification of housing (650 million EUR), biodiversity in the regions, risk prevention and resilience (300 million EUR), sustainable cities (measure related to the Programme d'Investissement d'Avenir[13] (PIA), including 57 billion EUR implemented between 2010 and 2017), and water networks and modernization of stations of sanitation including overseas (300 million EUR).
- Third, decarbonization of industry will receive 1.2 billion EUR.

13 www.gouvernement.fr/le-programme-d-investissements-d-avenir

- Fourth, the circular economy and short circuits will include 226 million EUR funding for investment in recycling and reuse (also supporting the plastic sector) and 274 million EUR for the modernization of sorting/recycling centers and waste recovery.
- Fifth, agricultural transition will be done through an acceleration of the transformation of the agricultural sector (organic, high environmental value, short circuits) with 400 million EUR, a plan in favor of protein independence (100 million EUR), the modernization of slaughterhouses, biosecurity in breeding, free range breeding and animal welfare (250 million EUR), the renewal of agro-equipment (250 million EUR), the modernization of agricultural technologies (related to the PIA), and the support of forests (200 million EUR). To a smaller extent, sea-related activities will also receive some support, with 50 million EUR dedicated to fishing, aquaculture, fish mongering, and 200 million EUR to the greening of harbors.
- Considering the infrastructure and green transport, strengthening the resilience of electricity networks will receive 50 million EUR; the development of daily mobility 1.2 billion EUR; the railways (network modernization, rail freight, and security) 4.7 billion EUR; the acceleration of work on transport infrastructure 550 million EUR; the support for demand for clean vehicles in the automotive plan (subsidy, conversion premium) 1.9 billion EUR; and the greening of the State vehicle fleet 180 million EUR.
- In the same way, green technologies will be supported to develop green hydrogen (2 billion EUR), to back the nuclear industry with skills development, industrial investments, modernization in subcontracting (200 million EUR), to help R&D in the nuclear sector (in relationship with the PIA), to support plans for the aeronautics and automobile industries (2.6 billion EUR), and to finance the development of key markets in green technologies like hydrogen, recycling and reincorporation of recycled materials, bio-based products and biofuels, and agro-equipment for ecological transition (3.4 billion EUR), and new climate products from Bpifrance (the French public investment bank) 2.5 billion EUR.

3.1.2 Competitiveness

To promote the development of high value–added activity in France and create jobs, the recovery plan also includes changes that will make the economy more competitive. Recovery is the key to economic sovereignty and technological independence. This is reflected in particular by 34 billion EUR dedicated to the following measures:

- On a fiscal viewpoint, the taxation of production will be lowered (20 billion EUR).
- The funding of companies with equity will be reinforced for SMEs (3 billion EUR).

- Technological sovereignty and resilience will be financed through several ways: support for the development of key markets like digital (cyber, cloud, quantum, edtech) and health (digital health and innovative therapies) with 2.6 billion EUR; innovation financing of strategic sectors with 1.95 billion EUR; support for the space industry with 515 million EUR; preservation of R&D employment with 300 million EUR; relocation and safety of strategic supplies with 600 million EUR; relocation of industrial projects with 400 million EUR; and equity investments (in relation with the PIA) with 500 million EUR.
- The support plan for export reaches 247 million EUR.
- The digital upgrading for the State, regions, and companies includes 385 million EUR for SMEs and 1.5 billion EUR for the State, regions, and public services (schools, justice).
- The support for cultural and creative industries, in relation with the PIA, includes 1.6 million EUR.
- The military order anticipations as part of the "aeronautics" plan includes 832 million EUR.

3.4.3 Regions (territoires) and Social Cohesion

To avoid an increase in inequalities in France due to the economic impact of the crisis, the recovery must also be a social and regional recovery. The recovery plan thus carries collective momentum through 36 billion EUR invested in the following actions.

3.4.3.1 Social cohesion

Considering job retention, the long-term partial activity and employee training in partial activity will receive 7.6 billion EUR. As for the younger population, learning assistance, professionalization contracts, and community-based service will receive 2.7 billion EUR; the hiring subsidy will reach 1.1 million EUR; the reinforced and personalized support 1.3 billion EUR; the boarding schools of excellence 50 million EUR, and the training in the professions of the future 1.6 billion EUR. The handicap hiring subsidy for disabled workers will reach 100 million EUR. As for professional training, the investment program in digitalization of training will be backed with 900 million EUR and the strengthening of intervention resources and the support of France Compétences and Pôle Emploi (French national employment agency) with 1 billion EUR. Research will be backed through the National Agency for research (ANR) with 400 million EUR, and funding of the university ecosystem, and innovation and valuation of research (in relation with the PIA) with 2.55 billion EUR. Considering health and dependence (the so-called "Ségur de la santé" plan) the long-term care public investment will reach 6 billion EUR. As for health cooperation, support for projects in the health security sector and access to vaccines reaches 50 million EUR. Finally, support for precarious people includes an increase in the back-to-school allowance, and universities' restaurant funding with 600 million EUR, and the financing of associations helping vulnerable people with 200 million EUR.

3.4.3.2 Regional/territorial cohesion

It will be financed through development of digital technology throughout the different regions (very high speed, digital inclusion) with 500 million EUR; support for local development actions, in particular overseas, with 250 million EUR; support for local authorities with 5.2 million EUR; recovery plan for the Banque des Territoires (social housing and real estate for small businesses) with 3 billion EUR; renovation of downtown shops with 150 million EUR; aid for the development of sustainable tourism with 50 million EUR; and modernization of the national road network with 350 million EUR.

3.4.3.3 The role of the regions

The regions will play a dual role. On the one hand, they will accompany the State in the implementation of the national plan, and on the other hand they will on their own initiate measures to help companies. Thus, out of the 100 billion EUR recovery plan, 16 billion EUR will be followed in the coming weeks (end 2020 and early 2021) by the regional prefectural authorities within the framework of regionalized envelopes. This co-piloting agreement for the recovery plan will be concluded at the same time as the draft State–Regions Plan Contract (CPER) 2021–2027, which includes a component of credits dedicated to the recovery over two years.

At the same time, France's 13 major metropolitan regions have adopted their own plan. For example, the Nouvelle-Aquitaine, France's largest region with its 84,000 km², which has been badly affected by the tourism and aeronautics crises, has urgently invested more than 120 million EUR in the 2020 and 2021 budgets. While these sums are relatively limited, they are a complement to the governmental measures that do not always meet certain specific needs. But longer-term plans have also been implemented. The Île-de-France region, France's richest one, will invest 10 billion EUR in environmental measures over the period 2020–2024.

3.4.4 Supplementary measures of November 4, 2020

As the country experienced the second episode of the Covid-19 pandemic, and with an economic recession estimated at −11 percent of GDP in 2020, the Fourth Amending Finance Law (PLFR 4), rectifying finance bill mobilized more than an extra 20 billion EUR to help companies and small businesses, employees, and precarious households. The aim is to respond to the economic consequences of the country's second lockdown.

In addition, following the speech of the President of the Republic on November 24, 2020, it is expected that the solidarity fund will evolve for companies that remain administratively closed. It will be open to all companies that remain administratively closed, regardless of their size. They will benefit from a right to choose between a monthly tax-free aid of up to 10,000 EUR, or a compensation of 20 percent of the monthly turnover achieved in the same period of the previous year with a ceiling of 100,000 EUR.

As long as these companies are closed, the solidarity fund will be maintained. This measure concerns 200,000 companies.

As the measures of the recovery plan will be enforced gradually until 2022, the first results are expected in the coming months. However, certain measures have already been adopted under the third amending finance law for 2020 (measures for youth employment, partial activity long-term, financial support for relocation in particular). Most of the other measures will be included in the finance bills for 2021 which were submitted to Parliament for examination in October 2020 and voted on by the end of 2020. The government will monitor the implementation of the revival Plan as a priority of the last part of the five-year term.

3.5 The financial support

According to Carletti et al. (2020, p.1), the Covid crisis "will test the resilience of the financial system and the regulatory reforms implemented after the global financial crisis of 2007–2009". Indeed, besides the domestic economic policies, the crisis "will stretch the limits of central bank intervention, and put to the test the incomplete Banking Union in the euro area". During the winter of 2008–09 the G20 countries attempted to avoid huge recession. Among the main measures that were taken we have to mention interest rate cuts, fiscal help, and of course the quantitative easing policy. Whereas at the G20 summit in April 2009, the developed countries implemented a 5,000 billion USD fiscal expansion to support jobs and growth and reform the banks, many countries decided to stick to their own schedules. This led to a major increase in budget deficits because of lower taxes. Jorda et al. (2013) showed that after the major recession caused by the financial crisis, the real risk-free interest rates may stay low for 5 to 10 years. But some factors may mitigate the lowering of the natural interest rates, namely the lower death toll of Covid-19 compared to previous major pandemics, the higher death toll among elderly people, who are no longer working, and the quantitative easing policy which may increase the public debt and reduce the saving rates. Jorda et al. (2020) studied the long run consequences of pandemics and concluded that these events are followed by several decades of depressed investment opportunities, low returns to assets, high saving rates. Meanwhile, the decline of the real interest rates may be mitigated by the death toll (if not too high) in the population, the age of the victims (elderly people tend to have a high saving rate and they do not belong to the labor force anymore), and the post-pandemic public debt increase.

3.5.1 Fiscal policy

When examining the decisions of the French government to fight the effects of the Covid-19 crisis, one can be impressed by the magnitude of the expenses. From the beginning of the crisis an emergency plan of 470 billion EUR was committed. It was followed a few months later by a recovery plan of 100 billion EUR, supplemented in November 2020 with an additional 20 billion EUR. But while these amounts may seem considerable, they do not reflect the impact on the public budget. For example, loans guaranteed by the state for an amount of 120 billion EUR are accounted for in the urgency plan. In addition, a part of the announced spending is based on the redeployment of funds. In fact, the 470 billion mobilized in 2020 compensated "only" 64 billion EUR of actual state spending. The situation is the same for the recovery plan that runs from 2020 to 2022. Therefore, in 2020 there is a sharp deterioration in the state budget, whose deficit exceeds 240 billion EUR against an initial target of 53.5 billion EUR. This is the consequence of a loss of revenue of nearly 100 billion EUR related to the fall in GDP, while additional spending was expected between 78 billion EUR and 86 billion EUR according to the estimates.

This deficit nevertheless raises two problems. In the short term, monetary policy is essential. By reinforcing quantitative easing measures (purchases of public and private debt), the ECB is helping to keep interest rates very low, which facilitates the financing of deficits through debt issuance. But in return, in the medium and long term, the increase in the debt ratio above 120 percent of GDP will lead to the problem of the sustainability of the French debt, and will also reopen the debate on the monetization of debt via the issuance of zero-coupon perpetual bonds. Moreover, Anderson et al. (2020) pointed out that in Europe France had the second highest rate of fiscal impulse deferral (8.7%) after Portugal at the end of 2020.

3.5.2 French state-guaranteed loans

To cope with the economic shock linked to the coronavirus crisis, the government has implemented an unprecedented mechanism to provide the necessary financing to companies facing a decline in activity. State-guaranteed loans ("Prêts garantis par l'Etat", PGE) are the central link in this system.

To allow businesses that do not have access to the EMP to also be supported, specific intervention tools have been created or strengthened: Economic and Social Development Fund (FDES), subsidized loans, repayable advances, and equity loans.

The state-guaranteed loan (PGE) is an exceptional guarantee scheme to support bank financing of companies, to the tune of 300 billion EUR. It is open to all companies until December 31, 2020 regardless of their size and legal form (for example companies, traders, artisans, farmers, liberal professions, micro-entrepreneurs, associations and foundations having an economic activity therein including certain real estate companies, companies in difficulty since January 1, 2020, and "young innovative companies"). Some firms are excluded, like the real estate companies, credit institutions, and finance companies, as they may apply to their usual bank for a loan guaranteed by the State to support their cash flow.

This large loan may represent up to three months of 2019 turnover, or two years of payroll for innovative companies or companies created since January 1, 2019. No repayment will be required for the first year; the company may choose to amortize the loan over a maximum period of five years.

Companies can take out a loan guaranteed by the State with their usual banking establishment or since May 6, 2020 with lending platforms having the status of crowdfunding intermediary. Essentially in this case, the EMP is governed by the same rules as when it is taken out with a bank. The loan amount can reach up to three months of 2019 turnover or two years of payroll for innovative companies or companies created since January 1, 2019. No repayment is required in the first year, and the company can choose to amortize the loan over a maximum period of five years.

The banks have pledged to massively distribute state-guaranteed loans at cost price to immediately relieve the cash flow of businesses and professionals. They will examine all inquiries addressed to them and provide them with a rapid response. However, all companies, in particular the largest ones, which do not meet their obligations in terms of payment deadlines, will not have access to this state guarantee for their bank loans. In addition, French banks have undertaken to postpone the repayment of corporate loans for up to six months, free of charge. It is possible to apply for several loans. The cumulative amount of these loans must not exceed 25 percent of turnover or two years of payroll for start-up or innovative companies. After examining the company's situation (eligibility criteria in particular), the bank gives a pre-approval for a loan.

State-guaranteed loans granted through a crowdfunding/crowdfunding platform are governed, for the most part, by the same rules as in the case of a state-guaranteed loan taken out with a bank. Moreover, there is a responsibility commitment for large companies. Indeed, a large company that requests a postponement of tax and social deadlines or a loan guaranteed by the State is not allowed to pay dividends in 2020 to its shareholders in France or abroad, and not allowed to buy back shares during 2020. The state-guaranteed loans are given to about 566,699 companies, i.e. about 20 percent of all the French enterprises. The main industries concerned are: retailing (28.5 billion EUR), manufacturing industry (20 billion EUR), scientific and technical activities (12 billion EUR), finance and insurance (11.6 billion EUR), building (10.3 billion EUR), and transportation and warehouses (8.2 billion EUR).

Businesses that have been unable to obtain a government-guaranteed loan from their bank can contact their department's credit mediator. If the mediation fails, they can refer the matter to the departmental committees for the examination of business financing problems (CODEFI) to request other financing mechanisms.

3.5.3 Other financing mechanisms

The Economic and Social Development Fund (FDES) is an intervention mechanism activated by CODEFI with a budget of 1 billion EUR that aims to support the financial and operational restructuring of companies in difficulty alongside private funders, mainly for companies with more than 250 employees.

Subsidized loans and repayable advances are a new discretionary intervention mechanism intended for companies with 50 to 250 employees and endowed with 500 million EUR. It is activated on the initiative of CODEFI. It is intended to be used when recourse to the EMP is not possible and the fiscal and social liability clearance plans are insufficient to allow the turnaround. Eligibility for the scheme is subject to certain conditions.

Participatory loans are intended for very small and small businesses (fewer than 50 employees) having difficulty obtaining an EMP, in order to enable them both to rebuild a cash flow and improve their balance sheet structure ("junior" loans, to be repaid in seven years). The companies concerned must contact the CODEFI in their department. After examination of the file and pre-decision by CODEFI, the company will be able to finalize its simplified application for a participatory loan on an online platform.

3.5.4 French debt management

An element specific to France may be important, despite the "whatever the cost" guideline announced by the government at the start of the lockdown on March 19, 2020. Indeed, the presidential elections will take place in 2022, and the identification of candidates will happen in 2021. In this regard, Chen et al. (2019) found that the way in which tax reforms are designed and implemented affect the likelihood of re-election of politicians. Among the most unfavorable factors for re-election are economic recession, type of tax (direct taxation, such as corporate tax), or the desire for fiscal rebalancing.

As for the French savings rate, close to 13 or 14 percent of gross disposable income since the beginning of this century, it had exceeded 15 percent in 2009 following the subprime crisis. It is estimated to exceed this threshold again in 2020, above all to the benefit of fixed income products, despite their weakness.[14] This level is regularly 1 or 2 points higher than the European average, but 2 or 3 points lower than the rates observed in Germany, the Netherlands, or Luxembourg.[15]

---

14 Source: www.banque-france.fr/statistiques/epargne-et-comptes-nationaux-financiers/epargne-des -menages
15 Source: https://ec.europa.eu/eurostat/databrowser/view/tec00131/default/table?lang=fr

3.6 Conclusion

Facing this crisis of unprecedented magnitude, not all governments have reacted in the same way. Unlike the Asian countries that were able to cope with the health crisis, France, like its European neighbors, experienced strong challenges to its health care system which led to two successive lockdowns, the first from March to May 2020 and the second from October to December 2020. In order to deal with the economic crisis that followed, and to avoid business bankruptcies as much as possible, the government has invested unprecedented amounts of money. An emergency plan of 470 billion EUR was followed by a recovery plan of 100 billion EUR, and in November 2020 new financial measures (PLFR4) were taken to face the second lockdown, hoping that there would not be a third or fourth one. But not all of these measures were implemented in 2020. To be more specific, the overall cost of the Covid-19 crisis for public finances in 2020 can be estimated at 186 billion EUR, due to revenue losses of 100 billion EUR caused by the contraction in activity and by the emergency measures implemented, which will have an impact of 86 billion EUR on the public finances in 2020. Consequently, the economy is experiencing a growing debt that will rise from 98 percent of GDP to 120 percent of GDP in 2021.

This crisis will therefore also weigh heavily on the 2021 budget, and even beyond that year, and it is essential that the situation of the French economy improves rapidly in order to limit both the social impacts of the crisis and its effects on France's financial situation, which has been steadily deteriorating over the last few decades. It should be recalled that, at the end of the subprime crisis, the public debt ratio was at 80 percent of GDP. Finally, the various announcements during November 2020 about the development of vaccines against Covid-19 were welcomed by the financial markets, giving hope for a way out of the crisis.

References

Anderson, J., Bergamini, E., Brekelmans, S., Cameron, A., Darvas, Z., Dominguez, M., Lenaerts, K. and Midoes, C. (2020), The fiscal response to the economic fallout from the coronavirus, Available on www.bruegel.org/publications/datasets/covid-national -dataset/#france

Carletti, E., Claessens, S., Fatas, A. and Vives, X. (2020), *The Bank Business Model in the post-Covid-19 World*, The Future of Banking 2. London: CEPR Press, Available on https ://voxeu.org/article/bank-business-model-post-covid-19-world

Chen, C., Dabla-Norris, E., Rappaport, J. and Zdzienicka, A. (2019), *Political costs of tax-based consolidations*. IMF working paper 19/298. Washington, DC: International Monetary Fund.

Jorda, O., Schularick, M. and Taylor, A.M. (2013), When credit bites back, *Journal of Money, Credit and Banking*, 45(2), 3–28.

Jorda, O., Singh, S.R. and Taylor, A.M. (2020), *Longer-run economic consequences of pandemics*, NBER working paper 26934.

4 The case of Germany

Frank Rövekamp

4.1 Introduction

In March 2020 the scale of the COVID-19 pandemic became evident and German authorities reacted swiftly, mobilizing unprecedented amounts of funds and modifying laws and regulations wherever deemed necessary to soften the crisis. Apparently lessons learned from the financial crisis of 2008/2009 were applied: then a similar approach prevented the world from slipping into a prolonged depression. As of December 2020, however, the crisis is not over and questions arise, whether the economic responses are having the intended effects considering the nature of the downturn, and what side effects the measures might have in the long term.

This chapter focuses especially on the issue of fiscal sustainability and the long-term effects of the COVID-19 economic crisis measures in Germany. For this purpose the unfolding of the pandemic will be reviewed with the health policy responses and the immediate economic consequences. Thereafter economic policy responses will be discussed. An evaluation of these measures and their potential long-term effects against the backdrop of the nature of the crisis will form the main part of the paper. The last section offers some reflections on the sustainability of crisis fighting.

4.2 The unfolding of the pandemic

The first COVID-19 case in Germany was confirmed on January 27, 2020. At that time the virus was still considered a thoroughly Chinese or Asian affair. German nationals were therefore evacuated from Wuhan in China on January 31. Infections increased slowly in February, but only toward the end of the month the awareness arose that the virus would seriously affect the whole society and economy. Daily infections rapidly increased in March and jumped to over 1,000 on March 12. In a speech by Chancellor Angela Merkel on March 18, a far reaching lockdown was announced, which fully took effect on March 22.[1] From that day on, only retail businesses offering essential goods for living

---

[1] Handelsblatt (2020a). The leading German economic daily paper "Handelsblatt" provides a chronology of the crisis, which is regularly updated.

DOI: 10.4324/9781003153603-4

like supermarkets could stay open; all other shops as well as restaurants, cafeterias, sports clubs, hairdressers, cosmetic studios etc. had to close. Mass events, including religious services were forbidden. There was no curfew, but no more than two people were allowed to meet in public, unless they belonged to the same household. Also mandatory social distancing was instituted requiring a minimum distance of 1.5 m between two individuals. The rules of social distancing also had to be followed by companies, which could stay open in this phase and continue with their production and other business activities.

Only in late April however did masks become mandatory on public transport and during shopping. Unlike many Asian countries there has been no tradition of wearing masks in Germany for people with a cold or hay fever or for people who want to protect themselves against infectious diseases like influenza. In the beginning it was even widely doubted that masks would have a significant positive effect even by medical experts.[2] The German federal state of Saxony was the first to order the wearing of masks on April 20, with other states following suit thereafter. This reflects the fact that individual Federal States in Germany are responsible for measures against infectious diseases, not the federation. Rules therefore often vary between states. Mask wearing eventually became widespread, but there is still a significant part of the population which disagrees with the rule and which considers masks a nuisance and a strong infringement of personal rights and freedom.[3]

The measures proved successful, however. The number of daily infections peaked at 6,922 on April 2 and thereafter steadily decreased. A stepwise easing of the measures went into effect from May 4. Schools could open again to some degree as well as essential services like hairdressers. Restaurants reopened on May 11. Customers had to register their names, addresses, and contact data in order to follow up on any potential infections, but this proved ineffective later, because the rule was not strictly followed, either by the restaurants or by the guests.

Also, after the easing of the lockdown the situation continued to improve with the number of daily infections falling below 1,000 from mid-May. Borders in the Schengen Area[4] were opened again and by June 15 a general warning against traveling abroad was replaced by travel warnings only to countries which were considered high risk areas.

On June 16, a government sponsored smartphone application was introduced in order to inform people about their infection risks. Strict data protection regulations in Germany, however, do not allow for a central collection of personalized data and so this app is dependent on voluntary input by the infected people themselves. This feature, combined with the still unsatisfactory number of users, has rendered the application rather ineffective so far.[5]

2 Medinside (2020-03-31).
3 SZ (2020-10-15).
4 The Schengen Area is formed by a group of 26 countries in Europe which have abolished passport and other controls at their borders.
5 SPIEGEL (2020-10-29).

The reopening of the borders came just in time for the holiday season in July and August and with hindsight may well have proven fateful. The German word for holiday, "Urlaub", has a much deeper significance and standing in German culture than the English translation can convey. "Urlaub" is considered a kind of natural entitlement and sacred – if anything, more akin to "Christmas" than simple "holiday". Not only is it accepted that people take about 3–4 weeks leave of absence from work and travel abroad during the summer season, often to southern countries like Spain and Italy, it is even "expected", unless one wants to take the risk of being considered rather odd by friends, colleagues, and neighbors. Therefore the main news during this time centered around the issue of how to safeguard an appropriate "Urlaub" despite the pandemic. Few media or politicians really dared to recommend not taking a holiday, let alone putting any restrictions on it. So despite some uneasiness people still flocked to foreign countries by the thousands. Free of charge COVID-19 tests for returnees were offered at airports and border checkpoints, putting a strain on the still limited testing capacities and causing delays in the issuing of results, thereby rendering them useless in many cases.[6]

The holiday season may have combined with a general feeling of an easing of the threat by the virus and may thus have prepared the ground for an increase again in infections. Also the rebounding economy may have contributed to an atmosphere of optimism and a certain carelessness along with it. Thus, the number of infections reached more than 1,000 per day again in early August and further increased steadily. October then saw a virtual explosion of infections going from 2,000 cases a day at the beginning of the month to 20,000 at the end. On October 28 therefore the Federation and the Federal States agreed on a second lockdown, albeit to a milder degree at first than in March and April. Restaurants, sports clubs, and similar services had to close again, but retail business and schools were exempted. This semi-lockdown was initially planned for one month, but infections failed to decrease. They even climbed to over 30,000 cases on some days in December. From December 16 measures were therefore tightened again with further restrictions on social contacts and the closure of retail shops and schools.

At the end of 2020 the total number of infections since the outbreak of the pandemic exceeded 1,700,000 cases. More than 33,000 of the infected persons succumbed to the virus (Figure 4.1).

4.3 Economic consequences of the pandemic and policy responses

The first shutdown in March and April had drastic consequences. The GDP in the second quarter fell by 11.3 percent compared to the previous year, the strongest

---

6 Tagesschau (2020-08-24).

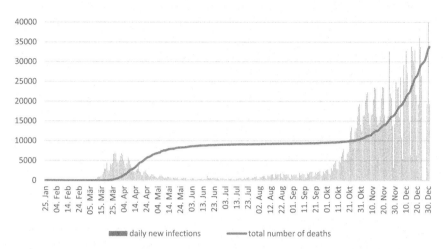

Figure 4.1 Daily new cases and total number of deaths related to COVID-19. Source: Johns Hopkins University, CSSE COVID-19 Dashboard.

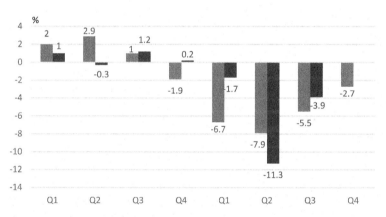

Figure 4.2 Quarterly GDP growth rate in Germany as compared to the previous year. Source: Statistisches Bundesamt (Federal Statistical Office).

decline in Germany after World War II, outpacing the decline of 7.9 percent in the second quarter of 2009 in the wake of the financial crisis (Figure 4.2).

Different industries were affected in different ways. Obviously all kinds of retail businesses, hotels, gastronomy, entertainment, airlines, and travel were hit hardest. Also the output in export oriented industries, like important machinery and automotive businesses dropped sharply. The German automotive industry is heavily reliant on the Chinese market. The outbreak of the pandemic occurred in China and economic activities there were still close to a freeze in that period with the car business suffering accordingly. As a consequence, some car factories as well as producers of the related automotive parts in Germany even closed their doors.[7] Other industries like logistics (related to online business), communications equipment (cameras, headsets etc.), bicycles, sewing-machines etc. had windfall gains which, however, were far from offsetting the downturn effects.

In this situation, the German government reacted with a range of financial and regulatory measures in order to cushion the crisis. The immediate goals were to preserve liquidity for businesses and to safeguard income for households. But later, the stimulation of aggregate demand also came into focus. Obviously the experience during the financial crisis of 2008/2009 and the European debt crisis from 2010 served as models. During the financial crisis rescue packages for the banks and other financial institutions as well as large-scale fiscal spending programs helped to control the situation and to implement a V-shaped recovery with growth rates already strongly rebounding in Germany in early 2010.[8] It was feared at that time that the crisis could develop in a similar way to the Great Depression of the 1930s, which was so deep and prolonged as fiscal and monetary interventions were nonexistent or weak and late in most countries.[9] These mistakes should not be repeated. Furthermore, the European debt crisis, which originated in Greece and threatened the break-up of the Euro area, significantly abated when the president of the European Central Bank Mario Draghi assured the financial markets in July 2012 that the ECB would support the integrity of the Euro "whatever it takes".[10] This "whatever it takes" mentality is also at work now during the pandemic: the ensuing economic crisis should be battled quickly, with any regulatory measure considered useful and with funds as large as deemed necessary.[11]

Therefore, in March various significant measures were already being devised including direct financial aid, tax relief, guaranties of employment, insolvency prevention, and other regulations.[12] Given the very detailed rules, it is not easy to get a comprehensive picture of the real extent of the measures. Guarantees, for example, only set up a framework and the extent of the state's obligations in the future remains unclear. Also, the total effects of various tax measures like the adjustment of advance payments or the extension of loss carry backs are difficult to quantify. Things are complicated further by the federal structure of Germany, where the Federal States often complement measures taken by the Federation, but each in different degrees and ways.

---

7 Fuest (2020), pp 45, 46

8 KfW (2010).

9 Kindleberger (1986).

10 KfW (2017).

11 This is well reflected for example in a speech by Olaf Scholz, the Federal Minister of Finance, made in the German parliament (Bundestag) on March 25, s. BMF (2020-03-25).

12 A comprehensive overview is given by KPMG (2020).

The extent of state intervention becomes clear, however, when illustrated with some examples.[13] The following measures serve the goal of preserving liquidity for businesses:

- A framework of 50 billion EUR was set to grant aid for struggling small and medium enterprises.
- A major package via the Economic Stabilization Fund (Wirtschaftsstabilisierungsfonds or WSF) consists of 400 billion EUR for state guaranties, 100 billion EUR additional financing for the state development bank KfW (Kreditanstalt für Wiederaufbau) and 100 billion EUR for the direct recapitalization of private companies. Using the last provision of the program, the German Federal State rescued the flagship airline Lufthansa, as the most prominent example, by injecting capital (dormant holding) to an amount of 4.7 billion EUR with options to increase the stake in the future and compounded by credit guaranties via the state development bank KfW.
- With the second lockdown in November 2020, further state aid was approved and extended to include self-employed people in the area of culture and entertainment to compensate for lost business. An individual business may receive a no-repayment-obligation subsidy of 75 percent of lost turnover under this scheme. The estimated costs are 4.5 billion EUR per week.[14]

Non-financial regulatory interventions also serve the goal of supporting businesses:

- A measure to avoid large-scale bankruptcies of businesses hit by the pandemic is the suspension of the obligation to file for insolvency, if the business is deemed to be fundamentally healthy under a set of criteria. The grace period was first set until September 30, 2020 and then it was further extended in steps to January 31, 2021.
- Another example of the legal protection of crisis-affected businesses are regulations to protect commercial tenants. Depending on certain conditions rent payments may be delayed until June 30, 2022.

The most important measure to shield the labor market from the effects of the slump, thus serving the goal of safeguarding household income, has been the short-time work scheme ("Kurzarbeit").[15] A basic version had already been introduced in 1956, allowing companies under certain conditions to reduce working hours and accordingly labor costs without laying off people. Under

---

13 BMF (2020-05-22).
14 BMF (2020-11-27).
15 Sinn (2020), pp. 37–39.

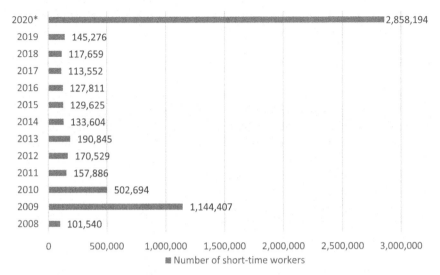

Figure 4.3 Number of short-time workers; 2008–2019 annual average, 2020 average January – November. Sources: Bundesagentur für Arbeit (Federal Employment Agency), ifo Institute.

this scheme working hours and salaries can be reduced flexibly even up to 100 percent. The individual employee on the other hand receives compensation for the loss of income via the Federal Employment Agency (Bundesanstalt für Arbeit) in the standard amount of 60 percent of the reduced net income. The scheme was widely praised during the financial crisis for avoiding a major increase in unemployment rates, often experienced by other countries in similar situations. Indeed, the sheer number of workers under the short-time scheme reveals the magnitude of the potential problem (Figure 4.3):

The original maximum six months-time limit for the short-time work scheme was temporarily extended to 24 months during the financial crisis of 2008/2009 and again during the current pandemic. This time also the standard subsidy was increased to cover 80 percent of the net compensation loss of the employees.

After implementing the measures to protect businesses and to preserve household income by safeguarding employment, the German government moved on, trying to further stimulate aggregate demand by a fiscal spending program in the magnitude of 130 billion EUR, which parliament approved on June 4, 2020. The main elements are as follows:[16]

- The biggest item is a reduction of value added tax from 19 to 16 percent (or from 7 to 5 percent for essential goods like basic food) for the period

16 Fuest (2020), pp. 64–67.

July 01 to December 31, 2020, in order to stimulate demand, especially for expensive goods like household appliances or even cars. This is projected to reduce state tax revenue by about 20 billion EUR.

- A subsidy for household electricity prices, which are very high in Germany because of extra charges for the promotion of renewable energies, amounting to about 11 billion EUR.
- Around 50 billion EUR to be spent for investments in the areas of digitalization and climate protection like the accelerated construction of the 5G network, subsidies for E-cars, hydrogen technologies, and building insulation.
- Other items of the fiscal package include, among others, subsidies for municipalities (9.9 billion EUR), further tax measures like special depreciations (8 billion EUR), and subsidies for families with children (2 billion EUR).

In addition to this, Germany also committed itself to contributing to the pandemic related European Recovery Fund, to be administered by the European Commission, with a volume of 750 billion EUR total. Half of the money is scheduled to go to EU member states especially hard hit by the crisis as non-repayment subsidies, and the other half as credits.[17] Germany's share in the EU COVID-19 programs will be about 185 billion EUR.[18]

Unlike the previous financial crisis, however, when the sharp downturn was already followed by a V-shaped recovery in early 2010, the economic crisis caused by the pandemic may well prove to be a more protracted matter. Although GDP in the third quarter of 2020 increased by over 8 percent as compared to the second, it was still about 4 percent below the previous year.[19] And the second lockdown from November will cause a downturn again.

Major bankruptcies and high unemployment have been avoided so far by the current set of measures. But given the fact that a return to normal economic conditions is not possible as long as the pandemic continues, are the measures sustainable? Furthermore how adequate are these measures in the long term?

4.4 On the sustainability of the economic policy responses

The fiscal and monetary crisis measures in the wake of the pandemic reached truly extraordinary dimensions. Already in May 2020 the Federal Ministry of Finance summed up the total volume of state credits, direct subsidies, tax relief, funds for recapitalization and guarantees to 1,177 billion EUR.[20] On

17 SVR (2020), pp. 171–173.
18 Fuest (2020), p. 69.
19 Destatis (2020-10-30).
20 BMF (2020-05-22). It should be pointed out, however, that there are considerable difficulties in reconciling this sum with the individual measures and their estimated cost. Transparency is clearly lacking as also pointed out by Sinn (2020), p. 144.

top came the fiscal spending program of 130 billion EUR, which is more than double the amount of similar programs during the financial crisis of 2008/2009.[21] Whereas it is not clear yet to what extent guarantees and other contingent payments will lead to actual public expenditures,[22] state debt in 2020 is scheduled to increase by 217 billion EUR. This compares to an originally planned balanced budget.[23] Also for 2021 new debt in the amount of 180 billion EUR is forecasted.[24]

As for the sustainability of the measures, it appears that Germany has sufficient fiscal capacity to deal with such amounts of debt for the time being. The debt to GDP ratio, which increased to 82.4 percent in 2010, fell to 60 percent in 2019, the maximum level allowed according to the so-called "Maastricht criteria" for Euro zone member countries.[25] This was guided by the so-called "debt brake", an austerity rule implemented into German Basic Law and thus even granted constitutional status in the wake of the financial crisis.[26] According to the "debt brake" the yearly fiscal deficit should not exceed 0.35 percent of GDP under normal circumstances. This can be modified in times of economic downturns and especially in times of outright crises like the current pandemic. But in these cases the government needs to provide a detailed plan on how and when the excessive debt will be repaid in the future. Germany took pride in this rule and in its balanced budgets in recent years.

In 2020, however, the debt ratio is projected to go up again to 71 percent.[27] The new fiscal deficit will be financed mostly by short-term government bonds and will come along with the mandatory repayment plan. Many economists argue, however, that Germany should have financed the new debt with long-term bonds, thereby making better use of the zero or even negative interest rates, and a newly invigorated discussion about the pros and cons of the "debt brake" has been set off.[28]

Furthermore, some argue there seems to be plenty of room to raise even more debt, not only for rescue measures, but also for long-term purposes like more investments in infrastructure and education.

It remains to be seen how these discussions will evolve, but the topic must be seen against the backdrop of the monetary policy of the European Central

---

21 Two fiscal spending packages at the end of 2008 and at the beginning of 2009 added up to 61.5 billion EUR, see Roos (2009).
22 Large parts of the guarantee, subsidy, and credit schemes still remain unused, see SVR (2020) p. 94.
23 Bundestag (2020-07-02).
24 Bundestag (2020-11-27).
25 Eurostat, Government finance statistics.
26 Grundgesetz, Art. 109.
27 Statista, Economy & Politics.
28 The issue is also openly contested among the influential government appointed five members of the German Council of Economic Experts (Sachverständigenrat), see SVR (2020), pp. 147–150.

Bank, which provides for the extremely low interest environment, thereby keeping debt servicing costs very low.[29]

If, however, gravity sets in again and inflation picks up at some point in the future and interest rates increase, the picture may change with potentially drastic consequences, given the high state debt ratios in some other countries of the Euro area. The prospect of inflation may seem remote, but as the pandemic works to reduce or restrict the supply of a range of goods and services while ample liquidity is provided by the rescue programs, the ingredients for a rise in prices are in place.[30]

In the light of potential contagion effects among the Euro area countries, the 750 billion EUR Recovery Fund of the EU may be the source of another sustainability problem (see Chapter 2 in this volume). For the first time the money is raised at the EU level, while liability stays with the member states in the end. The Recovery Fund has not taken all legislative hurdles yet and is designed so far as a one-off event, but there are voices already which call for the regular engagement of the EU in a similar fashion.[31] If a large member state like Italy needs to be bailed out in the future, Germany may be forced to provide a large share of the necessary funds one way or the other.

4.5 The nature of the crisis and the adequacy of the responses

As fiscal sustainability issues pose certain risks, but no immediate problem for Germany, the strong response to the economic crisis in the wake of the pandemic was informed by the apparent success of the measures during the financial crisis of 2008/2009 and the Euro area debt crisis of 2012. The "whatever it takes" approach allegedly prevented a slump into a 1930s style depression. This apparently also convinced erstwhile proponents of fiscal and monetary prudence even under crisis conditions such as German chancellor Angela Merkel. Thereafter, this time also a swift and big reaction was called for. But have the measures really hit the target considering the nature of the current crisis?

The financial crisis of 2008/2009 was a demand shock caused by a rapid loss of trust in the financial system. Consumers became very careful about spending

29 As with the other countries in the Euro area concerning monetary policy, Germany has to contend with the decisions of the European Central Bank. The bank has been very accommodating ever since the financial crisis began. The goal during the pandemic has been to prevent the crisis in the real economy from extending into a financial crisis. Therefore commercial banks can secure nearly unlimited liquidity at negative interest rates now. Furthermore the Pandemic Emergency Purchase Programme (PEPP) was introduced, which set up a framework of 1.85 billion EUR for the additional purchase of bonds and other public and private securities, see Neyer (2020) and Handelsblatt (2020b).

30 Also other factors like the slowdown of globalization and demographic changes may work toward this direction, see *The Economist* (2020), Goodhart and Pradhan (2020).

31 Reuters (2020-10-12).

money and the sharp downturn in export demand and ensuing downturn in investments exacerbated the situation. Furthermore things could not be fixed easily by monetary policy as the transmission mechanisms were rendered ineffective by the banking crisis. Rapid monetary easing by the reduction of interest rates and by asset purchase programs did therefore not stimulate demand appreciably but simply prevented banks from failing. Once, therefore, trust in the financial system resumed and domestic and export demand picked up again, the crisis was left behind and regular growth resumed.

The main characteristic of the current crisis on the other hand is an exogenous shock with a combined effect on supply and demand. On the supply side, with the closure of shops, many services cannot be provided and, if international supply chains do not fully function anymore or if social distancing reduces productivity, production of physical goods is affected. Also, the demand side is impeded not only by monetary effects like reduced income or precautionary savings but by the same physical barrier of social distancing. It is not clear, furthermore, when the pandemic will come to an end.

In this situation the goal of economic crisis fighting can obviously not be to return to "normal" conditions as quickly as possible. The issue is rather to weather the crisis as long as it takes without a major breakdown of important institutions, rapidly increasing unemployment and social unrest, while at the same time allowing for structural change – like an accelerated trend toward digitalization – which is occurring because of the crisis. To evaluate the measures taken, the following questions need to be considered:

1. Do the measures support critical institutions threatened by the crisis, which are fundamentally sound?
2. Do they prevent strong increases in unemployment?
3. Do they help preserve social stability by checking increasing inequality related to the crisis?
4. Do they support structural change toward industries and forms of employment evolving from the crisis?
5. Are they financially sustainable even over a longer period of time?

It should be noted that there is a strong likelihood of trade-offs between criteria 1–3 on the one hand and 4 and 5 on the other. Preserving institutions may run counter to promoting different industry structures, for example, and the cost for subsidies to keep employment may eventually become untenable.

How do the measures taken by the German government fare against these criteria?

Parts of the fiscal spending program need to be viewed rather critically. The VAT reduction, especially, has met with skepticism.[32] It appears contradictory to induce people to go shopping while at the same time trying to minimize

---

32 Fuest (2020), pp. 60–63.

social contact. A recent survey, furthermore, showed that the 3 percent reduction does not really induce people to purchase goods they would not buy anyway or to bring forward major investments in expensive appliances, cars, or similar items.[33] The 20 billion EUR may go to waste.

Some of the subsidies are also worthy of critical analysis. Whereas investments in a modern 5G network and digitalization may be considered positive in terms of the expected structural changes, subsidies in hydrogen technologies, E-cars, and other environment related projects seem to mix dual purposes and may thus miss the target of promoting growth by steering resources into potentially non-competitive fields.

A close look at the recapitalization undertakings of the Economic Stabilization Fund (WSF) also reveals the potentially problematic nature of some rescue measures. The Fund was established in March 2020 to support companies with a "special significance for the German economy" hit by the Corona crisis. It is modeled after the Financial Market Stabilization Fund (Finanzmarktstabilisierungsfonds FMSF), which was founded in October 2008 for the purpose of rescuing banks in the wake of the Lehman shock. In order to stabilize the financial system the FMSF acted quickly to recapitalize "systemic relevant" banks like Commerzbank, WestLB, and Hypo Real Estate. The idea was to sell the shares again after the crisis without a loss for the tax payer. But even today, some 12 years later, the FMSF is still the major shareholder in Commerzbank; its equity stake of 15.6 percent, once acquired for about 5 billion EUR, is worth around 1.5 billion EUR as of December 2020.[34] The implications of the state being stuck with a major equity share in a private financial institution are regularly part of political quarrels. This does not bode well for the undertakings of the Economic Stabilization Fund. For one it is even less easy to argue about "systemic relevance" for companies in the real economy than it is for financial institutions. A closer look reveals the issue: the WSF has spent about 9 billion EUR in credit and equity to support the German flagship carrier Lufthansa. It furthermore supports the travel conglomerate TUI with funds of about 5 billion EUR so far, FTI Touristik, another travel conglomerate, with 150 million EUR, and shipbuilder MV Werften Holding, which specializes in large passenger cruise ships, with 193 million EUR.[35]

Taken all together it seems questionable whether this portfolio constitutes a group of truly "systemic relevant" companies. On the contrary it may be expected that travel activities will not fully resume even after the pandemic as people get a taste for the potential of online conferences and holidays closer to home instead of in faraway places. This is underlined already by a fresh tug of war between the crisis companies Lufthansa and TUI about market share in the

33 SVR (2020), 119.
34 Finanzagentur Finanzmarktstabilisierung (2020).
35 Finanzagentur Wirtschaftsstabilisierung (2020).

area of touristic air flights, which are assumed will resume after the pandemic albeit at lower levels than before. It currently seems that neither company will profit from these maneuvers, raising strong doubts about directing taxpayers' money into this area.[36]

A further concern is that companies will apply for funds, seeing a chance of getting state aid although their difficulties started long before the pandemic.[37]

While hard to quantify the effects, these examples show that the trade-off between the preservation of more or less "systemic relevant" companies and proper adjustments for inevitable structural change may be large. The same is true for other measures: the suspension of the obligation to file for insolvency for ever longer periods of time may in the end create a large number of "zombie companies" which are not competitive anymore.[38] Likewise, the short-time working scheme, which certainly has been a very effective instrument in preventing large-scale unemployment and the accompanying social unrest in times of crisis, may become a hindrance to necessary structural change if prolonged for too long. In this connection especially the increase of the standard allowance for short-time work from 60 percent to 80 percent of net income may set incentives working against the goal of promoting structural change.

4.6 Conclusion: the trade-off between crisis fighting and sustainability

The total commitment of the German state to fighting the economic fallout of the Coronavirus pandemic stands at about 1.500 billion EUR or 43 percent of GDP – a truly huge, unprecedented sum. Certainly, this has prevented the German economy from collapsing, mass unemployment, and the ensuing social unrest. But there are also signs of overshooting. Many measures may work to preserve structures which even before the crisis were already slow in making the necessary changes. The balance appears tipped toward preserving "whatever it takes" instead of smoothing the way for structural change while protecting the really vulnerable. Unlike the financial crisis of 2008/2009, however, this crisis will not fade away quickly and the longer it takes the more the issue of the financial sustainability of the rescue packages may move into the foreground. This is exacerbated by the political struggles around the rescue measures, which tend to get worse over time. More and more requests appear which seem to be not so much driven by concerns to cushion the crisis, but

---

36 Handelsblatt (2020c).

37 An example is Thyssenkrupp, formed by the merger in 1999 of the old traditional steel conglomerates in the Ruhr area in Germany Thyssen and Krupp. It is engaged today in various industrial activities, but still has failed to put its steel business on a healthy footing. In an interview Martina Merz, Thyssenkrupp's CEO, confirmed talks about potential state aid, stating that the pandemic has wiped out the original restructuring plan, s. FAZ (2020-11-14).

38 In a survey of 120 German economists 86 percent raised concerns in this regard, s. FAZ (2020-10-19). Strong evidence, however, remains elusive so far.

rather by ideological positions. The crisis seems to be an opportunity to aim for pushing through long-cherished positions like the nationalization of certain industry branches or enacting strict requirements for the introduction of environmentally friendly technologies like E-cars.

The historian Peter Wetzler observed that military strategists have a tendency to prepare for wars which have already been fought. So the Japanese navy prepared for the Pacific War mostly with big battleships as these were crucial for winning the Russo-Japanese War of 1904/05 with the epic sea battle in the Tsushima Strait. Times changed, however, and the Pacific War did not see any large-scale battleship sea battles. Most of these dinosaurs fell prey instead to modern American carrier-based planes not on the radar screens of Japanese naval planners.[39] The result is known.

We may have a similar problem with economic crises.[40] Preparations are often geared toward the past instead of considering how the scenarios about future events may evolve. "Whatever it takes" may have worked during the financial crisis and the ensuing Euro area debt crisis, but the pandemic is a different and more protracted matter. Instead of throwing large sums at everything, the promotion of structural change by focusing on large investments in digitalization and education, on supporting the labor market and tax reforms, and on social security designed to cushion the transformation instead of cementing in non-competitive structures is extremely important. Better-focused crisis fighting could preserve considerable fire power and, moreover, preclude sustainability issues for a long time.

References

Bundesministerium der Finanzen (BMF) (2020-03-25). Rede von Olaf Scholz am 25. März 2020 im Deutschen Bundestag zur Bewältigung Corona-Krise. www.bundesfinan zministerium.de/Content/DE/Reden/2020/2020-03-25-BT-Rede-Corona.html, Retrieved November 29, 2020.

Bundesministerium der Finanzen (BMF) (2020-05-22). Kampf gegen Corona: Größtes Hilfspaket in der Geschichte Deutschlands. www.bundesfinanzministerium.de/Content /DE/Standardartikel/Themen/Schlaglichter/Corona-Schutzschild/2020-03-13-Milli arden-Schutzschild-fuer-Deutschland.html, Retrieved November 29, 2020.

Bundesministerium der Finanzen (BMF) (2020-11-27). Stark durch die Krise: Dezemberhilfe kommt, Überbrückungshilfe wird deutlich erweitert und verlängert. www.bundesfinanzministerium.de/Content/DE/Pressemitteilungen/Finanzpolitik/ 2020/11/2020-11-27-PM-dezemberhilfe-ueberbrueckungshilfe-III.html, Retrieved November 29, 2020.

Bundestag (2020-07-02). Zweiter Nachtragshaushalt beschlossen. www.bundestag.de/pre sse/hib/703976-703976, Retrieved November 29, 2020.

---

39 Wetzler (2020), p. 170.

40 This is also pointed out by the economic historian Albrecht Ritschl, who considers the crisis fighting of 2008 mostly directed toward the problems of 1929, see Ritschl (2012), p. 37.

Bundestag (2020-11-27). Bundeshaushalt 2021 beschlossen. www.bundestag.de/presse/hib /810198-810198, Retrieved November 29, 2020.

Destatis (2020-10-30). Statistisches Bundesamt. Bruttoinlandsprodukt im 3. Quartal 2020 um 8,2% höher als im Vorquartal. www.destatis.de/DE/Presse/Pressemitteilungen/ 2020/10/PD20_432_811.html, Retrieved November 29, 2020.

Eurostat. European Commission, Eurostat, Government Finance Statistics. https://ec.euro pa.eu/eurostat/web/government-finance-statistics/data/database, Retrieved November 30, 2020.

FAZ (2020-10-19). Volkswirte fürchten "Zombie-Unternehmen". www.faz.net/aktuell/ wirtschaft/unternehmen/volkswirte-fuerchten-zombie-unternehmen-17008261.html, Retrieved January 02, 2021.

FAZ (2020-11-14). Frankfurter Allgemeine Zeitung (FAZ). "Wir sanieren gegen die Uhr.", November 14, 2020, p. 28.

Finanzagentur. Finanzmarktstabilisierung. Sondervermögen Finanzmarktstabilisierungsfonds. www.deutsche-finanzagentur.de/de/finanzmarkt-stabilisierung/, Retrieved November 30, 2020.

Finanzagentur. Wirtschaftsstabilisierung. Sondervermögen Wirtschaftsstabilisierungsfonds. www.deutsche-finanzagentur.de/de/wirtschafts-stabilisierung/, Retrieved November 30, 2020.

Fuest, Clemens (2020). *Wie wir unsere Wirtschaft retten – Der Weg aus der Corona-Krise*. Berlin: Aufbau Verlag.

Goodhart, Charles and Pradhan, Manoj (2020). *The Great Demographic Reversal*. London: Palgrave Macmillan.

Grundgesetz. Grundgesetz der Bundesrepublik Deutschland, Art. 9. https://dejure.org/ gesetze/GG/109.html https://dejure.org/gesetze/GG/109.html, Retrieved January 03, 2021.

Handelsblatt (2020a). Coronavirus: So hat sich die Lungenkrankheit in Deutschland entwickelt. www.handelsblatt.com/politik/deutschland/covid-19-in-deutschland-coronavirus-so-hat-sich-die-lungenkrankheit-in-deutschland-entwickelt/25584942 .html?ticket=ST-3801993-hct5mR3s7rUtsnhBVPRv-ap4, Retrieved December 01, 2020.

Handelsblatt (2020b). EZB im Kaufrausch, December 11/12/13, 2020, pp. 6, 7

Handelsblatt (2020c). Finanzhilfen verschärfen Preiskampf, December 8, 2020, p. 20

Kindleberger, Charles P. (1986). *The World in Depression, 1929–1939*. Berkeley, CA: University of California Press.

Kreditanstalt für Wiederaufbau (KfW) (2010). Paukenschlag im 2. Quartal: Deutsches BIP steht 2010 vor Rekordzuwachs; Belebung bei Unternehmensinvestitionen, www.kfw .de/Download-Center/Konzernthemen/Research/PDF-Dokumente-Investbarom eter/KfW-Investbarometer-September-2010.pdf, Retrieved November 29, 2020.

Kreditanstalt für Wiederaufbau (KfW) (2017). Economics in Brief: Five years of "whatever it takes": three words that saved the Euro. www.kfw.de/PDF/Download-Center/Konz ernthemen/Research/PDF-Dokumente-Volkswirtschaft-Kompakt/One-Pager-2017 -EN/VK-No.-139-July-2017-Whatever-it-takes_EN.pdf, Retrieved November 29, 2020.

KPMG (2020). Germany – Government and institution measures in response to COVID-19. https://home.kpmg/xx/en/home/insights/2020/04/germany-government-and-i nstitution-measures-in-response-to-covid.html, Retrieved November 29, 2020.

Medinside (2020-03-31). Corona: Das sagen Experten über Masken. www.medinside.c h/de/post/corona-das-sagen-experten-ueber-masken, Retrieved November 28, 2020.

Neyer, Ulrike (2020). Die geldpolitischen Maßnahmen des Eurosystems in der Corona-Krise. *Perspektiven der Wirtschaftspolitik*, 21(3), 273–279.

Reuters (2020-10-12). EU moving towards fiscal union with pandemic recovery plan: German FinMin. www.reuters.com/article/us-eu-economy-germany-idUSKBN26X13H, Retrieved November 30, 2020.

Ritschl, Albrecht (2012). War 2008 das neue 1929? Richtige und falsche Vergleiche zwischen der Großen Depression der 1930er Jahre und der Großen Rezession von 2008. *Perspektiven der Wirtschaftspolitik*, 13 (Special Issue), 36–57.

Roos, Michael W.M. (2009). Die deutsche Fiskalpolitik während der Wirtschaftskrise 2008/2009. *Perspektiven der Wirtschaftspolitik*, 10(4), 389–412.

Sinn, Hans-Werner (2020). *Der Corona-Schock – Wie die Wirtschaft überlebt*. Freiburg: Verlag Herder.

SPIEGEL (2020-10-29). Was bringt die Warn-App? www.spiegel.de/netzwelt/apps/was-bringt-die-warn-app-a-c516f63e-f44c-45ef-871e-b6025355e73b, Retrieved November 28, 2020.

Statista. Europäische Union: Prognose zur Staatsverschuldung in den Mitgliedstaaten von 2019 bis 2022. https://de.statista.com/statistik/daten/studie/207261/umfrage/prognose-der-staatsverschuldung-von-ausgewaehlten-europaeischen-laendern/, Retrieved November 30, 2020.

SVR (2020). Sachverständigenrat zur Begutachtung der wirtschaftlichen Entwicklung (SVR). Corona-Krise gemeinsam bewältigen, Resilienz und Wachstum stärken. Jahresgutachten 2020/1. Wiesbaden.

Süddeutsche Zeitung (SZ) (2020-10-15). Die Krux mit den Maskenverweigerern. www.sueddeutsche.de/wirtschaft/maske-einkaufen-handel-maskenverweigerer-1.5072991, Retrieved November 28, 2020.

Tagesschau (2020-08-24). Corona-Pflichttests bald Geschichte? www.tagesschau.de/inland/testkapazitaeten-corona-101.html, Retrieved November 28, 2020.

The Economist (2020). Briefing Inflation – Prognostication and prophecy, December 12th – 18th 2020.

Wetzler, Peter (2020). *Imperial Japan and Defeat in the Second World War: The Collapse of an Empire*. London: Bloomsbury Academic.

5 The case of Italy

Claudio Cozza[1] and Leopoldo Nascia[2,3]

5.1 Covid-19 pandemic outbreak in Italy

5.1.1 The Covid-19 pandemic timeline in Italy

Less than one month after the first case officially acknowledged by the WHO in Wuhan province of China, Covid-19 hit Europe on February 21, 2020, with the first registered case in Codogno (Lombardy Region), Italy. Within a few days the surrounding towns registered a large increase in new cases of Covid-19. Italian government policy shifted quickly from limitations on access to Italy of people from China to domestic containment measures. The initial containment measures quarantined ten towns around Codogno, with significant restrictions on mobility, while the virus was still circulating across the country, with hundreds of new cases in Lombardy and Veneto. After a few days these measures were extended to all Northern Italy and finally, on March 9, the government put the whole country into lockdown with significant mobility restrictions, closure of every education institution, every kind of public space, and of the borders of the country. On March 21 the government expanded lockdown measures to all "non-essential" productive activities because the pandemic was not yet showing any significant slowdown.

Only from May 4 on did the government gradually lifted the most significant restrictions. From May to the second half of August the pandemic slowed down with just some hundreds of daily new cases in the country. The government lifted mobility restrictions and partially lifted social distancing limitations. Toward the end of August, mainly due to the return of people from summer holidays, the number of Covid-19 cases again started to increase. At the end of September, two weeks from school re-opening, the pandemic curve rose up. The daily number of new positive cases reached levels that were six times higher than at the peak in the first wave, mainly due the higher number of diagnostic

---

1 Parthenope University of Naples.
2 ISTAT, Istituto Nazionale di Statistica.
3 The opinions expressed in this publication are those of the authors. They do not purport to reflect the opinions or views of the affiliating institutions.

DOI: 10.4324/9781003153603-5

Table 5.1 Share of companies with turnover set to zero in March–April 2020, by sector of economic activity

Overall economy	*14.6%*
Sports activities and amusement and recreation activities	58.2%
Travel agencies and tour operators	57.1%
Accommodation services	50.9%
Artistic activities	42.5%
Gambling and betting activities	36.6%
Restaurants	35.4%

Source: own elaboration on ISTAT (2020b).

tests performed by the health system. However, increased hospitalizations, and the greater number of intensive care units (ICUs) used by Covid-19 patients meant that the number of deaths only peaked close to the same number recorded in the first wave.[4] Conversely from the first wave, the new pandemic outbreak also hit some Central and Southern regions of the country, usually with local health systems less efficient than in the northern regions.[5] During September, the government approach showed some relevant changes in respect to those in March. Compared to the first wave, the mitigation strategy was very flexible with the government classifying in each region the applicable emergency level, and the typology of restrictions, according to a set of regional weekly indicators.[6] The fear of a prolonged recession and conflict within government slowed down the ability to quickly set in place restrictions, despite the warnings from eminent members of the scientific community who forecasted the risks of the ongoing second wave.[7] The restrictions were imposed gradually: only on November 4 did the government adopt some stringent restrictions which were limited to some regions only. These measures were milder than those in March, even in the regions hit more severely by the pandemic, both in terms of stringency and duration (Figure 5.1). Only in December did the pandemic curve slow down

4 In November the pandemic reached nearly 40,000 new daily cases and more than 500 daily deaths.

5 During the peak of the second wave eight regions had the status of "red zone" with the highest level of restrictions, namely Lombardy, Piedmont, Autonomous County of Bolzen, Aosta Valley, Tuscany, Abruzzo, and Campania.

6 The list of 21 regional indicators has been provided in the DPCM of April 26, 2020, www.governo.it/ sites/new.governo.it/files/Dpcm_img_20200426.pdf. During the second wave of the pandemic the government imposed restrictions in each region according to these indicators.

7 Giorgio Parisi, the president of Accademia dei Lincei forecast the impact of the second wave on 21/10/2020: www.huffingtonpost.it/entry/misure-drastiche-o-a-meta-novembre-500-morti-al -giorno-di-g-parisi_it_5f8ffeaec5b686eaaa0cbfcf?utm_hp_ref=it-accademia-dei-lincei. Around 100 scientists and professors sent a letter to the Prime Minister requesting the immediate introduction of a stringent lockdown on 23/10/2020: www.huffingtonpost.it/entry/covid-100-tra-prof-e-scienziati-scrivono-a-conte-e-mattarella-subito-misure-drastiche_it_5f92aefdc5b61c185f493035

COVID-19: Government Response Stringency Index

This is a composite measure based on nine response indicators including school closures, workplace closures, and travel bans, rescaled to a value from 0 to 100 (100 = strictest). If policies vary at the subnational level, the index is shown as the response level of the strictest sub-region.

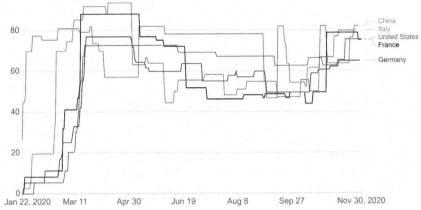

Source: Hale, Webster, Petherick, Phillips, and Kira (2020). Oxford COVID-19 Government Response Tracker – Last updated 2 December, 00:01 (London time)
Note: This index simply records the number and strictness of government policies, and should not be interpreted as 'scoring' the appropriateness or effectiveness of a country's response.
OurWorldInData.org/coronavirus • CC BY

Figure 5.1 The Italian government response stringency index

with less pressure on hospitals and ICUs, with some supplementary restrictions applied for the Christmas holidays.

5.1.2 Government response to mitigate the pandemic

The pandemic outbreak caught the country unprepared for the rapid diffusion of the contagion. The government opted for a strict lockdown to deal with the crash of the health system. The Italian lockdown was the most stringent among western democratic countries and in some degree also in respect of the Chinese one. Italy's response to the pandemic has been very quick and has earned the respect of the other EU countries and it contributed positively to controlling the first wave of the pandemic. The quick response in respect of mobility restrictions prevented the pandemic severely affecting the whole country. The effective reproduction number[8] (Rt), the major indicator measuring the dynamics of pandemics in Italy, was less than one after 39 days, a shorter reduction period than France (50) and the United Kingdom (54), although slightly longer than Germany (37) and Spain (34).[9]

---

8 The aim of mitigation strategies is to reduce the Rt to below one, where each positive-tested individual infects fewer than one other individual.

9 OECD/European Union (2020).

The pressure of the pandemic outbreak on the health system has been huge from the beginning of the first wave. Between February and May 2020 Italy recorded more than 33,000 confirmed Covid-19 deaths, and the number of daily hospitalizations peaked at 33,000 in April and at nearly 4,100 ICU cases out of a total of 5,184 available ICUs in the whole country.

Moreover, the pandemic severely hit the northern regions of the country with a huge increase in the death rate and the risk of the collapse of the regional health system in Lombardy. In March and April 2020, the death rate in the northern regions of the country increased in relation to the rest of the country, in comparison to the average for 2015–2019, by 93.9 percent and 74.3 percent, respectively, confirming the high degree of territorial concentration of the pandemic.[10] The concentration of the pandemic in a few regions required a large amount of relocation of patients, especially in cases of severe respiratory risk. For some weeks the saturation levels of ICUs in Lombardy was close to the 100 percent with extraordinary pressure on the insufficient numbers of medical personnel required to tackle the emergency.

The pressure on the health service increased again in October. The number of daily hospital cases was close to 39,000 at the end of November, with around 3,800 daily cases in ICUs (Figure 5.2).

Despite the larger number of available hospital beds and ICUs, the larger number of medical personnel, and the greater availability of personal protection

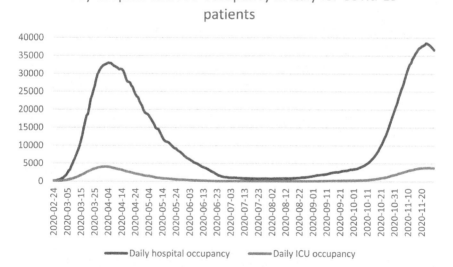

Figure 5.2 Hospital beds and ICU occupancy during the pandemic in Italy. Source: European Centre for Disease Prevention and Control.

10 ISTAT (2020a).

equipment (PPE) for hospitals and for the population in general, the second wave of the virus had a huge impact in terms of the number of deaths and pressure on the health system.

The number of recorded deaths due to Covid-19 by December was close to 60,000 from the beginning of the pandemic, 25,000 of which occurred during the second wave, a share close to 10 percent of the total yearly deaths in the country.

5.1.3 The impact of Covid-19 on the public health system

The Italian public health system is designed to provide universal services to the population, in cooperation with the private health sector. The organization is decentralized, and regional governments are in charge of providing local health services. The Ministry of Health has the role of coordinating the regional systems which have a large degree of managerial autonomy.

The Covid-19 pandemic outbreak tested the resilience[11] of the national health system that was still suffering from the budget cuts of the post-2008 austerity measures and a widening gap with the other major EU countries. According to OECD estimates, Italy reduced the share of GDP to finance the public health system from 7 percent of GDP in 2009 to 6.4 percent in 2019 and from $151b to $141b, measured in constant prices (base = 2015).[12] Conversely, Germany, France, and the United Kingdom increased public financing of health services in terms of shares of GDP and in absolute terms in the same years.

The Italian hospital system on the eve of the pandemic outbreak had a lower capacity than the EU average: 3.1 hospital beds per 1,000 population and 8.6 ICUs per 100,000 population in Italy compared with 5.0 hospital beds and 12.9 ICUs in the EU on average.[13]

Thus, the 180,000 available beds in hospitals and the 5,184 intensive care units were at risk of sudden saturation due to the pandemic outbreak.[14] Moreover, the staff employed by the health service, who were at the forefront of the response to the pandemic, were still suffering from the fall between 2012 and 2017 of 20,000 personnel out of a total of around 670,000.[15]

5.1.4 Government financing and the strategy to
increase the health system capacity

March and April 2020 were also characterized by shortages for medical staff of PPE such as face masks and other protective equipment, shortages of ICUs, hospital beds, and of diagnostic tests.

11 See OECD, European Commission (2020: 21–25) for the concept of resilience.
12 Data available in https://stats.oecd.org/
13 Source: OECD Health Statistics 2020; Eurostat New Cronos Database.
14 Corte dei Conti (2020).
15 There was a huge contraction of permanent positions between 2012 and 2017 only partially compensated by the increase in temporary positions. Additionally, around 11,000 doctors emigrated according to the estimates of the Corte dei Conti (2020).

Domestic production of PPE and ventilators and equipment required for ICUs was marginal and requirements were largely dependent on imports from abroad. Moreover, the temporary trade barriers and transport limitations quickly imposed by the other EU countries compromised the supplies of protective equipment and required the setting-up of new channels of supply from the government.

The lack of adequate containment protocols and of PPE in hospitals and long-term care facilities caused widespread contagion between patients and medical personnel. According to the Covid-19 monitoring bulletin of the Istituto Superiore di Sanità, the institution in charge of monitoring the pandemic, as of June 1, 28,319 health personnel were Covid-19 positive out of 233,607 cases in Italy.[16] The contagion among hospital staff increased the difficulty of dealing with the increasing number of patients.

The priority of the government strategy was to quickly strengthen the public health system with additional medical staff and to streamline purchasing procedures to deal in a timely manner with the shortage of medical supplies and intensive care units equipment. The simplification of standards for PPE production and innovative public procurement through subsidizing companies to set up new production activities for PPE was a key feature of the government strategy.

In March two emergency laws, DL 14/2020 and DL 18/2020,[17] made available additional budget sums of €770m to hire new personnel in the health system and to postpone the retirement of current medical personnel. The emergency laws included a fast recruitment procedure for medical staff which extended also to students close to the end of their medical specialization schools, to medical staff living abroad, and to retired health workers.

The public health system has hired 29,433 additional health professionals since March 2020 to combat Covid-19 (across all contract types and facilities), including 6,330 doctors and 13,607 nurses.[18]

Emergency legislation in March created the office of "Commissario Straordinario per l'Emergenza"[19] to centralize the purchase of PPE and ICU equipment in an effective and timely manner. The new office launched a fast-track public procurement policy to purchase equipment for an additional 5,000 ICUs, namely 1,800 high intensity ventilators and 3,200 turbine-based ventilators, to double the existing capacity. The policy included a set of incentives to increase the productivity of domestic producers of ICU equipment with the cooperation of the public sector. Public–private cooperation was a key feature

16 The bulletin is downloadable at www.epicentro.iss.it/coronavirus/bollettino/Infografica_1giugno %20ITA.pdf
17 DL 14/2020.
18 OECD, European Commission, 2020: 78.
19 The Commissario Straordinario was the body in charge of managing and allocating medical supplies to the hospitals in the country. It replaced the role of regional governments that were in charge by law to manage the regional health systems.

of the policy involving large domestic companies reconverting their productive capacity into PPE production. The public sector provided the machinery, raw materials, and certifications for the private business paid to manufacture PPE in domestic outlets. Moreover, the Commissario Straordinario office was responsible for the management of the logistics in respect of the timely importation of the PPE and diagnostic tests during the first months of the pandemic outbreak. At the end of November 2020, the number of operating ICUs was 8,836 with the potential to increase that number to 11,199 according to the estimates of the Commissario Straordinario.[20]

Moreover, the government managed the transformation of hospital wards into ICUs, supported the creation of field hospitals, also in cooperation with the army, and relocated patients to hospitals with spare capacity.[21] During the first wave the government designed a contact tracing procedure managed by the local health system offices. However, even by October contact tracing was only partially effective and was unable to deal with the quick increase of positive cases.

According to the estimates of the Ufficio Parlamentare di Bilancio[22] (UPB, Parliamentary Budget Office, the independent body in charge of the audit of public expenditure), the additional funding for the public health system amounted to €7.8bn, of which €4.6bn was managed centrally by the government. The strengthening of the regional health services to provide assistance to patients and to reduce the pressure on the Emergency Room departments of hospitals, although financed with a budget of almost €1.5bn, was only partially implemented and was not yet effective during the second wave of the pandemic.

Finally, the budget law under discussion in December, assigned for 2021 some €4bn of additional funding to the health system. The budget law measures are largely aimed at financing the emergency, the wages of the health personnel and the purchase of the vaccine, with only €1m allocated directly to reinforce the health system.

5.2 The impact on production and public spending/welfare policy

5.2.1 *The impact of the economic lockdown on the overall business sectors*

The fall in Italian GDP in 2020 is expected to be around 10 percent mostly due to the sharp decrease between March and April (see Figure 5.3), during the spring lockdown. During the first half of 2020, the fall in GDP was dramatic, at −17.8 percent. In the following months, the relaxation of the restriction

---

20 www.invitalia.it/chi-siamo/area-media/notizie-e-comunicati-stampa/conferenza-stampa-commis sario-26-novembre-2020
21 OECD (2020).
22 Ufficio Parlamentare di Bilancio (2020).

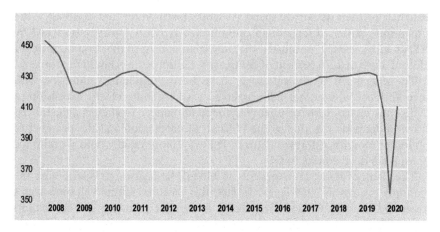

Figure 5.3 Italian GDP, 2008-2020 (third quarter). Source: ISTAT (2020d).

measures gave new space to renewed production activities. After the publication by ISTAT of preliminary GDP estimations of the third quarter, showing a recovery of 16.1 percent in relation to the second quarter, the new estimation in respect of the yearly 2020 GDP decrease is limited to −8.2 percent. However, the second wave of the pandemic has aggravated the crisis. In the last quarter of 2020 the limitations to trade, mobility and some services suggest a worsening of the GDP not yet included in the available estimates in July and in the update in September of the Economic and Financial Document of the Department of the Treasury.[23] This is in line with the trend in other countries most affected by the pandemic.

The GDP reduction, during spring, was mostly due to the specific measures undertaken by the Italian government to stop the pandemic: many economic activities were temporarily closed; as a result, some companies have never resumed their activities; and entire sectors – such as transport, tourism, and cultural activities – have continued diminishing throughout the whole of 2020.

While the lockdown in spring (between March 9 and May 4) caused an interruption in activities, especially of smaller companies, lockdowns in autumn have been limited to specific regions or sectors, with very heterogeneous consequences.

Overall, the spring lockdown gave rise to the suspension of activities for 2.1m companies, equal to 48 percent of the total, which employed 7.1m personnel, around 30 percent of the total.[24]

23 Ministero dell'Economia e Finanza (2020).
24 Parliamentary audition of Roberto Monducci, ISTAT, April 28, 2020 www.istat.it/it/files//2020/04 /Istat_Audizione-DEF_28aprile2020.pdf

Looking at macro-sectors, construction and service companies had more than half of their activity suspended, while for industry and commerce the suspension accounted for around one third of activity. A survey launched by ISTAT in May 2020[25] estimated that in March and April the drop in turnover affected more than 70 percent of companies, causing serious liquidity problems.

The effects on work and wages have been temporarily addressed with unconditional subsidies for self-employed workers and with the expansion to SMEs and micro-firms of unemployment insurance. Domestic demand has shown a dramatic fall, due to the collapse of production and the prospect of job losses; moreover, foreign demand fell even more rapidly with world trade in a sudden deep contraction.

The Bank of Italy[26] estimates that it will take at least three years before the economy returns to 2019 levels. In fact, this crisis has affected all dimensions across the national economy especially household spending and the export trade of Italian companies. In the first half of the year the collapse of world trade deeply affected Italian exports which fell by over a third in value. Even more serious was the fall in business investment, influenced by uncertainty and high corporate debt, due to a decade of stagnation after the 2008 crisis. Conversely, disposable income fell in the first two quarters by only 6.6 percent, thanks to the government's income support measures.

5.2.2 The unequal impact across sectors and on key players during the lockdown

The Italian production system had not fully recovered from the effects of the 2008 and 2011 crises when in 2020 it had to face another crisis. Therefore, the unequal impact of the pandemic across sectors can be estimated on the basis of very recent national statistics, developed during the pandemic.

In May 2020, just after the end of the lockdown period, one third of Italian manufacturing companies declared to ISTAT[27] that they were "at risk of failure" due to the fall in demand, a widespread condition especially in traditional sectors (textiles, wood and furniture, ceramics, etc.); another third declared that they were beginning a process of change and reorganization.

Not all economic sectors have been helped by government intervention, and this has been especially due to the prevalence in Italy of many informal sectors. Thus, small traditional companies, especially companies with low profit margins and facing higher barriers to access the credit market, might not survive the pandemic crisis, especially in some service sectors like tourism, cultural, and transportation services. Conversely, larger companies have the opportunity to take advantage of the expansive fiscal policy of the government

---

25 ISTAT (2020b).
26 Banca d'Italia (2020).
27 ISTAT (2020c).

and are able to grow with new market opportunities. In addition, larger companies, which are often the most internationalized, have tended to postpone some strategic investments. These companies also availed of the opportunity to reorganize their internal processes and to accelerate their digital transformation. Some smaller companies that did not close, instead, simply went on with the same type of activities as before. The joint occurrence of these strategies – the closing of many micro and small companies, "business as usual" for a minority of small companies, and reorganization for larger companies – represents the basis for an even more pronounced inequality among companies in the future.

Concerning firm size, the ISTAT statistics (2020b) show that the 45 percent of companies with a minimum of three employees stopped their activities during the spring lockdown. However, this share increases to almost 50 percent if looking only at micro–firms (those with three to nine employees), which represent the large majority of companies in the Italian economy; conversely, only 19.2 percent of medium companies and 14.5 percent of large companies stopped their activity during the lockdown. The main reason for this difference is due to the inability of a large share of micro (15.3 percent) and small (11.6 percent) companies in adapting their working spaces according to government rules of distancing. In addition, according to medium and large companies, a larger share of their working places were quickly re-adapted or could be adapted to distancing rules, with only a tiny minority of companies unable to do so.

The second feature determining company survival or closure related to the sector they belonged to. More than 70 percent of companies declared a strong reduction in turnover between March and April, and the degree of reduction strongly varies across sectors (see Figure 5.1). In particular, service sectors related to travel and entertainment activities have seen a dramatic reduction in business activity.

The adaptation to government rules on distancing have adopted especially a form of "smart working". This is another cause of inequality among sectors. According to the ISTAT statistics, the share of activities that cannot be moved to smart working varies dramatically. For companies in the NACE section J (Information and communications), only one fourth of personnel cannot be moved to smart working; at the other extreme, the distribution companies in the NACE section I (Accommodation and Food Service Activities) are characterized by all employees being unable to use smart working. In between, Italian manufacturing companies (NACE section C) reflect the overall economic situation: almost 80 percent of the employees cannot use smart working options at all, and only a very tiny minority of manufacturing companies can put more than half of their employees into smart working.

Another crucial issue is financial constraints. If liquidity problems are obviously more relevant for smaller companies, a strong heterogeneity across sectors exists, too. Overall, more than 50 percent of companies declare they will face mid-term liquidity problems, with the share going up in the construction and *Made in Italy* manufacturing sectors. For example, 64.5 percent of

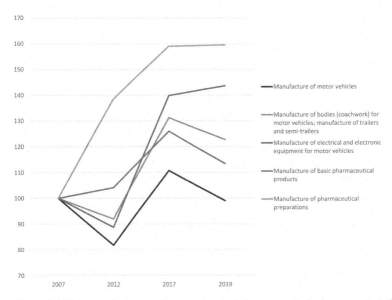

Figure 5.4 Volume of exports of automotive and pharmaceutical sub-sectors in Italy, 2007–2019, 2007=100. Source: authors' elaboration on ISTAT-Coeweb database.

furniture firms and 62.6 percent of wearing apparel firms claim they will soon face liquidity problems.

Over recent months, public policies in Italy have especially tried to limit the effects of the expected shock on the industrial system. Similarities can be, in fact, detected with regard to the previous financial crisis of 2007–2008. As a result of that crisis, according to ISTAT (2017) between 2011 and 2014 about 194 thousand Italian companies left the market (–4.6 percent), with a reduction in employees amounting to 800 thousand (–5 percent). Beside this strong reduction in firm numbers, the financial crisis had a big impact on the positioning of Italian companies in global value chains (GVCs)[28]. As a result, key sectors of the Italian industrial system have been altered. The Italian automotive industry has made a shift in GVCs by assuming a greater role as global supplier of components for the car industry, while losing shares in the final markets of cars (in Figure 5.4). Although car production is still important in the national economy, employing around 66,000 workers in 110 companies in 2017, it has a lower export orientation than the car electrical components industry. In particular, after 2008, the latter has largely increased its share of exports, shifting the functional role of the Italian automotive industry into GVCs and increasing the country's specialization in production of some parts of the automotive

28 See Coveri, Cozza, Nascia, and Zanfei (2020) for a detailed discussion about GVCs and industrial policy.

production chain, namely electrical components and bodies for motor vehicles. The traditional car industry, which used to be highly concentrated and dependent on the Italian domestic market, has thus moved toward a specialization pattern focused on motor vehicle components for export for further assembly abroad, while the national production of cars is stable (its volume in 2019 equal to that in 2007).

Conversely, the pharmaceutical sector undertook a different path in Italian industry in the 20th century. Especially by the end of the century, the increase in mergers and acquisitions (M&As) left Italy with no lead company in the pharmaceutical industry and a decreasing role of foreign oligopolistic giants in the country. Most pharmaceutical production is done for export and the top Italian companies – albeit large – are far smaller than their foreign counterparts. Overall, it seems a more balanced industrial structure, thanks to the fact that no real lead company is operating in it (in Figure 5.4).

These changes are relevant as they suggest a further acceleration in this trend might happen as a response to the Covid-19 crisis. The dependency of the Italian economy on more and more distant supply chains will increase and make existing firms more efficient. On the one hand, this is a common evolutionary mechanism where only the best companies will remain in the market. On the other side, this mechanism will imply an extraordinary loss of jobs and, especially, of competences. Not by chance but because of business decisions, the pharmaceutical sector in Italy (again, as shown in Figure 5.4) is nowadays more stable but also smaller and marginal in the global industry. For example, the only Italian company (IRBM) involved in the production of vaccines against Covid-19 is relatively small and necessarily linked to a foreign center of excellence (Oxford University) and a foreign multinational company (Astra Zeneca). It is likely also that other Italian sectors, like the automotive sector, will follow the same path after reorganization due to the Covid-19 crisis.

5.2.3 Public policies and welfare policies to mitigate the impact

Between March and August 2020, the government passed four national laws to mitigate the impact of the social and economic effects of the Covid-19 pandemic: "Decreto Cura Italia" [DL 18/2020, later converted into law 27/2020]; "Decreto Liquidità" [DL 23/2020, law 40/2020]; "Decreto Rilancio" [DL 34/2020, law 77/2020]; and "Decreto Agosto" [DL 104/2020 then converted into law in mid-October]. These four laws over the period March–August 2020 have deployed resources of over €100bn, mostly in respect of higher business costs. There are also important off-balance sheet allocations, such as guarantees given to banks and companies, which represent a financial commitment but not real public expenditure, unless business failures occur. In the six-month period, therefore, government expenditure in the budget laws was the equivalent of the last three years expenditure. This level of expenditure is comparable to that of other European countries struggling with the effects of Covid-19.

New additional supports to companies were introduced in the fourth quarter of 2020, when a second wave of Covid-19 started. There have been problems in the implementation of these measures, especially because of the decentralization of some administrative procedures, with Italian regions behaving very differently from others. In addition, cooperation between regional and national public administration has been poor.

Over a third of the resources allocated by the Italian government in the pandemic period, about €34bn, have been committed to support workers. In more detail, 70 percent of the benefits went to typical workers, a quarter to the self-employed, while "universal measures" received less than 5 percent of the total resources.

For typical workers, the widened unemployment insurance support, Cassa Integrazione Guadagni, has been the main tool for protecting the income of employees and to ensure the continuity of production after lockdown, with coverage extended until the beginning of 2021. In practice, however, this measure has helped preserve the productive capacity of companies and it should be understood as being like cross support for companies and employees.

Typical workers received support from the renewal of unemployment regulations while also benefiting from widening the eligible beneficiaries of social safety provisions. Furthermore, the government approved measures amounting to €6.2bn to support small companies and freelance workers. It also introduced a one-off income support measure for other categories of workers – self-employed and professionals – with amounts on average of 500 euros per month. Conversely, the government also imposed a suspension of lay-offs until March 2021.

The government has introduced various other measures amounting to €1.3bn to support households including a new "emergency income" (REM) addressed to households in difficulty. The UPB[29] documents show how the government interventions reached a third of Italian families and provided on average almost half of their monthly disposable income before the crisis.[30]

5.3 Beyond purely health policy: industrial policy under Covid-19

5.3.1 *Government policy to support companies during the emergency and the post emergency policies for growth*

During the first weeks of the pandemic outbreak, the Italian government, as well as public opinion, was already focusing on emergency measures. However, as weeks went by, these measures started becoming mid-term policies for growth and recovery. If that overall strategy is correct and in line with demands coming from the European Commission, it has to be underlined that

29 Ufficio Parlamentare di Bilancio (2020).
30 In the study by Pianta, Lucchese, and Nascia (2021) there is a detailed description of the economic policies during the pandemic in Italy.

the boundaries between the two types of measures are blurred. In other words, it is hard to distinguish policies aimed at compensating for the direct effect of the current crisis, from policies mostly meant with a long-term perspective. This confusion seems problematic, as it implies a dangerous expectation of solving, with emergency funds, the decline of Italian industry occurring over the last decades.

During the lockdown of economic activities, several measures were launched to provide liquidity to companies through State guarantees to banks and credit institutions, allocating over €8bn for this purpose. Aid to companies has also comprised support for fixed costs other than those relating to personnel (€12bn), a cut in the 2019 IRAP (the "regional tax on productive activities") and on the first installment of the 2020 advance, amounting to a total of €3.9bn. These measures have especially supported smaller firms, while only 24 percent of the large companies requested support (ISTAT, 2020b). These measures also had a contradictory outcome: companies that have not lost value added during the crisis had an unexpected advantage for their balance sheets. Since IRAP is a tax on business value added aimed also at financing the public health system, the loss of tax revenue from IRAP is greater than the cost of many other measures aimed at supporting the population.

The capitalization of companies has also been taken into account: the so-called "Relaunch Decree" provided for the establishment of a €44bn fund managed by Cassa Depositi e Prestiti (CDP, the State-owned investment bank). The objective of this fund was to relaunch Italian companies in difficulty but with prospects of future profitability, especially those active in strategic sectors. It also refinanced SACE (the State-owned export credit agency) with €30bn, with the aim of facilitating the granting of State guarantees on credit lines to medium and large companies. A "Fund for the safeguarding of employment levels and the continuation of business activity" was also created, with loans amounting to €100m, aimed at joint stock companies with at least 250 employees and in a state of economic and financial difficulty, representing an instrument of public intervention to resolve the approximately 150 industrial crisis cases of the MISE (Ministry of Economic Development).

Among fiscal incentives, there were minor interventions to reduce the cost of rents, electricity, and the adaptation of workplaces, especially in terms of safety. In addition, some tax and social security obligations of companies were suspended – as well as the related penalties – amounting to €1.3bn.

The government furthermore provided specific aid to the sectors most affected by the crisis, in particular tourism, catering, cultural activities, with resources allocated in the budget amounting to over €4bn. Among the measures envisaged there is also €2bn for the transport sector, which has suffered a collapse in revenue, and almost €1bn in favor of agriculture, publishing, justice, and sport. In support of the real estate industry achieving environmental sustainability, the government approved a massive enlargement of tax credit benefits for energy efficiency housing redevelopment and the anti-seismic renovation of homes, with €1bn allocated for 2021 and about €3bn for 2022.

Government intervention also included the implementation of innovation policies. However, these have been quite limited and are represented by incentives for "start-up" companies, innovative small and medium-sized enterprises, and for companies hiring on a permanent basis in the South. There is an increase of €200m in grants by MISE for venture capital and €500m for technology transfer between universities, research centers and companies. In total, less than €4bn – out of the €100bn committed – is dedicated to innovation and post-pandemic development. It should be emphasized that the interventions in respect of companies were carried out without an overall strategy in place and without stringent conditional criteria for granting benefits.

During the second wave the government, namely through the "Ristori Decree" DL 137/2020, allocated approximately €6.2bn to extend the duration of the prohibition on lay-offs; to grant refunding to some economic sectors hit by the crisis, namely tourism and transport, including a partial cancellation of the IMU (the regular property tax) without including any relevant conditionality.

Some measures, Legislative Decree 18/2020, Legislative Decree 23/2020, and Legislative Decree 34/2020 reduced the tax obligations of businesses with the suspension of payments with some tax exemptions to prevent further liquidity shortages. From a public budget perspective, these exemptions entail a total loss of revenue in 2020 of €4.3bn, which is almost completely concentrated on IRAP (€3.9bn), which has been provided to all businesses without any conditions attached.

5.3.2 The absence of an industrial policy

The lack of a clear industrial policy in Italy has been an ongoing problem at least since the 1980s. The current difficulties in facing the Covid-19 crisis and reorganizing the national industrial structure cannot be separated from the privatization waves of the 1990s. With privatization, past Italian governments decided to leave industrial policy entirely to market dynamics. Equally during this crisis, the government allocated grants and subsidies to the business sector without any conditionality. This approach differed from other European countries that required some compliance with employment and innovation objectives as being contingent on providing support to large companies. Especially in case of unresolved industrial crises, public economic support should be contingent on the beneficiary companies striving toward common interest objectives.[31]

However, in the political debate and in the setting-up of the Italian Recovery Plan,[32] it is more and more evident that the government should

---

31 See Lucchese, Nascia, and Pianta (2016) and Pianta, Lucchese, and Nascia (2016) for alternative detailed proposals for Italian industrial policy, or Rullani, Cozza, and Zanfei (2016) for the new role of industrial policies in the knowledge-based economy.

32 The Italian recovery plan was still under discussion at government level as of mid-January 2021; a preliminary version has been outlined in section 4.

set some strategic priorities for industrial policy. On the one hand, the policy should define which industries are strategic industries for the country's future. On the other hand, the adoption of an industrial policy focused solely on the annual estimation of GDP growth is the same short-term perspective that has limited Italian industry over these years. The government should, in line with and beyond European demands, propose a vision for Italy's industrial policy over the mid-term (5 to 10 years). In addition, the national budget should be allocated with the same mid-term perspective, without being constrained by GFP fluctuations in the short term. Public investment in key sectors (R&D and innovation, infrastructure, health, education), as also demonstrated by the strategies of other countries (China above all), needs a wider and longer scope. This is especially as countercyclical R&D investment can represent a new source of competitive advantage, as it has been for some EU firms in respect of the 2008 financial crisis.[33]

After the 2008 crisis, Italy faced a very similar situation and did not adopt any significant industrial strategy. As stated before, Italian industrial decline has continued, especially losing key positions in several GVCs. The current Covid-19 crisis, however, more explicitly demonstrates that the absence of an industrial policy makes the country more vulnerable to global shocks. Without regaining core competences in key industrial sectors, subsequent crises might be even more difficult to face. While the 2008 crisis was perceived by public opinion as merely financial – although we have seen its strong impact on the industrial system – maybe Covid-19 has the "advantage" of showing directly to the entire country how the absence of an industrial strategy is "the" political problem for Italy, today.

Finally, a national industrial strategy should also go beyond the typical old dichotomy between profit maximization (of the private sector) and production maximization (of the public sector). What is today needed is a "knowledge maximization" and the pandemic has shown this clearly: on the one hand, the problem of "vaccine patents" ownership, with giant global corporations owning competences and undertaking research, using enormous amounts of public money; on the other hand, highlighting how much advanced countries have lost, during the last decades, industrial competences, as in the case of inability to produce face masks and other PPE just after the first pandemic outbreak. As stated by Coveri et al. (2020: 475):

> the COVID-19 emergency has shown that de-specializing in some key segments of healthcare equipment manufacturing is detrimental to the overall efficiency of the system and to its resilience in particular. For example, only a few Italian companies still have the knowledge to rapidly set up fully equipped ICUs if necessary, despite the long lasting Italian industrial tradition in the biomedical sector.

33 See Cincera, Cozza, Tübke, and Voigt (2012) on this.

5.4 Financing the recovery through public spending in deficit

The Italian public debt, already huge before the introduction of the Euro currency, was put under further pressure after the 2008 crisis and the subsequent austerity policies of the last ten years. The burden of public debt and the risk of State insolvency determined the restrictive fiscal policies that increased the fiscal pressure and reduced the budget for public spending. The underfinancing of the national health system, which undermined the capacity to face the Covid-19 pandemic, comes from the implementation of restrictive austerity policies that slowed down more GDP growth than the public debt.

The policies to recovery from the recession of 2008 were based on the notion of monetary stability throughout a mix of public budget cuts and new taxation, the so-called austerity program. That approach lasted for around ten years in Italy, under the strict surveillance of the ECB and the European Commission. In reality, the country had to deal with ten years of recession and stagnation until the eve of the pandemic. The public budget measures of 2008 aimed at recovering from the recession, although compliant with the Euro treaty rules, had to face two years later an even stricter monetary discipline imposed by the European Commission after the Greek default. The pressure to reduce the public debt to GDP ratio was the main driver of ten years of austerity policies that resulted in a worse public debt to GDP ratio due to the depressive effects of public budget cuts. Moreover, the public budget constraints affected the political debate and favored the growth of pro-sovereignty anti-euro political parties.

Although in 2019 Italian debt was the largest in Europe, the growth trend of public debt in Italy between 2008 and 2019 was the lowest in the 19 Euro countries. In Italy, public debt between 2008 and 2019 recorded an increase of 39 percent, while the Euro-area (19 countries) recorded an increase of 50 percent.[34]

After many years of primary public spending surpluses, equal to 1.8 percent in 2019, in 2020 Italy had to deal with a public spending deficit although without a significant increase in the interest costs on the public debt.[35] The public debt to GDP ratio rose from 134.8 percent in 2019 to 158 percent in 2020.[36] The worsening of the public sector finance arises also from the contraction in tax revenues that fell by 8.1 percent in 2020. The public sector deficit fell from 2.2 percent of GDP in 2018 to 1.6 percent in 2019 and suddenly increased in 2020 due to the emergency measures to 10.1 percent of GDP.

---

34 Elaboration on Eurostat New Cronos data (General government gross debt [SDG 17 40]). Yearly data in current prices.

35 Ministero dell'Economia e Finanza (2020).

36 The public debt to GDP ratio rose from 106.2 percent in 2008 to 116.6 percent in 2009, and the policy measures undertaken had to comply with the Maastricht treaty rules. Nonetheless, the sovereign debt crises of 2010 after the Greece debacle also involved Italy and started ten years of austerity measures.

However, the worsening of the public debt indicators is a common point for European countries that had to tackle a huge recession and deficit spending measures to support the welfare of their populations and production.

The pandemic outbreak at the beginning apparently hit only Italy, but in one month had hit all EU countries, giving rise to a generalized increase in public budget expenditures. There were worsening public financial indicators in nearly all European Union countries. The traditional strict financial stability rules, adopted in the aftermath of Greek insolvency, were no longer fit for purpose in Covid Europe and gave rise to conflict between the Southern EU countries hit severely by the pandemic already under the burden of large public debts, and the northern EU countries with more positive public financial indicators reluctant to embrace solutions like mutual European public debt. The conflict, also gave rise to the prospect of a sudden dissolution of the European Union; months of negotiation ended in an agreement signed on July 21 by the European Council aimed at supporting the countries with financial difficulties.

The Next Generation EU program, financed directly by the European Union through the Recovery and Resilience Facility (RFF) – amounting to €672.5bn, of which €312.5bn represents grant assistance – is the policy measure aimed at addressing the development of each country through the adoption of initiatives compliant with the European Commission recommendations. The amount of financing for Italy is determined by the GDP per capita and the unemployment rate before the Covid-19 pandemic. Italy will receive €63.8bn of grants and €127.6bn of loans, between 2021 and 2022, for initiatives that should end in 2026.

The Italian recovery plan – named "Piano Nazionale di Resistenza e Resilienza" (PNRR) – will have to jointly comply with the general European priorities, namely environmental transition, digital transition, innovation and competitiveness, social resilience and sustainability, and with the recommendations formulated by the European Council to Italy in 2019 and 2020. The European debate about the Recovery Fund had its origins in a suggested alternative approach to the recovery rather than a new set of austerity measures. The PNRR should be a set of measures needed to stimulate the growth of GDP and to improve the public debt to GDP ratio in the medium term. Unlike 2008, the economic recovery policy pattern is oriented to stimulate domestic demand and to support investment in the public and private sector in order also to comply with the requirements coming from sustainability.

The program requires the putting in place of a national strategy to be approved by the European Commission in 2021. The Italian government released the national guidelines for the PNRR at the end of October,[37] and during December the government was discussing the final version of the PNRR.

---

37 The guidelines are downloadable at: www.agenziacoesione.gov.it/news_istituzionali/piano-nazional e-di-ripresa-e-resilienza-sfide-missioni-azioni/

The PNRR should focus on six objectives: green revolution and digital transition (€74.3bn); digitalization, innovation, competitiveness, and culture (€48.7bn); infrastructure for sustainable mobility (€27.7bn); education and research (€19.2bn); gender equality, social, and territorial cohesion (€17.1bn); and health (€9bn).

In mid-December, the PNRR is still provisional and under discussion, including the funding allocation among different priorities. The PNRR is very ambitious and should be the key element of the political agenda for the next three years. There are still some uncertainties about the ability of the public sector to manage the plan and to implement every chapter according to the conditions prescribed by the European Commission. It is difficult to understand what system of selection in respect of the projects will be put in place, and how it will be effective and able to trigger growth in the country. The risk of a return, in the near future, of spending constraints in line with the Stability Pact would have the effect of triggering an irremediable conflict with the European Union.

The PNRR should return a huge growth of GDP in order to compensate for the debt increase. The forecasts of the last finance document of the government have been formulated in accordance with an expansive monetary policy of the ECB for the next three years, with low interest rates and the reduction of the public debt to GDP ratio scheduled only in the medium term. The economic policy of the government is oriented to spend in two years the funds of the PNRR to stimulate growth. However, the industrial policy pattern, as highlighted in the previous paragraph is still showing many weaknesses. The monitoring of the implementation of the PNRR and the inclusion of conditional access to grants for the productive sector are necessary measures to achieve an efficient impact on the productive system. As highlighted in some articles, the public financing of R&D in Italy is well below the European Union average and has suffered from austerity policies.[38] The last budget and the stimuli laws approved during 2020 did not record R&D as a priority. Public research and universities have received little funding in comparison to other sectors.

5.5 Conclusions and open issues

Italy was the first European country to face the Covid-19 pandemic. Especially at the beginning of the crisis, Italy had to tackle an unprecedented emergency isolated from the other European countries. The government was quickly able to manage an extensive lockdown to mitigate the pandemic outbreak and to set up an effective system to support the national health system. Nonetheless, the national health system was largely underfinanced and unprepared for a large-scale emergency, which showed many weaknesses due to years of budget cuts, lack of reforms, and staff shortages. The first wave had a huge impact on

38 Nascia, Pianta, and Isella (2017) and Nascia, Pianta, and La Placa (2018).

mortality rates in the country – more than 35,000 deaths – and on the social, education, and economic system, due to a prolonged lockdown and restrictions on mobility and on many production activities. Emergency legislation supported the health system to overcome the shortage of hospital beds, of ICUs and of PPE, and enlarged capacity to face the sudden pressure of pandemics. Conversely, during autumn the second wave showed a lack of willingness to return to a stringent lockdown to prevent another large-scale pressure point on the health system. The government adopted a very gradual approach in introducing mobility and social distancing restrictions, so as not to slow down the recovery of production and to avoid school closures. Only under the threat of saturation of hospital capacity in November did the government impose a stringent lockdown on some regions and only after the number of deaths was greater than 500 a day. The perspective in December was to introduce new restrictions for the Christmas holidays and to start the campaign to vaccinate the whole population from January, although there are risks of a third large-scale wave of Covid-19, and all the vaccines are not yet officially approved by the pharmaceutical regulatory authorities.

The fall in Italian GDP in 2020, according to preliminary data, is equal to 8.8 percent,[39] with a partial recovery in 2021 of 3.4 percent, forecasted by the EU Commission.[40] During the first half of 2020 the fall in GDP reached −18.1 percent, and a partial recovery in the third quarter of the year has been impacted by the second wave of the pandemic.[41]

The impact of the pandemic is unequal in its effects between sectors and between firm sizes with more inequality also forecasted between companies in the future.

The impact of Covid-19 is greater on the most informal sectors of the economy, on small and traditional companies, and on tourism, culture, and transportation services. Larger companies and the industries that were not affected by the restrictions, like pharmaceuticals and digital platforms, have the opportunity to profit from an expansive fiscal policy, with a low degree of conditionality to access the benefits issued by the government during the emergency. Despite the production restrictions, larger companies are prepared to benefit from universal measures, like the cut in IRAP, and have the ability to maximize the allocation of public subsidies on an international level. Smaller companies in some cases had to deal with long periods of inactivity, of profit loss with a likely higher rate of failures in the future. Other small companies were able to return to the same type of pre Covid-19 activities.

Thus, the joint effect of business strategies related to business size and sector, the wider diffusion of "smart working", and financial constraints are the basis for a wider gap between the smaller and the larger companies.

---

39 Istat (2021).
40 European Commission (2021). The forecast does not include the Next Generation EU impact.
41 Istat (2021).

The government has introduced various measures to support individual income, including safety nets addressed not only to traditional permanent employees, but also to atypical workers, individual firms and professionals. The conditional rules for eligibility to receive individual supports were less stringent than in the past with a reduction of the "formal" progressivity of the interventions, and also the inclusion of income typologies usually excluded by the welfare system.

A clear articulated public industrial policy in Italy has not been in the political agenda for many years. The most recent public programs like Industria 4.0, which were focused on technologies and state support to local companies, have been progressively limited to comply with EU law. The lack of a long-term industrial policy is a major weakness and the Covid-19 crisis could be the opportunity to generate a strategic overview of development based not only on quantitative GDP growth. The grant and support measures provided to the business sector during 2020 have not been made contingent in pushing the business sector into public interest missions like R&D investments, macroeconomic targets, and sustainability.

The new pattern of public–private partnership, tested during the pandemic for the manufacturing of face masks and ventilators, based on the direct involvement of the government purchasing equipment and raw materials and private business involved in their manufacturing, increased productivity and oriented manufacturing into goods required for the national policy. This is not replicable on a large scale and it represents a kind of "state acknowledged" private capitalism with many outstanding issues for the structure of the economic system.

Furthermore, the Decreto Rilancio released between the two Covid-19 waves does not include a long-term strategy, with only a few measures addressed toward sustainability. The budget law under discussion in December had the same structure as in the past in respect of industrial policy, with some additional measures focused on the emergency and a few innovations toward the vision of long-term development.

The pandemic crisis has caused a fall in State income especially from VAT, while the financing of the health system, businesses, and households has significantly increased public expenditure with the debt to GDP ratio reaching 158 percent in 2020. Italy is currently operating outside of the Maastricht parameters and it is not feasible to schedule an abrupt return to the old public financial constraints without a collapse of the economy.

The success of the Italian government in relaxing the Euro-area financial constraints and to reaching agreement on the European Recovery Plan, which is based on a mix of conditional grants and loans, provides a new opportunity to overcome the current emergency strategy and the austerity approach which has affected growth in the last ten years.

The major economic novelty in the near future is the "Piano Nazionale di Ripresa e Resilienza", the PNRR, which was under discussion in Parliament in December, and should be the major strategy to ensure a long-term view for the development of the country after its approval by the EU Commission. The future of the country is closely connected to the successful implementation of the PNRR. In fact, in the forecasts by the DEF the success of the PNRR is the key element to ensuring a GDP growth able to support the return by Italy within financial stability parameters, and to reform the structure of the country within the targets of sustainability and modernization.

Nonetheless the PNRR has to face risks relating to the quality of the projects they fund, from the "structural fund syndrome" that traditionally affects the Italian public administration of being usually able to spend only part of allocated EU structural funds, and finally, to the threat of a return of high interest rates with an increase in the burden of the public debt on the government finance.

Moreover, the success of the PNRR and of the Recovery Fund at European level is a crossroad for the future of the European Union. The Recovery Fund is the opportunity to achieve a key player role for the European Commission in the national economies and to reduce the center–periphery polarization that is bringing European Union institutions into question in many countries. Especially for the near future, the approach of the European institutions will be crucial in preventing a return to the old austerity policies that would suddenly place Italy at risk of debt default with the associated risk of the implosion of the Euro-area and of the European Union. In the event of a return in 2021 or 2022 to the spending constraints of the Stability Pact this would undermine the future of the European institutions in an irremediable way.

References

Banca d'Italia (2020). Proiezioni macroeconomiche per l'Italia, luglio 2020.

Cincera, M., Cozza, C., Tübke, A., & Voigt, P. (2012). Doing R&D or not (in a crisis), that is the question …. *European Planning Studies*, 20(9), 1525–1547.

Corte dei Conti (2020). Rapporto 2020 sul coordinamento della finanza pubblica.

Coveri, A., Cozza, C., Nascia, L., & Zanfei, A. (2020). Supply chain contagion and the role of industrial policy. *Journal of Industrial and Business Economics*, 47(3), 467–482.

European Commission (2021). European Economic Forecast Winter 2021 (Interim), Institutional Paper 144, February 2021.

ISTAT (2017). Rapporto sulla competitività dei settori produttivi, febbraio.

ISTAT (2021). Stima preliminare del PIL-IV trimestre 2020, 2 febbraio 2021.

ISTAT (2020a). Decessi per il complesso delle cause. Periodo gennaio–agosto 2020.

ISTAT (2020b). Statistica Report. Situazione e prospettive delle imprese nell'emergenza sanitaria Covid-19. 15 giugno 2020. Roma.

ISTAT (2020c). Nota mensile sull'andamento dell'economia italiana, luglio 2020.

ISTAT (2020d). Quarterly National Accounts, December 2020.

Lucchese, M., Nascia, L., & Pianta, M. (2016). Industrial policy and technology in Italy. *Economia e Politica Industriale*, 43(3), 233–260.

Ministero dell'Economia e Finanza (2020). Nota di aggiornamento del documento di economia e finanza 2020, 5 ottobre 2020.

Nascia, L., Pianta, M., & La Placa, G. (2018). *RIO Country Report, Italy 2017*, JRC Science and Policy Report, European Commission, Joint Research Centre, Institute for Prospective Technological Studies.

Nascia, L., Pianta, M., & Isella, L. (2017). *RIO Country Report 2016, Italy*, European Commission, Joint Research Centre, Institute for Prospective Technological Studies.

OECD (2020). Health Statistics 2020 in https://data.oecd.org/health.htm.

OECD/European Union (2020). *Health at a Glance: Europe 2020: State of Health in the EU Cycle*. OECD Publishing, Paris.

Pianta, M., Lucchese, M., & Nascia, L. (2021). La politica economica del governo Conte al tempo del coronavirus in Politica in Italia 2020, *Il Mulino*.

Pianta, M., Lucchese, M., & Nascia, L. (2016). *What is to be Produced? The Making of a New Industrial Policy in Europe*. Rosa Luxemburg Stiftung, Brussels.

Rullani, E., Cozza, C., & Zanfei, A. (2016). Lost in transition: Systemic innovations and the new role of the state in industrial policy. *Economia e Politica Industriale*, 43(3), 345–353.

Ufficio Parlamentare di Bilancio (2020). *Rapporto sulla programmazione di bilancio 2020*, Luglio 2020, Roma.

6 The case of the UK

Alex De Ruyter and David Hearne

6.1 Introduction

Thus far, the UK has been hit harder by the Covid-19 crisis than most of its peers. The country has one of the highest per capita death tolls in the developed world and experienced a larger economic contraction during the first half of 2020 than most of its peers. While this might be taken as *prima facie* evidence that something has gone awry in the country's fiscal and monetary response, the reality is more complex. In particular, the economic costs of Covid-19 are intrinsically linked to the medical and organisational response to the disease itself. In considering all of these, it is worthwhile being cognisant of some of the unique challenges faced by the UK. In particular, long before the pandemic had even begun to emerge, 2020/21 promised to be years of economic upheaval due to the UK's decision to leave the European Union.

This chapter is therefore structured as follows. We begin by outlining the organisational response to the pandemic and the UK's socio-economic background. This provides necessary context within which to understand and assess the UK's fiscal and monetary responses. We continue by outlining each of these in turn, assessing their efficacy and making a broad comparison with the recession of 2008/9. Finally, we turn to how the UK's decision to leave the EU might have contributed to shaping the economic upheaval of recent months. The chapter conclusion then sets this in context to facilitate comparison with both other European states and East Asia.

6.2 The organisational/medical response

In common with many of their European peers (and in contrast to much of East Asia, notwithstanding the initial reticence of the Chinese authorities when faced with the emergence of the virus), authorities in the UK were slow to realise the severity and nature of what they faced. Evidence suggests that there were over 1300 separate instances whereby the SARS-CoV2 virus entered the UK, the overwhelming majority of which emerged from Spain, France and Italy (Pybus, Rambaut, & COG-UK-Consortium, 2020). While largely a reflection of Britons' international travel patterns, this does suggest that had

DOI: 10.4324/9781003153603-6

travel restrictions and greater testing been imposed earlier, much of the economic damage arising from the spread of the virus would have been avoided.

More generally, the absence of significant testing capability was a key hindrance. Where South Korea and Germany were able to effectively test in order to identify the spread of the disease (and thus act in a targeted fashion to limit this), the UK was not. In spite of the evidence coming out of Italy, which was by far the hardest hit country in Europe during the earliest (European) phase of the pandemic, serious remedial action was not taken until mid-March. The failure to learn from Italy, which was around two weeks ahead of the UK in terms of its death toll, was a key policy error. By the time serious action was taken, some have estimated that the country was seeing in excess of 100,000 new cases per day (Jit et al., 2020).

After apparently vacillating between advocating a "herd immunity" strategy and adopting measures to suppress the virus, a "national lockdown" was implemented on 23 March, following exhortations to work from home and the closure of an array of hospitality venues during the previous week. The high infection level and challenges in ensuring full compliance with aspects of the policy (which we touch on further in the following section) meant that this lasted rather longer than elsewhere. In the UK, economic policy therefore was acting to mitigate a much larger shock than in countries where the initial response was quicker and hence more effective. The UK also faced certain structural challenges, which were exacerbated by prior policy. England in particular has a relatively high population density, with London being rivalled only by Paris in Europe, for size and international connectivity. Moreover, a relatively high proportion of the UK's domestic consumption involves "social" spending, as broadly defined (Keogh-Brown, Wren-Lewis, Edmunds, Beutels, & Smith, 2010), which is vulnerable in a pandemic.

6.3 The socio-economic background

Other structural challenges specifically relate to past policy choices and all feed in to the efficacy and scope of the fiscal and monetary responses to the crisis. Here, we discuss two crucial aspects to this. Firstly, per capita healthcare spending in the UK is lower in real terms than in a number of its neighbours[1] (Eurostat, 2020a). The UK also has notably higher levels of obesity than elsewhere in Europe (Eurostat, 2019) and areas with extremely poor health outcomes. Secondly, we discuss key aspects of the UK labour market and policy, which make an important contribution to the challenge of controlling Covid-19 while simultaneously minimising the economic damage from this.

Partly as a result of its lower spending, the UK has fewer healthcare personnel per capita than some of its peers (Eurostat, 2020b). Where Germany

---

1 For example, in PPP terms, per capita health spending is 17 percent higher in Ireland, 25 percent higher in France and 48 percent higher in Germany (Eurostat, 2020a).

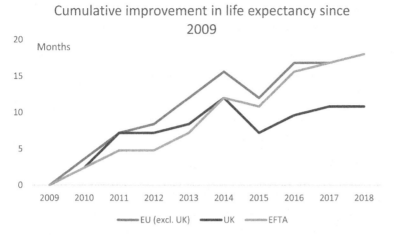

Figure 6.1 Improvements in life expectancy in Europe. Source: (Eurostat, 2020c).

entered the public health crisis with some 25,000 ventilators and over 28 critical care beds per 100,000 people, the UK made do with around 8,000 ventilators (of which some 5,000 were in the hands of the NHS) and 6.6 critical care beds per 100,000 (Buck & Ghiglione, 2020). This, in effect, reduced the number of patients that the UK was able to sustain before breaching critical care capacity. The UK faces well-documented challenges with social care funding and, as can be seen in figure 6.1 above, has enjoyed slower increases in life expectancy than most other European states (Eurostat, 2020c). It is therefore unsurprising that the UK saw such a dramatic rise in non-Covid deaths during the April peak (Office for National Statistics, 2020a) and this undoubtedly testifies to the country's struggle to deal with an unexpected health emergency. In combination with population density and the labour market issues outlined below, this ultimately meant that the approach pursued by Sweden was much less feasible in the UK (where critical care capacity was not breached, in spite of the absence of some of the strict legal measures seen elsewhere).

However, perhaps more important are the labour market issues specific to the UK. The country's much-vaunted flexible labour market has high overall employment rates, with the country's employment rate reaching record highs prior to the onset of Covid-19 (Office for National Statistics, 2020b). However, the pandemic has exposed an Achilles heel: Britons face significant barriers to self-isolating (and hence breaking chains of transmission related to employment). Statutory sick pay in the UK is set at £95.85 per week – very low relative to average earnings (Office for National Statistics, 2019). For the median full-time employee, this represents an 83.6 percent reduction in income. In a household with two working adults, a period of sickness (or, equivalently, isolation) can therefore involve a prohibitive loss of income. Worse still, for the 5 million who are self-employed there is no recourse to statutory sick pay at all.

Beyond this, there is a significant incentive to work (and therefore travel) in the face of illness. Estimates suggest that in excess of 20 percent of the labour force are in precarious forms of work (Booth, 2016) and, following plant closures related to deindustrialisation, precarious and insecure work has tended to replace formerly secure jobs in a unionised workforce (Armstrong, Bailey, de Ruyter, Mahdon, & Thomas, 2008; Bailey & de Ruyter, 2015). Those who feel insecure in their employment or are unable to suffer a loss of income without significant ill effects are naturally vastly more likely to work through illness. Moreover, a substantial body of employees – almost 8 million (Office for National Statistics, 2020e) – on an ostensibly "permanent" contract are not covered by unfair dismissal provisions (which have a two year qualifying period). Worse, such precarity is particularly common among the workforce who care for the most vulnerable (Northern Ireland Statistics and Research Agency and Office for National Statistics, 2020).

As a result, there was a pressing need and desire to reduce infections from such a high level and a national "lockdown" broadly akin to those enforced elsewhere was imposed. While somewhat less strict than similar measures imposed in France, Spain and much of Hubei, the economic impact was rather similar with GDP declining by over 20% year-on-year in the second quarter of 2020. Statistics suggest that the UK was not an outlier in terms of changes to movement (Google, 2020) with large falls in traffic activity in line with European norms (L. Thomas, 2020). This unprecedented experiment led economic activity to shrink by more than one quarter virtually overnight (Office for National Statistics, 2020c). In many regards, what is remarkable is that in spite of draconian restrictions, GDP did not fall much further. In common with elsewhere in Europe and further afield, the fiscal and monetary responses were swift and aggressive.

6.4 Fiscal policy

In common with other governments across Europe and further afield, government borrowing has increased dramatically, with borrowing in April (the first month of the 2020/21 fiscal year) almost equalling the entirety of borrowing during the previous fiscal year. Thus far, in the four months of April–July borrowing reached £150.5bn ($194bn, €164), with expectations that borrowing will exceed £300bn for the full year (Office for National Statistics, 2020d). This dwarfs most recent potential comparisons, although borrowing in 2009 reached £160bn (the equivalent of approximately £190bn after adjusting for inflation). However, the present expectation is for government borrowing to decline sharply from its current exceptional levels (Office for Budget Responsibility, 2020).

The shutdown of much economic activity by government fiat threatened to precipitate a wave of business insolvencies and redundancies. Rapid action needed to be taken to avoid the worst of this. In common with elsewhere in Europe, the set-piece at the centre of the fiscal response was a scheme whereby the Treasury effectively took on the wage bill of a substantial proportion of the labour force. Officially known as the "Coronavirus Job Retention Scheme" (henceforth CJRS), this allowed employers to furlough staff, who would then have 80 percent of their salary paid by the government up to a maximum of £2500 per month – roughly the median salary of full-time employees in the UK. Employers were free to "top up" this payment up to 100 percent of salary, and many who were in a financial position chose to do so. The primary condition of participation was that the employee could undertake no work (voluntary or paid) for their employer.

Unlike Germany, which via the *Kurzarbeit* scheme has a wealth of previous policy experience with such measures (and therefore a clear delivery mechanism, see Chapter 4 in this volume), the UK has not used such programmes previously. Similar impediments exist to lump-sum transfers (as practised by the US). As a result, the scheme had to be designed and delivered from scratch. The fact that this was done so quickly was an undoubted achievement. At its peak, the scheme was paying in excess of 8.8m salaries and, remarkably, some 9.6m jobs were furloughed at some point during the scheme, representing almost one third of all employee jobs (Her Majesty's Revenue and Customs, 2020). In particular, the Treasury acted with speed and skill to overcome the administrative challenges of setting up the scheme (designing systems for company enrolment etc.) and actually rolling out the payments. Astonishing though it may seem to readers, the UK has very little information on who is resident in the country, although rather more information is known on taxpayers.

It was quickly decided that, speed being of the essence, the scheme would effectively operate as a "reverse PAYE[2]" system. This served a twin purpose. Firstly, it acted to effectively enable the government to hold the economy *in stasis* for an initial period of three months. There is no question that, by doing so, it substantially reduced the number of redundancies that were made and will also have reduced company bankruptcies somewhat. Secondly, it ensured that the purchasing power of a substantial segment of the population was protected. In this regard, it seems to have functioned as an (admittedly temporary) extremely generous but very partial unemployment benefit.

While perhaps unavoidable, the focus on speed meant that the system had certain obvious holes. Due to the use of the PAYE system, individuals who had just started a new job were effectively excluded. In particular, in order to make the payment, the employer needed to have notified HMRC that the new starter was on payroll by the cut-off date.[3] In important ways it lacked conditionality. There was no onus on companies who made use of the scheme to ensure

---

2 Pay as you earn.
3 Initially this was set as 28 February, although was later retrospectively altered to be 19 March. Nevertheless, a substantial number would still not be covered – since many employers only notify HMRC

that employees were not subsequently made redundant. Insofar as the aim was to avoid redundancies, this seems counterintuitive (although there was always the risk that conditionality would have reduced take-up). Secondly, unlike the *Kurzarbeit* scheme, there was no onus on either employer or employee to undertake training (whether at the state's expense or otherwise). In practice, this might have been a challenging endeavour for many since schools and pre-schools were shut to the majority of pupils of much of the period. Moreover, it isn't clear whether training providers would have been able to deliver on the scale required given that many were grappling with enforced campus closures and rapid escalation of online learning for their existing student base. In spite of these challenges, this feels like a missed opportunity.

Moreover, the scheme was significantly inflexible during the early period, being effectively binary: either working or furloughed. Later, the scheme was extended in duration and altered to permit employees to come with short-time (with the government making up 80 percent of the remainder of their salary). Partly as a result of the need to act quickly and ensure that the scheme was easily available to as many employers as possible, there was remarkably little policing, which has led to concerns over the scale of payments lost to fraud and administrative error. For all its specificities, the scheme ultimately functioned rather similarly to its counterparts elsewhere in Europe.

Where the fiscal response in the UK differs notably from its continental counterparts is in what occurs after the initial period. Where both France and Germany have extended their equivalents, the UK began winding the scheme down in August[4] and it was initially planned to fully cease in November. Events, however, have dramatically intervened to effectively force the UK's finance ministry into a series of policy changes. Initially, when infection rates remained relatively low during August and through to early September, proposals were put forward to replace the scheme with a much less generous set of support measures. These quickly became inadequate as infections increased through September and October. Indeed, given the impact of infection control measures (substantially reduced capacity in some cases, extra staff time cleaning etc.) on profitability, it is unclear whether more support might be necessary. The government's initial response was to move toward a system in which local areas where the infection rate was higher would be placed under greater restrictions.

Initially, these took the form of restrictions on household socialising. However, as these proved inadequate (and exceptionally difficult to enforce in settings such as restaurants, bars and pubs) additional restrictions on business functions became necessary. Given increasing evidence of the nature of the

---

of changes to the payroll once a month (typically at the end). Secondly, the delay in moving the cut-off date is likely to have led to a small number of new starters losing the position in the interim.

4   Specifically, during August, employers had to make both employer's National Insurance contributions and any employer pension contributions. In September, employers have to pay 10 percent of the employee's salary in addition to this, while in October the salary contribution ramps up to 20 percent.

virus's spread, it is unclear whether opening many types of indoor venues will be feasible at all during the winter months. This situation was exacerbated by two major factors. Firstly, the government ignored advice from senior scientists to impose a short blanket lockdown while the infection rate was still modest but rapidly increasing (during late September). Secondly, there was a complete refusal to countenance mandatory closures of any educational settings (including education for over-16s) *en masse*. In this regard, the UK has actually been even more lax than Sweden.

Moreover, because the initial expectation was of increasing parsimony from the Treasury, many businesses planned on that basis. The rapidly increasing infection rate during the early autumn months – parallel to that observed elsewhere in Europe – quickly meant that events overtook government plans and threatened to completely overwhelm the health service, particularly in certain areas of the country. As a result, a second "national lockdown" was imposed from the start of November. While it mandated the closure of non-essential retail businesses (which of course includes accommodation, food and hotels), it did not impact any educational settings (including universities). This closure – perhaps inevitably – led to the last-minute restart of the previous job retention scheme, which was now extended until the end of March 2021, bringing the UK much more into line with the European norm.

Naturally, there is some academic controversy over the optimal way to proceed in the medium term. It is clear that, in the long run, there is no place for a policy that essentially pays a substantial portion of the workforce to remain out of work. This would represent a staggering waste of resources, actively working to shrink the economy (both by paying individuals not to work and by transferring resources away from successful companies and productive employment).

Equally, it is clear that demand in many sectors and regions is going to remain curtailed for the duration of the pandemic. What we do not know is how much of this represents permanent structural change and how much represents a sharp but temporary drop in demand that will be reversed once the pandemic ends. Of course, there is also uncertainty over what that "end" might look like and how far away it might be. If safe and effective treatments or vaccines swiftly emerge, this might be sudden. However, this is far from guaranteed at present.

In any event, we know that there will be permanent structural change as a result of the pandemic. There will be long-term structural change in consumption patterns and production. At present, however, it simply is not possible to discern what these will be. As a result, there is a risk that the complete withdrawal of employment protection measures will lead to a wave of redundancies from jobs that – in six months' time – will turn out to be viable. In such circumstances there is a real risk of unemployment hysteresis (Blanchard & Summers, 1987) and "scarring", particularly for younger workers. This suggests that the optimal outcome would be some form of targeted and conditional intervention to extend aspects of the scheme, with careful work done to ensure that employees' skills are not allowed to atrophy. In practice, this would take the form of an ongoing furlough scheme with mandatory work-based training. The government might also want to consider limiting it to certain sectors using an enhanced benefits system to support industries and individuals that fall outside of these groupings.

Other interventions have been more political. The Coronavirus Job Retention Scheme completely excluded the self-employed. Insofar as the aim of the scheme was to avoid redundancies and hold the economy in stasis, this made sense. However, many felt that there was an injustice in giving generous support to protect employee jobs without any counterpart for the self-employed. While perhaps true from the perspective of fairness, it is not clear what the *economic* justification for implementing such measures might be, beyond merely injecting demand into the economy. The self-employed are, by definition, not at risk of redundancy although, in common with any business, they do face the risk of bankruptcy. Nevertheless, perhaps due to political pressures, an equivalent scheme (based on the income from self-employment gained during the 2018/19 tax year) was duly introduced. In economic terms, this effectively amounts to a rather crude injection of cash into the economy.

Although it helped avoid unnecessary redundancies in the three-month period during which lockdown was implemented, the Coronavirus Job Retention Scheme failed to fully protect companies from the adverse consequences of being unable to trade. In particular, many face a host of fixed costs (including rents, utilities bills and ongoing servicing costs, among others). While a variety of other government schemes to support businesses have been made available, these have primarily (but not exclusively) taken the form of loans and the deferral of taxes (which amount to a loan from the state). These include the Coronavirus Business Interruption Loan Scheme, the Bounce Back Loan Scheme and a separate scheme for larger businesses. Both the Business Interruption Loan Scheme and the Bounce Back Loan Scheme are aimed at smaller and medium firms and are delivered through mainstream lenders (predominantly major retail banks).

In each case, the first 12 months are interest-free (interest payments are covered by the government). There are two key differences, however: the Business Interruption Loan Scheme typically deals with much larger amounts – up to £5m – for an otherwise sound loan application that has been rejected on the grounds of security. In this case, the government guarantees lenders 80 percent of the loan amount, with the business providing security for the remaining 20 percent. In contrast, the Bounce Back Loan Scheme appears targeted at much smaller firms, with a maximum payment of £50,000 (or 25 percent of business turnover, whichever is lower). In this case, the government guarantees 100 percent of the debt. In practice, the need to act quickly and a desire to minimise "red tape" has meant that businesses self-certify their eligibility and creditworthiness. As a result, serious concerns have been raised over the alleged extent of fraud within the scheme and it appears likely that a substantial proportion of loans will be written off (D. Thomas & Morris, 2020).

Moreover, concerns are already mounting about the long-term consequences of unwanted increases in business indebtedness.

Finally, a plethora of schemes have sought to target particular businesses and sectors. These include (but are not limited to) a temporary reduction in the UK's property transactions tax (known domestically as the Stamp Duty Land Tax), a subsidy to encourage an increase in restaurant usage during August, a temporary reduction in the UK's value-added-tax on certain items and a series of reliefs on certain taxes (which function as grants). The latter of these primarily relates to property taxes paid by businesses in certain sectors (notably hospitality and leisure as well as some educational establishments). Finally, there has been a temporary (and quite modest) increase in certain social protection benefits (including unemployment benefit) as well as a significant rise in certain spending – notably around healthcare.

6.4.1 Effectiveness and comparison to financial crisis

There are clear differences between the two crises and these clearly affect the nature of the government responses to each. In the UK, the size of the 2020 contraction dwarfs that of 2008/9 (or, indeed, any recession in living memory). However, much of this is due to the fact that activity was – in effect – deliberately suspended during the second quarter of 2020. At present it is not clear what the long-term effects (and economic damage) will be. After all, many countries and regions see the virtual suspension of much economic activity during August every year. In contrast, the 2008/9 recession was clearly precipitated by systemic failures within the financial system. In particular, a rise in defaults on US mortgages following the rapid deflation of what is today widely regarded as a housing bubble, triggered a remarkable collapse in liquidity throughout the banking system.

As losses in the financial services sector quickly mounted the result was twofold: a sharp retrenchment (most obviously borne out in a dramatically reduced appetite for risk) and an astonishing fall in inter-bank lending. In turn, a decline in lending to new borrowers, by as much as 79 percent relative to its peak in some cases, ensued (Ivashina & Scharfstein, 2010). As key financial institutions faced bankruptcy, the government took extraordinary measures to protect the core financial system. This saw government effectively nationalise certain financial institutions and, although not typically included in figures on government debt, the move was staggering in terms of the liabilities ultimately taken on by government.

The evidence on recoveries from financial crises is mixed. It is widely argued that recoveries from financial crises are typically slow (Kannan, 2012) and some theoretical modelling also suggests slower productivity and output growth in their wake (Queralto, 2020). Nevertheless, this view is not universally held. Bordo and Haubrich (2017) suggest that, contra to widespread belief, recovery from financial crises is typically rapid. They suggest that the factor constraining recovery from the 2008/9 recession is, in fact, the level of residential investment. This thesis seems unlikely to fully explain the experience of the UK, however, where productivity growth has been lacklustre over the past decade in spite of growing investment in residential real estate and a clear recovery in the housing market (albeit with a clear regional divide).

In contrast, the 2020 recession, while exceptionally deep, was also artificial in the sense of being imposed by fiat. Insofar as the economy could truly be held *in stasis*, economic activity could then be resumed as before. Of course, this is not a strategy that can effectively persist for any great period of time. The fiscal costs are astronomical and it is clear that the longer people are either away from work or working in challenging environments the more permanent any damage becomes as skills atrophy. Nevertheless, reductions in social consumption are both necessary and inevitable for the duration of the pandemic. Even if no legal restrictions are introduced, a large portion of the UK's population are relatively vulnerable (the UK has in excess of 12 million pensioners and a number of younger individuals have health conditions that render them more vulnerable), which will naturally act to supress social consumption.

There is no obvious strictly *economic* rationale for most of these schemes and many also deliver serious concerns over value for money (Harra, 2020). In particular, encouraging increased use of social venues (restaurants) during the midst of a pandemic appears a poor use of public funds. While there is a clear desire to help protect livelihoods, this amounts to a temporary industry-specific subsidy. In many sectors, such temporary subsidies make some sense: notably where there are major sunk costs in the form of investment in plant and machinery or human capital (such that closure would render that investment permanently lost). Domestically, where there are concerns over international competition,[5] especially in the presence of increasing returns to scale, it can make sense to subsidise an industry. The hospitality industry is one in which this is clearly not the case. There are no international competitors, no obvious increasing returns to scale and few barriers to entry. The closure of restaurants will not lead to a permanent loss of capacity in the sector. A more equitable and efficient solution would be to increase the levels of unemployment benefit (and reduce conditionality) for the duration of the pandemic.[6] This would substantially protect demand by ensuring that those with the highest propensity to consume do not face catastrophic falls in income.

While the desire to avoid a sharp fall in property prices (and thus trigger a fall in consumption via wealth effects) is clear, cutting property transaction taxes

---

5 The archetypal example being an automotive or aerospace factory. It is much easier to justify building a new model in an existing factory where much of the investment (in both physical and human capital) has already been made. Closure due to a temporary loss of demand can lead to permanent loss of capacity: when demand increases again, the location then needs to compete with international alternatives from a much less favourable position.

6 In the absence of a clear definition, this would be left to government to define but wording to the effect of "in any event, until at least [date]" might be used with the latter likely to be March 2021. This would give some certainty to those affected.

is a relatively inefficient way of supporting consumption. Firstly, this tax cut is likely to be highly regressive (property ownership is strongly correlated with overall wealth and the lowest value properties and first-time buyers already face much lower tax rates on property transactions). This raises issues of both equity and efficiency, since the poor have a much higher propensity to consume than the wealthy. This is even more concerning as there are longstanding issues around the high cost of residential property (particularly in and around certain regions) in the UK. If there are concerns around real-estate investment in the presence of lower property values then these can be addressed directly. More generally, a more effective means of boosting consumption would be a temporary cut in Value Added Tax, which would generate some additional consumption and induce consumers to bring forward spending. This was an important action taken during the 2008/9 recession that helped to mitigate some of the fall in consumption.

Fiscal support should therefore concentrate on mitigating the worst of these effects, supporting industries which are particularly vulnerable to long-term damage from short-term shifts (those with high barriers to entry and increasing returns to scale). An effort was made to do this during 2008/9 via initiatives such as the "scrappage scheme", whereby government targeted support at the automotive industry. In retrospect, this had some benefits but was also rather inefficient (writing off large amounts of productive capital) and poorly targeted – much of the benefit went to manufacturers outside the UK. While the government acted aggressively and effectively in 2008/9, it is likely that fiscal support was reduced too quickly given the tepid nature of the ensuing recovery and the fact that interest rates remained around the lower bound. This was particularly true for the period from 2011/12 onwards when the Eurozone crisis coincided with a period of quite aggressive fiscal contraction.

6.5 Monetary policy

One of the challenges of the 2020 recession across much of the developed world is the absence of conventional monetary policy tools with which to react. In common with most of Europe, the UK entered the 2020 recession with interest rates close to zero. Indeed, the Bank Rate, formerly known as the repo rate, only rose above 0.5 percent (the level to which it was first cut in 2009) in mid-2018. As a result, there has been dramatically less scope to use interest-rate cuts to stimulate demand than has been the case in the recent past. Rates were reduced from 0.75 to 0.1 percent in March, although discussion as to the potential benefits of further reductions continues.

More significantly, the Bank of England[7] drew on the knowledge gained during the 2008/9 recession regarding unconventional tools. The Bank

---

7 The name is something of a misnomer as the Bank of England is the central bank for the UK in its entirety.

undertook quantitative easing (a policy tool first used during the recession induced by the financial crisis), purchasing £200bn of gilts on the secondary market. In June 2020, the Monetary Policy Committee agreed to increase this by a further £100bn. As the second (more partial) national lockdown was imposed in early November, the Bank decided to undertake another round of QE, increasing its balance sheet by £150bn on top of the earlier measures. As a result, the Bank of England will shortly own some £895bn of bonds – a very substantial portion of the total government debt. Since in the UK, the Bank is an arm of the state, this results in the rather paradoxical situation in which the state owns vast sums of money to itself.

The intended purpose of quantitative easing is to reduce interest rates on government bonds (particularly long-term interest rates). Once Bank Rate is reduced to (near) zero, this is the major route whereby interest rates in the wider economy can be impacted. However, while hugely successful in its stated (narrow) aim, the extent to which this impacts the real economy remains a matter of academic debate. More generally, the Bank has acted aggressively to ensure that there is no shortage of liquidity. The Term Funding Scheme was relaunched with additional incentives for SME lending. Originally launched in 2016 to reinforce pass-through of an interest-rate cut, the scheme enabled banks and building societies to borrow funds at close to Bank Rate for four years. The scheme worked by charging a fee to lenders that varied depending on the growth of their net lending, in order to stimulate lending to the real economy. Simultaneously, the amount that could be borrowed was partly tied to the amount that they grew net lending (Nardi & Nwankwo, 2018). The relaunch of the scheme in 2020 contained additional incentives to lend to SMEs (defined as non-financial businesses with turnover of below £25m).

In particular, banks are given an "Additional Allowance" to draw upon, which increases at a rate of five times any increase in lending to SMEs plus one times the rate of increase in lending to other borrowers. The fee structure is similar to the original Term Funding Scheme. This, in effect, made available a large quantity of funding for lending into the real economy at Bank Rate (0.1 percent) and has supported the provision of liquidity into the real economy. Capital buffers for banks have also been temporarily reduced, further supporting lending. In addition, the Bank is an integral part of the Covid Corporate Financing Facility, through which large firms (whose debt prior to the pandemic was investment grade), which would otherwise face critical issues with cash flow, can access liquidity via the issue of commercial paper.

6.5.1 Effectiveness and comparison to 2008/9

There has been no repeat of the 2008/9 "credit crunch". Indeed, whether due to the Bank's actions or otherwise, there has been no obvious shortage of liquidity during the pandemic. What is less clear is the extent to which there might, in the absence of the steps taken by the Bank of England, have been a shortage of liquidity or difficulties within the financial system. Nevertheless, the steps taken by the Bank in providing emergency liquidity can be reasonably adjudged successful. What is less clear is the extent to which monetary policy actions have actually been able to support the real economy. Given that interest rates going into the pandemic were near their lower bound, the onus has therefore fallen squarely on the shoulders of unconventional policy (as well as very modest interest-rate cuts). The question is therefore how successful has QE been at supporting the real economy?

Bernanke and Reinhart (2004) note that QE can act via several channels, notably via the portfolio balance effect. The purchase of gilts under QE is financed via the direct creation of money. The portfolio balance effect contends that insofar as money is an imperfect substitute for other financial assets, investors (who otherwise would be left holding more money in their portfolio of assets than they would like) will seek to use this excess money to purchase alternative assets – essentially "rebalancing" their portfolios to achieve the optimum outcome. This, in turn, will bid up prices (and reduce yields) of alternative (riskier) assets. There is some evidence that this has occurred: while there might be debate as to the extent to the substitutability of various asset classes with gilts, it is incontrovertible that asset prices (particularly of property) have risen very substantially over the past decade. That being said, while mortgage rates for prime borrowers with large amounts of collateral are near record lows, interest rates for risky borrowers (particularly those looking to invest) remain considerably higher.

Insofar as QE is effective at reducing interest rates on alternative asset classes, it should act as a spur to investment and, to a lesser extent, consumption.[8] However, the efficacy of this will be dependent on several factors. Akin to "normal" interest-rate changes, there are then several (more familiar) ways in which lower long-term interest rates increase consumption and investment. Faced with this increase in wealth (insofar as it is believed to be permanent), individuals consume more.[9]

Insofar as domestic assets yield a lower return than those elsewhere, there is also the likelihood that policy will lead to a depreciation in the exchange rate, thus boosting GDP via an increase in net exports. This does appear to have occurred, to a degree, in practice. However, since what matters is the *relative* rate of return, with most of the world's major central banks all engaging in QE to various degrees, these actions have (at least partly) offset each other in this regard. There is a degree of agreement among most developed countries not

---

8 There is vigorous debate over the manner in which this latter effect manifests itself, and considerable questions over its magnitude. Many theorize a "life-cycle" effect, whereby consumers attempt to smooth their expected consumption over time. In practice, limited information and borrowing constraints have a significant bearing on our ability to do this. In any event, a reduction in interest rates certainly acts to reduce the cost of consumption in the present time period vis-à-vis the future.

9 This also acts to increase individuals' ability to borrow against assets that have appreciated in value. Witness the phenomenon of "equity release" mortgages that became prevalent in the UK and elsewhere prior to 2008.

to engage in competitive depreciations, so this would appear to be a (perhaps welcome!) domestic side effect of QE (as is the case with changes in the Bank Rate) rather than a primary intended transmission channel.

Perhaps the most pertinent question is not whether QE works at all but rather the extent to which it works. On this, there is little consensus, although it has been suggested that under certain circumstances and in conjunction with other actions, it might offer the equivalent of an interest-rate cut of up to 3 percentage points (Bernanke, 2020). However, given the apparently low "natural rate" of interest and the volume of QE already undertaken by the Bank of England prior to the pandemic, it is questionable how much stimulus additional policy has (and can) realistically provide. More generally, given the uncertainty generated by the pandemic (in addition to the uncertainties around the UK's departure from the European Union), it is unclear whether the effects of even more conventional monetary policy on investment would be strong. In the 2020 pandemic, at least within the UK, much of the burden of adjustment has fallen upon fiscal policy, to a much greater extent than during previous economic shocks.

The contrast with the 2008/9 financial crisis is stark. Towards the very beginning of the crisis – on 14 September 2007 – Northern Rock experienced the first run on a British bank in 140 years. The remarkable scenes of mid-September were in many regards a portent of what was to come. Northern Rock was particularly vulnerable to a reduction in short-term liquidity, and particularly to the (relatively sudden) reduction in demand for securitised loans. Faced with an inability to raise funds from the money market (very short-term debt), the Bank of England stepped in and provided emergency liquidity to Northern Rock. Deposits were guaranteed by the government from 17 September and this event (amongst others) was instrumental in the later establishment of the Financial Services Compensation Scheme.

The collapse of Lehman Brothers in the United States is viewed by some as marking the beginning of the financial crisis proper, although it is probably more accurate to suggest that it marked the moment at which its severity dramatically escalated. In any event, liquidity dramatically dried up during the third and final quarters of 2008. In the UK, the Bank of England stepped in via the Special Liquidity Scheme[10] to provide emergency liquidity to the banking sector. Furthermore, the Bank of England also provided – at the time in secret – £36.6bn of liquidity to RBS and £25.4bn to HBOS. Further support was forthcoming as the crisis intensified. Interest rates (the primary monetary policy tool at the time) were cut dramatically and the Bank launched its first QE programme.

The Bank and Treasury largely acted in lockstep throughout the crisis to ensure that the banking sector did not collapse (with potentially

---

10 The Special Liquidity Scheme was actually launched in April 2008 and permitted banks to temporarily swap illiquid (but high quality) assets such as mortgage-backed securities for UK Treasury bills (a safe and highly liquid asset). The events of September 2008 led to the drawdown period being extended in order to allow banks to continue to access the scheme.

catastrophic consequences for the real economy). The public sector ended up taking ownership of significant parts of the financial sector. While the provision of liquidity was the chief contribution of the monetary policy domain, there can be no doubt that the wider actions of both the Bank and Treasury together averted an even more serious downturn. Nevertheless, the public sector ended up bearing significant risk and these events raised serious issues of moral hazard. While we hope that this has gradually been corrected (and that major financial institutions can fail in an orderly manner that minimises financial contagion), some challenges remain. British banks (alongside a number of their international counterparts) have significantly greater capital buffers than prior to the crisis and these are regularly stress-tested. However, the ideal shape of financial regulation remains an area of active debate.

6.6 Brexit

Finally, the Brexit context of the UK's departure from the EU Single Market and Customs Union on 1 January 2021 will have an impact on efforts to counter the impact of the virus going forward. Given that the free trade agreement reached between the UK Government and the EU is essentially a simple zero-tariff, zero-quota trade agreement for goods, the corollary of exiting the Single Market has meant that substantive new non-tariff trade barriers have come into place, including customs checks, sanitary and phyto-sanitary checks and other security checks and restrictions on the freedom of movement of people. The UK's Brexit trajectory then, has (and will continue to) impact on combating the virus in several aspects.

First, the imposition of new trade barriers impacts directly on the smooth operation of supply chains, with pharmaceuticals and medical supplies being a key example, as these products have to contend with being held up in ports of entry to the UK so as to be subject to the requisite checks above. The Pfizer-BioNTech vaccine for example is manufactured in Belgium and hence the UK Government has espoused transporting vaccines by air so as avoid "congestion in ports" (Healey, 2020). Such checks invariably will lengthen the time it takes to move goods between the UK and the EU, undermining the viability of manufacturing supply chains. As such, they will have particularly critical impact on semi-finished pharmaceutical products that have a highly-limited transport life.

Second, Brexit, by imposing direct economic costs to the UK in the form of higher unemployment, reduced business investment and profitability and inflation induced by Sterling depreciation, will have a negative impact on government coffers in the form of reduced tax revenues. Hence, this will increase pressure on the UK Government to increase borrowings, or otherwise reduce spending/increase taxes elsewhere in the economy just to maintain a given volume of fiscal response measures to counter the pandemic. The governing Conservative Party is not known for championing government intervention in the economy and pressures are already growing to cut back spending. In this context, Rishi Sunak, the UK Chancellor of the Exchequer's spending review announcement in November 2020 foreshadowed these sentiments, with its announcement of spending reductions across UK Government departments for 2021–22 onwards (HM Treasury, 2020).

Finally, Brexit, by disrupting the economies of scale and scope attained by acting in concert with 27 other EU member states, has weakened the UK's ability to maximise economic leverage in countering the virus. This was evident early on the pandemic when the UK Government declined to take part in an EU bulk-purchase of personal protective equipment (PPE) that would have secured volume-discounts in pricing. The UK Government claimed that it had not been informed, a statement disputed by the EU. That the UK Government's 2020 Spending Review allocated an additional £15 billion for PPE (an eye-watering sum) on top of initial outlays[11] only further exposes its poor record in demonstrating value for money on Covid19-related expenditure. In a similar fashion, exclusion from or reduced involvement in EU R&D funding programmes such as Horizon 2020 and the Socrates/Erasmus mobility scheme will only hinder scientific collaboration, imposing indirect economic costs on the UK.

6.7 Assessment/Conclusion

In conclusion then, the UK's response to Covid-19 has been mixed at best. On the one hand, the unprecedented use of fiscal policy to provide direct support to businesses and workers to counter the economic damage caused by a national lockdown is to be commended. However, it was also apparent that had the UK Government acted quicker to implement social restrictions then the impact of a lockdown could have been reduced, lessening the volume of assistance required. In a similar fashion, the UK's failure to implement an effective test, trace and isolate system early on in the pandemic only served to further intensify the undue impact of the virus on human life and economic wellbeing. With over 80,000 deaths attributed to Covid-19 at the time of writing, the human toll in the UK has been severe. The impact of the virus was further exacerbated because of underlying structural weaknesses of the economy and labour market in particular that rendered the UK almost uniquely vulnerable to Covid-19; namely, a high share of employment in social consumption sectors, and a flexible labour market with a high incidence of precarious jobs for which adequate sick pay provisions were sorely lacking. Going forward, concerns remain as to the impact of the UK Government scaling back support as 2021 progresses When coupled with the impact of a hard Brexit on the UK economy, it could be argued that the prognosis over the immediate coming years looks bleak.

11 https://theconversation.com/drafts/150875/edit

References

Armstrong, K., Bailey, D., de Ruyter, A., Mahdon, M., & Thomas, H. (2008). Auto plant closures, policy responses and labour market outcomes: A comparison of MG Rover in the UK and Mitsubishi in Australia. *Policy Studies, 29*(3), pp. 343–355. doi:10.1080/01442870802160051 Retrieved from https://doi.org/10.1080/014428708 02160051

Bailey, D., & de Ruyter, A. (2015). Plant closures, precariousness and policy responses: Revisiting MG Rover 10 years on. *Policy Studies, 36*(4), pp. 363–383. doi:10.1080/0144 2872.2015.1073248 Retrieved from https://doi.org/10.1080/01442872.2015.1073248

Bernanke, B. S. (2020). The new tools of monetary policy. *American Economic Review, 110*(4), pp. 943–983. doi:10.1257/aer.110.4.943 Retrieved from www.aeaweb.org/articles?id=10.1257/aer.110.4.943

Bernanke, B. S., & Reinhart, V. R. (2004). Conducting monetary policy at very low short-term interest rates. *American Economic Review, 94*(2), pp. 85–90. doi:10.1257/0002828041302118 Retrieved from www.aeaweb.org/articles?id=10.1257/0002828041302118

Blanchard, O. J., & Summers, L. H. (1987). Hysteresis in unemployment. *European Economic Review, 31*(1), pp. 288–295. doi:10.1016/0014-2921(87)90042-0 Retrieved from www.sciencedirect.com/science/article/pii/0014292187900420

Booth, R. (2016). More than 7m Britons now in precarious employment. *The Guardian.* Retrieved from www.theguardian.com/uk-news/2016/nov/15/more-than-7m-britons-in-precarious-employment

Bordo, M. D., & Haubrich, J. G. (2017). Deep recessions, fast recoveries, and financial crises: Evidence from the American record. *Economic Inquiry, 55*(1), pp. 527–541. doi:10.1111/ecin.12374 Retrieved from https://onlinelibrary.wiley.com/doi/abs/10.1111/ecin.12374

Buck, T., & Ghiglione, D. (2020). European countries search for ventilators as cases surge. *Financial Times.* Retrieved from www.ft.com/content/5a2ffc78-6550-11ea-b3f3-fe 4680ea68b5

Eurostat. (2019). Body Mass Index (BMI) by sex, age and educational attainment level. Retrieved from https://ec.europa.eu/eurostat/databrowser/view/hlth_ehis_bm1e/defa ult/table?lang=en

Eurostat. (2020a). Healthcare expenditure statistics. Retrieved from https://ec.europa.eu /eurostat/statistics-explained/index.php/Healthcare_expenditure_statistics#Healthcare _expenditure.

Eurostat. (2020b). Healthcare personnel statistics - Nursing and caring professionals. Retrieved from https://ec.europa.eu/eurostat/statistics-explained/index.php?title=Hea lthcare_personnel_statistics_-_nursing_and_caring_professionals#Healthcare_personnel

Eurostat. (2020c). Life expectancy at birth. Available from: tps00205.https://ec.europa.eu/ eurostat/web/products-datasets/-/tps00205

Google. (2020). See how your community is moving around differently due to COVID-19. Accessed, 2021 Retrieved from www.google.com/covid19/mobility/

Harra, J. (2020). COVID-19 "Eat Out to Help Out" (EOHO) scheme.

Healey, D. (2020). Covid vaccine could be flown to UK on military planes to avoid Brexit delays. *The Courier.* Retrieved from www.thecourier.co.uk/fp/news/politics/scottish -politics/1792432/covid-vaccine-brexit-delays/

Her Majesty's Revenue and Customs. (2020). Coronavirus job retention scheme statistics: August 2020. Retrieved from www.gov.uk/government/statistics/coronavirus-job-r etention-scheme-statistics-august-2020

HM Treasury. (2020). *Spending Review 2020*. London: HMSO. Retrieved from https://as
  sets.publishing.service.gov.uk/government/uploads/system/uploads/attachment_data/
  file/938052/SR20_Web_Accessible.pdf

Ivashina, V., & Scharfstein, D. (2010). Bank lending during the financial crisis of 2008.
  Journal of Financial Economics, *97*(3), pp. 319–338. doi:10.1016/j.jfineco.2009.12.001
  Retrieved from www.sciencedirect.com/science/article/pii/S0304405X09002396

Jit, M., Jombart, T., Nightingale, E. S., Endo, A., Abbott, S., Group, L. C. f. M. M. o. I. D.
  C.-W., & Edmunds, W. J. (2020). Estimating number of cases and spread of coronavirus
  disease (COVID-19) using critical care admissions, United Kingdom, February to March
  2020. *Eurosurveillance*, *25*(18), p. 2000632. doi:10.2807/1560-7917.ES.2020.25.18.2000
  632 Retrieved from www.eurosurveillance.org/content/10.2807/1560-7917.ES.2020
  .25.18.2000632

Kannan, P. (2012). Credit conditions and recoveries from financial crises. *Journal of
  International Money and Finance*, *31*(5), pp. 930–947. doi:10.1016/j.jimonfin.2011.11.017
  Retrieved from www.sciencedirect.com/science/article/pii/S0261560611001835

Keogh-Brown, M. R., Wren-Lewis, S., Edmunds, W. J., Beutels, P., & Smith, R. D.
  (2010). The possible macroeconomic impact on the UK of an influenza pandemic.
  Health Economics, *19*(11), pp. 1345–1360. doi:10.1002/hec.1554 Retrieved from https:/
  /onlinelibrary.wiley.com/doi/abs/10.1002/hec.1554

Nardi, B. G., & Nwankwo, C. (2018). The Term Funding Scheme: design, operation
  and impact. London. Retrieved from www.bankofengland.co.uk/-/media/boe/files/
  quarterly-bulletin/2018/term-funding-scheme-web-version.pdf?la=en&hash=547FD
  DCF2F459CBF463E0A12CE1700AA9D4E727B

Northern Ireland Statistics and Research Agency, & Office for National Statistics. (2020).
  Quarterly labour force survey, April–June, 2020. SN 8671. Retrieved from http://doi
  .org/10.5255/UKDA-SN-8671-3

Office for Budget Responsibility. (2020). Coronavirus analysis. Retrieved from https://obr
  .uk/coronavirus-analysis/

Office for National Statistics. (2019). *Annual Survey of Hours and Earnings, 1997–2019* [Data
  set]. Retrieved from www.ons.gov.uk/employmentandlabourmarket/peopleinwork/e
  arningsandworkinghours/bulletins/annualsurveyofhoursandearnings/2019

Office for National Statistics. (2020a). Analysis of death registrations not involving
  coronavirus (COVID-19), England and Wales: 28 December 2019 to 10 July 2020.
  Retrieved from www.ons.gov.uk/peoplepopulationandcommunity/birthsdeathsandm
  arriages/deaths/articles/analysisofdeathregistrationsnotinvolvingcoronaviruscovid19en
  glandandwales28december2019to1may2020/28december2019to10july2020

Office for National Statistics. (2020b). Labour market overview, UK: May 2020. Retrieved
  from   www.ons.gov.uk/employmentandlabourmarket/peopleinwork/employmenta
  ndemployeetypes/bulletins/uklabourmarket/may2020

Office for National Statistics. (2020c). Monthly gross domestic product: Time series.
  Retrieved from www.ons.gov.uk/economy/grossdomesticproductgdp/datasets/gdpm
  onthlyestimateuktimeseriesdataset

Office for National Statistics. (2020d). Public sector finances, UK: July 2020. Retrieved
  from www.ons.gov.uk/economy/governmentpublicsectorandtaxes/publicsectorfinance
  /bulletins/publicsectorfinances/july2020

Office for National Statistics. (2020e). *Quarterly Labour Force Survey, October - December, 2019*
  [Data set]. Retrieved from http://doi.org/10.5255/UKDA-SN-8614-1

Pybus, O., Rambaut, A., & COG-UK-Consortium. (2020). Preliminary analysis of SARS-
  CoV-2 importation & establishment of UK transmission lineages. Preprint at https://

virological.   org/t/preliminary-analysis-of-sars-cov-2-importation-establishment-of-uk-transmission-lineages/507

Queralto, A. (2020). A model of slow recoveries from financial crises. *Journal of Monetary Economics*, *114*, pp. 1–25. doi:10.1016/j.jmoneco.2019.03.008 Retrieved from www.sciencedirect.com/science/article/pii/S0304393219300546

Thomas, D., & Morris, S. (2020). A giant bonfire of taxpayers' money. *Financial Times*. Retrieved from www.ft.com/content/41d5fe0a-7b46-4dd7-96e3-710977dff81c

Thomas, L. (2020). French, Italian economies hurt most under second lockdowns. *Reuters*. Retrieved from https://uk.reuters.com/article/uk-europe-economy-data-graphic/french-italian-economies-hurt-most-under-second-lockdowns-idUKKBN28014Y

Part III

Monetary and fiscal policies in Asia

7 The case of China

Lifeng SU

7.1 Introduction

In early January 2020, the COVID-19 epidemic first broke out in China, and the number of infected people nationwide increased rapidly. After March, other countries around the world had their own outbreak periods of the COVID-19 epidemic, including Italy, Britain, France, the United States, Brazil, India etc. According to the statistics of the World Health Organization, on December 31, 2020, the cumulative number of infected people worldwide was 81.48 million, and the cumulative death toll was 1.80 million. Almost all countries in the world have been affected by the COVID-19 epidemic, their economies have fallen into recession, and the financial markets of developed countries have also experienced a huge decline.

The main content of the remainder of this chapter is divided into six parts. The first part introduces the extent of the outbreak of COVID-19 and the associated public health crisis. In the second part, the author summarizes the impact of the COVID-19 epidemic on China's economy; China's monetary and fiscal policies during the epidemic are introduced in the third part and the fourth part respectively. The fifth part compares and analyzes the differences in China's policy responses during this epidemic and during the 2008 global financial crisis (GFC). The sixth part provides an overall assessment and outlook on China's monetary policy and fiscal policy.

7.2 The extent of the outbreak of COVID-19 and the public health crisis

On January 20, according to the data from the National Health Commission of China, there were only 291 COVID-19 cases in China. Because there was insufficient COVID-19 detection reagent at the time, the estimated number of infected people was far higher. Subsequently, infection rate statistics became more accurate.

In respect of the epidemic, the Chinese government imposed strict containment measures, including the extension of the national Lunar New Year holiday, the lockdown of Wuhan city and Hubei province, large-scale travel

DOI: 10.4324/9781003153603-7

restrictions at the national level, social distancing, compulsory mask wearing, and a 14-day quarantine period for returning migrant workers from the interior provinces etc. Chinese people have also been willing to consciously abide by the government's regulations in respect of epidemic control. In terms of specific treatment measures, the central government dispatched a large number of medical personnel to Wuhan city and Hubei province to treat pneumonia patients and prevent the spread of the COVID epidemic.

In about a three-month period, the COVID-19 epidemic in China was basically brought under control (see Figures 7.1 and 7.2). Although there were several small-scale outbreaks in Beijing in early June, in Dalian of Liaoning province in early July, in the Kashgar area of Xinjiang Uygur Autonomous Region in late October, the epidemic did not spread because China had acquired sufficient experience in epidemic control.

At the Twelfth Lujiazui forum held on June 18, *Liu He*, the vice premier of the State Council of China, in charge of the economic and financial departments of central government, said that "China has achieved significant phased achievements in coordinating the COVID-19 epidemic control and resumption of work, production, and business activities, and marginal improvement in various economic indicators", and "we are still under great pressure of the economic downturn, but the situation is gradually changing in a better direction".

After the second quarter, new COVID-19 cases were mainly people entering China from abroad. In the fourth quarter, there were several sporadic cases of infection in Heilongjiang, Inner Mongolia, Tianjin, Shanghai, Beijing, Dalian of Liaoning province, and other places. We estimate that it was mainly due to infected imported cases or viruses occurring via cold-chain logistics. COVID-19 basically did not affect the daily activities of most people. China's social and economic activities have currently returned to normal.

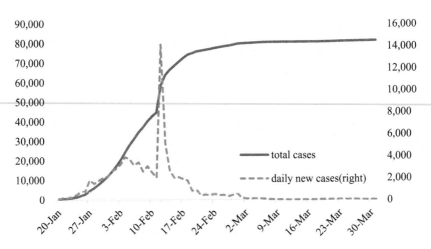

Figure 7.1 China's cumulative infected cases and daily new cases of COVID-19 Before April 1, 2020.

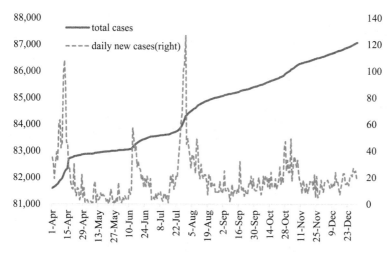

Figure 7.2 China's cumulative infected cases and daily new cases of COVID-19 after March 31, 2020.

7.3 The impact of the COVID-19 epidemic on China's economy

In the first quarter of 2020, the sudden outbreak of COVID-19 had an unprecedented negative impact on China's economic and social development. On the supply side, large industrial enterprises reduced production, and some micro-, small- and medium-sized enterprises (MSMEs) even stopped production completely. Due to concerns about the risk of infection, the negative impact on the services sector was greater, with offline trading activities strongly suppressed. The tourism, accommodation and catering, film and entertainment sectors stagnated, and the transportation, wholesale, and retail sectors were also greatly impacted.

7.3.1 Double impact on supply side and demand side in the first quarter

According to the data from a questionnaire survey of 23,524 enterprises conducted by China Merchants Bank in late April, the capacity utilization rate of MSMEs (fewer than 50 employees) was 42.5 percent, that of large and medium enterprises (more than 100 employees) was 73.3 percent, and of the whole sample was 45.7 percent. The main sectors with lower capacity utilization rates included education, culture, entertainment and sports, residential services, leasing and business services, accommodation and catering, and construction.[1]

---

1 Among the enterprises surveyed, 87.9 percent had fewer than 50 employees, and 70.5 percent had less than RMB 5 million operating revenue. From the perspective of sector type, the surveyed enter-

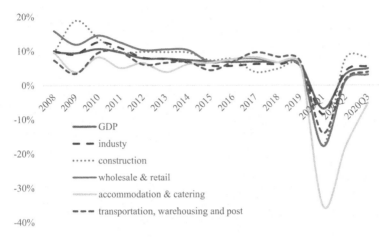

Figure 7.3 The year-on-year growth rate of gross value-added of various sectors in China.
Source: National Bureau of Statistics of China.

In terms of the gross value-added (GVA) of sectors from the National Bureau of Statistics of China, the accommodation and catering sector was impacted the most, with a year-on-year decrease of 35.3 percent in the first quarter of 2020, and still an 18 percent and 5.1 percent decrease in the second and third quarters respectively (as shown in Figure 7.3).

On the demand-side, due to the shutdown of some MSMEs, it was difficult for workers to find jobs, and unemployment increased, especially for farmer-turned-migrant workers. The growth rate of total retail sales of social consumer goods was −20.5 percent in the first two months of 2020 whereas it was +8.0 percent in 2019. The cumulative completion of fixed assets investment decreased by 24.5 percent in the first two months, compared with a 5.4 percent increase for the whole year of 2019. The total amount of international imports and export continued its downward trend of recent years. In the first quarter of 2020, the gross domestic product (GDP) of China fell by 6.8 percent year-on-year, and the GDP of Hubei province fell by 39.2 percent, which were the largest economic contractions since China commenced implementing the Reform & Opening-up policy in 1978.

Since April, industrial enterprises began to advance the resumption of work and production, and China's economy began to rebound. After April, because

prises are mainly concentrated in the tertiary broad sector, accounting for 85.6 percent. The number of enterprises in wholesale and retail, leasing and commercial services, information and software, and research and technology sectors together accounted for 71.1 percent of the sample. The secondary broad sector accounted for 14.1 percent, mainly manufacturing and construction enterprises. From the perspective of regional distribution, the surveyed enterprises are mainly concentrated in economically developed areas, especially in Guangdong, Beijing, Shanghai, Jiangsu, Shandong, and Zhejiang, with a total of 15,774 enterprises in six provinces and cities, accounting for 67.1 percent of the total.

the Chinese government had basically controlled the spread of the COVID-19 epidemic, the risk of infection gradually eased and economic activity rebounded significantly. From the point of view of the data, the decline range of each indicator gradually narrowed as shown in Table 7.1.

7.3.2 China's economic recovery since the second quarter

By June 2020, the public's concern about the risk of infection was very small, and investment and commodity consumption had relatively fully recovered. It should be recognized that in some service sectors requiring face-to-face inter-actions, such as aviation, tourism, hotels, catering, film and entertainment, the potential risk of infection is obviously greater. Therefore, the public and the government are still highly cautious about such interactions, and the recovery of these sectors was obviously slower. Because MSMEs and low-income groups are more vulnerable to the epidemic, they have suffered a greater and more lasting impact during the epidemic. In the economic recovery process, the recovery of their business activities and incomes has been relatively slow.

China's economic growth has shown strong resilience. In the first three quarters of 2020, the GDP grew slightly by 0.9 percent year-on-year, and the second and third quarters witnessed growth of 3.2 percent and 4.9 percent year-on-year respectively, which was much better than expected. Economic

Table 7.1 The impact of the COVID-19 epidemic on China's economy

	Investment in fixed assets	Total retail sales of consumer goods	Total imports and exports	Industrial value-added
Cumulative year-on-year growth rate of the demand-side and the supply side				
2013	19.6%	13.1%	7.6%	9.7%
2014	15.7%	12.0%	3.4%	8.3%
2015	10.0%	10.7%	−8.1%	6.1%
2016	8.1%	10.4%	−6.8%	6.0%
2017	7.2%	10.2%	11.4%	6.6%
2018	5.9%	9.0%	12.6%	6.2%
2019	5.4%	8.0%	−1.0%	5.7%
2020-02	−24.5%	−20.5%	−11.0%	−13.5%
2020-03	−16.1%	−19.0%	−8.5%	−8.4%
2020-04	−10.3%	−16.2%	−7.6%	−4.9%
2020-05	−6.3%	−13.5%	−7.9%	−2.8%
2020-06	−3.1%	−11.4%	−6.3%	−1.3%
2020-07	−1.6%	−9.9%	−4.8%	−0.4%
2020-08	−0.3%	−8.6%	−3.6%	0.4%
2020-09	0.8%	−7.2%	−1.8%	1.2%
2020-10	1.8%	−5.9%	−0.8%	1.8%
2020-11	2.6%	−4.8%	0.6%	2.3%

Source: National Bureau of Statistics of China.

indicators released in mid-November showed that China's production activity had returned to normal. In the first ten months, the industrial value-added turned to positive growth of 1.8 percent year-on-year, and the decline in consumption, investment, and export demand had gradually narrowed (as shown in Table 7.1). The government was expecting a full resumption of domestic demand in the fourth quarter.

In October 2020, the International Monetary Fund released the world economic outlook report (International Monetary Fund, 2020), which predicted that China's economy would grow by 1.9 percent in 2020.

Detailed data about the impact of the COVID-19 epidemic on China's economy are shown in Table 7.1.

Currently, the successful control of the epidemic has made China the least affected country among the major economy countries. The future development of the Chinese economy will still mainly be affected by some medium- and long-term trend factors, such as changes in the number and structure of the labor force, the transformation of the demand structure, the reduction of the debt leverage ratio, the changes in technology upgrading speed, and the external environment, such as the development of economic globalization and changes in Sino–US relations, etc.

In mid-May, the meeting of the Political Bureau of the Communist Party of China (CPC) Central Committee proposed that "China accelerates the establishment of a 'dual circulation' development pattern in which the domestic economic cycle plays a leading role while the international economic cycle remains its extension and supplement". This implies that China's future economic development will pay more attention to the leading role of domestic demand.

During the COVID-19 epidemic, the Chinese government adopted a series of policies to reduce the negative impact of the epidemic on the financial market and the real economy. These policies can be categorized into monetary policies and fiscal policies. The monetary policy mainly focuses on dealing with the short-term and medium-term impact of the epidemic, while the fiscal policy focuses on coping with the adverse impact of the epidemic on economic growth in the long run.

7.4 China's monetary policy after the COVID-19 outbreak

At the National People's Congress in late May, in his government work report, Li KeQiang, Premier of the State Council, stated that China will pursue a prudent monetary policy in a more flexible and targeted way, using a variety of tools, such as required reserve ratio (RRR) reductions, interest rate cuts, and central bank lending to banks to enable M2 money supply and aggregate financing for the real economy to grow at notably higher rates than last year (Li KeQiang, 2020).

After the COVID-19 outbreak, the monetary policy tools used by the People's Bank of China (PBOC) can be divided into two categories: one is those tools to adjust the amount of base money, the other is the tools to adjust the interest rate. The former can also be divided into short-term liquidity injections and medium- and long-term base money supply. From January to August, the monetary policies adopted by the PBOC are as shown in Table 7.2.

7.4.1 Quantitative monetary measures

In order to stabilize expectations and effectively respond to the COVID-19 disruptions, the PBOC acted decisively to inject short-term liquidity into the financial market. On February 2, the final day of the Spring Festival vacation, the PBOC announced stronger-than-expected liquidity injection measures to stabilize market expectations. It then injected short-term liquidity of RMB 1.7 trillion into the financial market on February 3 and 4, the first two working days after vacation. However, when the financial market stabilized, large amounts of short-term liquidity were taken back. In February, the PBOC withdrew liquidity of RMB 577.5 billion (Monetary Policy Analysis Group of the People's Bank of China, 2020a).

Previously, on January 31, 2020, in support of winning the fight against the effects of the outbreak, the PBOC released the *Notice on Providing Special Central Bank Lending to Support the Prevention and Control of COVID-19* (No.28 [2020]). The aim was to provide low-cost special central bank lending amounting to RMB300 billion to major national banks and some locally incorporated banks in ten key provinces (municipalities), such as Hubei, to support the provision of credit by financial institutions at favorable rates to key enterprises directly engaged in the production, transportation, and sale of key medical supplies and daily necessities in the fight against the virus (Monetary Policy Analysis Group of the People's Bank of China, 2020a).

The RMB 300 billion worth of special central bank lending was provided to nine national banks and 31 locally incorporated banks in ten provinces (municipalities). List-based management was adopted for major enterprises, which were selected by the National Development and Reform Commission, the Ministry of Industry and Information Technology, and the provincial governments. It was required that the funds be used for the production and business operations of sectors related to pandemic containment(Monetary Policy Analysis Group of the People's Bank of China, 2020a).

On February 26, 2020, the PBOC increased relending and rediscount quotas by RMB 500 billion, and commercial banks were required to issue loans at rates no higher than the one-year LPR plus 50 basis points, which supported the resumption of work and production. At the same time, cuts were made to the interest rates of relending designated for the agricultural sector and small businesses by 0.25 percent to 2.5 percent. Therefore, low-cost and inclusive funding support was provided for the orderly resumption of work and production, debt repayment, capital turnover, the expansion of the funding scale, and other urgent issues confronting enterprises were also addressed(Monetary Policy Analysis Group of the People's Bank of China, 2020a).

Table 7.2 China's monetary policies after the COVID-19 outbreak

policy tools		date	policy content
Quantitative monetary policy instruments	Short-term liquidity injection	Open market operations (OMOs)	February 3 to 4	From February 3 to 4, the first two working days after the Chinese Spring Festival vacation, the PBOC conducted a RMB1.7 trillion short-term repos injection into the banking system through OMOs. The net fund injection reached RMB 1.12 trillion in this week.
			February	The PBOC recovered RMB 577.5 billion through OMOs repos in four weeks.
	Medium- and long-term funds input	Cuts in the required reserve ratio (RRR)	January 6	The PBOC lowered the RRR for financial institutions by 0.5 percentage points, releasing over RMB800 billion of long-term funds.
			March 16	The PBOC implemented a targeted RRR cut of 0.5-2.5 percentage points to eligible institutions for inclusive finance, and thereby released approximately RMB550 billion in net long-term funds.
			April 3	The RRR cut at 1 percentage point for rural financial institutions was carried out in two phases, with a cut of 0.5 percentage points each time, on April 15 and May 15 respectively. About RMB400 billion of long-term funds were freed up by the cuts.
		Special central bank relending and rediscount	January 31	The PBOC provided low-cost special central bank lending of RMB 300 billion to major national banks and some local banks in ten key provinces, including Hubei, to support the provision of credit by financial institutions at favorable rates to key enterprises directly engaged in the production, transportation, and sale of key medical supplies and daily necessities in the fight against the COVID-19 virus.
			February 26	RMB 500 billion of central bank lending and discount quotas was introduced to support work and production resumption in an orderly manner.
			April 20	Another RMB 1 trillion of central bank lending and discount quotas was introduced to support economic recovery and development. Financial institutions were encouraged to increase their credit supply to the agro-linked sector, foreign trade, as well as sectors severely hit by the COVID-19 epidemic.

			June 1	The PBOC launched two monetary policy instruments that directly support the real economy to bolster the development of SMEs, to stabilize businesses, and to secure employment. Firstly, the PBOC provided RMB 40 billion central bank loans to ease the pressure on small and micro enterprises to repay the principal and interest.
			June 1	Secondly, the PBOC provided RMB 400 billion central bank loans to solve financing problems of small- and medium-sized enterprises (SMEs).
Interest rate instruments	Interest rate cuts	Repo interest rate	February 3	The PBOC cut the 7-day repos interest rate 10 basis points to 2.40 percent.
			March 30	The PBOC cut the 7-day repos interest rate 20 basis points to 2.20 percent
		Interest rate on excess reserve	April 7	The interest rate on excess reserves deposited in the central bank by financial institutions was cut from 0.72 percent to 0.35 percent.
		MLF[1] interest rate	February 17	The PBOC cut the 1-year MLF interest rate 10 basis points to 3.15 percent
			April 15	The PBOC cut the 1-year MLF interest rate 20 basis points to 2.95 percent, and this remains the same to-date
		LPR[2]	February 20	The PBOC cut the 1-year LPR 10 basis points to 4.05 percent
			April 20	The PBOC cut the 1-year LPR 20 basis points to 3.85 percent, and this remains the same to-date

Source: PBOC.

Note: 1. Medium-term lending facility (MLF) refers to the monetary policy tool that the PBOC utilizes to provide the medium-term currency base. It was established by the PBOC in September 2014. Commercial banks and policy banks (i.e. under the direct leadership of the State Council of China) that meet the requirements of macro-prudential management can apply for this funding through bidding. The loans are issued subject to the provision of collateral and high-quality bonds such as treasury bonds, central bank bills, policy financial bonds, and high-grade credit bonds can be provided as qualified collateral.

2. The loan prime rate (LPR) refers to the rates panel banks quote based on their own actual loan interest rates for prime clients, by adding some basis points to the interest rate of the MLF.

On April 20, the PBOC again increased the quota for relending and rediscounts by RMB 1 trillion, which was to be used to issue preferential loans to the vast number of MSMEs. Financial institutions were encouraged to increase their credit supply to the agro-linked sector, foreign trade sector, as well as sectors severely hit by the epidemic(Monetary Policy Analysis Group of the People's Bank of China, 2020b).

The RMB 500 billion and RMB 1 trillion worth of central bank lending was provided to over 4,000 locally incorporated financial institutions nationwide. According to the statistics of the PBOC in late November, as of end-June, the program of RMB 300 billion special central bank lending and RMB 500 billion of central bank lending and central bank discounts had been fully implemented. Over 80 percent of the RMB 1 trillion of central bank lending and central bank discounts had been put into place by end-September, which played a vital role in supporting pandemic containment as well as supporting the resumption of work and production(Monetary Policy Analysis Group of the People's Bank of China, 2020c).

The main monetary policy measures adopted by the PBOC are to provide low-cost special relending and rediscount funds (generally one-year term) to support enterprises' orderly resumption of work and production. As MSMEs are most seriously affected by the epidemic, the relending and rediscount funds issued by the PBOC are required to mainly provide loans to MSMEs. From February to June, the total amount of such funds reached RMB 2.24 trillion. The detailed amount is shown in Table 7.2.

Besides the central bank relending and rediscounts, from early 2020 to May 2020, the RRR was cut three times in order to maintain adequate liquidity, releasing long-term funds in the amount of RMB1.75 trillion. In the longer run, from 2018 to April 2020, the PBOC cut the RRR ten times, releasing long-term funds in the amount of RMB 8.4 trillion, and the average RRR fell from 14.9 percent in early 2018 to 9.4 percent currently. Furthermore, starting April 7, 2020, the interest rate on excess reserves deposited in the central bank by financial institutions was cut from 0.72 percent to 0.35 percent. The purpose of all the above-mentioned policies is to boost the banks' credit support for MSMEs, enhancing the financial institutions' efficiency in capital use, bringing down social financing costs, and shoring up the real economy(Monetary Policy Analysis Group of the People's Bank of China, 2020b).

The PBOC has also released base money to a certain extent through relending and rediscounting, whereas the reduction of the deposit RRR has the effect of contracting the balance sheet, so the total assets have been stable at about RMB 37 trillion since the beginning of 2020 as shown in Figure 7.4.

7.4.2 Interest rate measures

Another tool used was to cut interest rates. There are mainly three kinds of interest rates. First, the open market reverse repo rate was cut by a total of 30 basis points to 2.20 percent. Second, the medium-term lending facility (MLF)

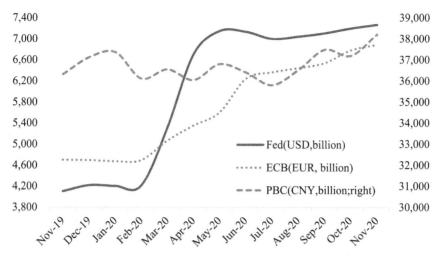

Figure 7.4 Total assets of Fed, ECB, and PBOC in the last 12 months. Source: Fed, ECB, PBOC.

rate was cut by 30 basis points to 2.95 percent. Currently, the MLF has become the main tool for the PBOC to conduct monetary policy operations. After June 2017, the MLF funding has been always on a one-year term. Third, the loan prime rate (LPR) was lowered by 30 basis points to 3.85 percent. The interest rate cut was completed in mid-April, and the low interest rate level has continued to-date. Since August 2019, the purpose of the LPR reform is to enhance the transmission efficiency of monetary policy to loan interest rates and reduce the capital cost of the real economy.

Since the third quarter, the benchmark interest rate has remained stable. Until late November, the one-year MLF rate and the LPR remained at 2.95 percent and 3.85 percent respectively. However, the market interest rate has risen slightly, as shown in Figure 7.4. This shows that the growth rate of the money supply is expected to decline after the third quarter.

In general, in response to the outbreak of the epidemic, the PBOC had put about RMB 4 trillion (1.75 trillion plus 2.24 trillion, around 4 percent of 2019 GDP) into the financial system since late January, and has cut the benchmark interest rate by 30 basis points. The most important concern of the PBOC is the financing of MSMEs seriously affected by the epidemic, including finance availability and cost of financing.

From the perspective of market interest rates, we also compare the changes in treasury bond yields (one-year and ten-year) of China, the United States, and Eurozone over the 12-month period beginning November 2019, as shown in Figure 7.5.

As can be seen from Figure 7.4, after the outbreak of the epidemic, China's one-year treasury bond yield decreased by about 100 basis points, and gradually

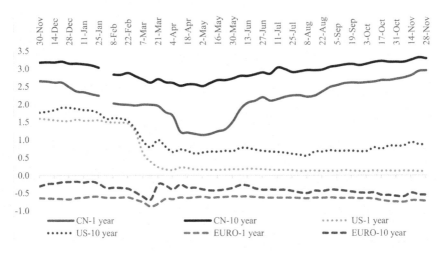

Figure 7.5 Treasury bond yield of US, China, and Eurozone in the last one year. Source: Fed, ECB, PBOC.

rose after the mid-May. By mid-September, it had returned to the same level as the previous year. The ten-year yield declined slightly and has now returned to its original level. The Eurozone bond yield trajectory is similar to that of China. However, the market interest rate in the United States has remained at a low level after March. Compared with before the epidemic, the short-end interest rate has been cut by about 110 basis points, and the long-end interest rate by about 90 basis points.

In conclusion, the monetary policy measures adopted by the PBOC are relatively more moderate, the increase in asset purchases limited, the policy interest rate is rarely reduced, and the current interest rate is still far above zero. The PBOC has repeatedly stressed that the monetary policy adopted after the epidemic would pay more attention to its transmission effect, namely that the impact should directly reach the real economy.

Affected by the COVID-19 epidemic, as part of a package of counter-cyclical policies, monetary policy needs to make efforts to promote the resumption of work and production, and economic growth. On June 18, Yi Gang, governor of the PBOC, said at the Lujiazui forum that the central bank would expand money aggregates through quantitative monetary policy tools to solve the financing difficulties of MSMEs, that monetary policy would also maintain reasonable and sufficient liquidity, that the PBOC is expected to increase loans by RMB 20 trillion (around 20 percent of 2019 GDP) in 2020, and that the growth rate of M2 will be about 12 percent(Yi Gang, 2020). Yi Gang (2020) said that the central bank would also guide the continuous decline of market interest rates through the reform of market-oriented interest rates, and strive to solve the problem of costly financing for MSMEs.

At the Lujiazui forum in June, Guo ShuQing (2020), vice governor of the PBOC, said, "the scale and intensity of fiscal and monetary stimulus measures that have been introduced by developed countries are unprecedented, and while they have played an important role in the initial stage, their marginal utility is gradually diminishing"; "large economies should take the initiative to consider the spillover effect of their own policies and consciously balance their internal and external impacts", and "the Chinese government cherishes its monetary and fiscal policies in a normal state very much, and we will not carry out such policies as unlimited quantitative easing, monetization of the fiscal deficit and negative interest rates".

7.5 China's fiscal policy after the COVID-19 outbreak

At the meeting of the Political Bureau of the CPC Central Committee held on April 17, in order to support China's economic development, the government upgraded measures from the original "ensuring stability on the six fronts" (that is ensuring stability in employment, financial operations, foreign trade, foreign investment, domestic investment, and expectations), to a more specific "ensuring security in the six areas " (that is ensuring job security, basic living needs, operation of market entities, food and energy security, stable industrial and supply chains, and the normal functioning of primary-level governments). At the National People's Congress in late May, Premier Li KeQiang continued to emphasize the "ensuring security in the six areas" in his government work report delivered at the third Session of the 13th National People's Congress on May 22, 2020(Li KeQiang, 2020). Until recently, several economic and financial departments under the central government have stressed the importance of "ensuring security in the six areas" on various occasions.

7.5.1 Policies and measures before the National People's Congress

In the early stage of the COVID-19 outbreak, the fiscal departments continued to increase funds for epidemic control. According to the data released on the website of the Ministry of Finance, as of February 24, 2020, financial sectors at all levels had paid RMB 100.87 billion to control the spread of the epidemic. In late February, the Ministry of Finance issued a series of taxes and fees reduction policies and measures, aimed at alleviating the difficulties of enterprises, promoting the orderly resumption of work and production of enterprises, and supporting the stabilization and expansion of employment. These measures are mainly for those micro-, small-, and medium-sized enterprises.

For example, from March 1 to the end of May, small firms in Hubei province were exempted from value-added tax (VAT), and the tax rate in other regions will be cut from 3 percent to 1 percent; tax payments will be postponed, and fiscal interest subsidies will be increased; the income obtained by small taxpayers in transporting epidemic prevention and control supplies will be exempted from VAT, etc. In addition, the government also reduced or exempted enterprise social insurance premiums, including endowment insurance, unemployment insurance and work-related injury insurance premiums. The government also encouraged state-owned property owners to reduce rent for small and medium-sized firm tenants.

7.5.2 Policies and measures announced at the National People's Congress

Because of the COVID-19 epidemic, the National People's Congress was postponed from early March to late May; however the implementation of fiscal policies must follow certain legal and administrative procedures. As a result, the central government's fiscal assistance and stimulus measures did not begin until early June. These measures included enlarging the budget deficit, increasing the issuance of government bonds and greater fiscal expenditure, and further cuts in taxes and fees etc. as shown in Table 7.3.

In the government work report of Premier Li KeQiang (2020), the formulation of policies in the economic field is as follows. The government

Table 7.3 China's fiscal policies for COVID-19 control

On May 22, in a government work report, fiscal policies measures proposed by Premier Li KeQiang

Policy measures	Content
Enlarge fiscal deficit	Deficit-to-GDP ratio this year is projected at more than 3.6 percent (previous projection 2.8 percent), with a deficit increase of RMB 1 trillion over last year.
Increased government bond issuance	Issue RMB1 trillion of special government bonds for COVID-19 epidemic control; it is planned to issue RMB 3.75 trillion of local government special bonds, an increase of RMB 1.6 trillion over that of 2019.
Further cuts in taxes and fees	Lower the value-added tax rate and enterprise endowment insurance rate; delay the payment of income tax for small & micro enterprises and individual businesses, and extend the policy of phased reduction and exemption of social security contributions.
Increased fiscal transfers	The newly increased fiscal deficit funds and funds from special government bonds for COVID-19 epidemic control, totaling RMB 2 trillion have been all allocated to local governments. The central government will also provide additional funds to ensure job security, basic living needs, and the normal functioning of primary-level governments.
Strengthening fiscal budget balance	In order to hedge revenue falls, the government will reduce non-essential expenditure and ensure expenditure in basic livelihoods and key areas. The government will also strengthen the budget balance and government debt management to enhance fiscal sustainability.

Source: Compiled by the author.

will further cut taxes and fees, reduce enterprises' production and operating costs, expect additional savings of more than RMB2.5 trillion for enterprises throughout this year, increase financial support to keep business operations stable, ensure that MSMEs have significantly better access to loans and that overall financing costs drop markedly.

From June 15 to July 31, a total amount of RMB 1 trillion special treasury bonds for COVID-19 control was issued. The issuance of special bonds of local governments was completed by the end of September. These two types of funds are invested in new infrastructure construction, new urbanization construction, transportation, water conservation, and other major engineering construction fields.

In his government report, Li KeQiang(2020) said that priority would be given to new infrastructure and new urbanization initiatives and major projects, and efforts would be made mainly in the following three areas. Firstly, to step up the construction of new types of infrastructure, and developing next-generation information networks. Secondly, to strengthen the development of new types of urbanization, improving public facilities and services in county seats, and beginning the renovation of 39,000 old urban residential communities. Thirdly, to redouble efforts to develop major transportation and water conservation projects.

Overall, in order to control the epidemic and support the reopening of the economy, China's central government and local governments directly increased fiscal expenditure by RMB 3.6 trillion, accounting for 3.6 percent of 2019 GDP. In addition, the government will cut taxes and fees for enterprises by RMB 2.5 trillion in 2020. The sum of these two measures is about RMB 6 trillion, accounting for around 6 percent of 2019 GDP. According to the data of the State Taxation Administration of China, in the first three quarters of this year, RMB 1,365.9 billion of taxes and fees reduction were added in support of containing the COVID-19 epidemic and for economic and social development.

In contrast, China's direct and indirect financial assistance allocations are the smallest, accounting for only 6 percent of GDP, while the EU and the United States expenditures have reached 10 percent and 15 percent of GDP, respectively.

7.6 Comparison of monetary and fiscal policies between the 2008 global financial crisis and the COVID-19 epidemic in China

7.6.1 Comparison of output trends in the two crises

The COVID-19 epidemic broke out first in China, and as a result of the strict containment measures that directly inhibited production activities and domestic demand, China's GDP shrank by 6.8 percent in the first quarter of 2020. Since the spread of the COVID-19 epidemic in China was basically under control within three months of its outbreak, and with the normalization of economic activity, real GDP growth rebounded by 3.2 percent and 4.9 percent year-on-year respectively in Q2 and Q3. China's economy had recovered to the level of Q4 of 2019 in Q2 of 2020.

In 2008, the global financial crisis first broke out in the United States and then spread among developed countries, and the Chinese economy was affected through declining external demand channels. At that time, China was in a period of rapid economic expansion after China's accession to the WTO, so the impact on the growth rate of China's GDP was very small as shown in Figure 7.6.

7.6.2 Comparison of macroeconomic policy in the two crises

Although the impact of the 2008 GFC on China's economic growth was relatively small, the monetary policy and fiscal policy launched by the government at that time were relatively stronger as shown in Table 7.4.

The year 2008 witnessed the shift of China's macroeconomic policy from tightening to easing. In the first half of 2008, the official expression of China's macroeconomic policy was "prudent fiscal policy and tight monetary policy"(Monetary Policy Analysis Group of the People's Bank of China, 2009). Specifically, in the first half of the year, the PBOC raised the benchmark interest rate five times and raised the deposit RRR eight times to curb the pressure of economic overheating and inflation.

However, after Q3 of 2008, in order to deal with the impact of the global financial crisis, the macroeconomic policy guidance statement of the Chinese government changed to "positive fiscal policy and moderately loose monetary policy". In Q4, the PBOC cut the benchmark interest rate five times, the one-year deposit rate by 189 basis points, and the one-year loan rate by 216 basis points (as shown in Table 7.4 and Figure 7.6). In addition, the PBOC also cut

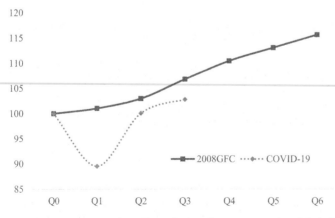

Figure 7.6 Output trend in China during the past two crises. Note: The base periods are the 3rd quarter 2008 and 4th quarter 2019, respectively. Source: World bank, National Bureau of Statistics of China.

Table 7.4 China's monetary and fiscal policy: 2008 GFC and COVID-19 pandemic compared

policy tools		2008 GFC	COVID-19 pandemic
monetary and financial policy	lowered RRR	In 4th quarter of 2008, the PBOC lowered the RRR four times and by 2 percent (from 17.5 percent to 15.5 percent), and thereby released RMB 800 billion (2.5 percent of 2008 GDP) base money.	Since early 2020, the RRR was lowered three times and by 2.5 percent, and the PBOC released RMB 1.75 trillion (1.8 percent of 2019 GDP) base money.
	cuts in interest rates	PBOC cut the 1-year deposit rate 189 bps, from 4.14 percent to 2.25 percent, and the 1-year loan rate 216 bps, from 7.47 percent to 5.31 percent.	The benchmark interest rate was reduced 30 basis points.
	loans of financial institutions	In 2009, RMB 10.5 trillion (around 30 percent of 2009 GDP) of new loans were issued, which is almost twice as much as in 2008, and 2.6 times as much as in 2007.	In the first half of 2020, new loans reached RMB 12.1 trillion (around 12 percent of 2019 GDP), an increase of 25 percent (y/y).
fiscal policy	public investment programs	In November 2008, the State Council issued 10 measures to expand domestic demand, and decided to invest RMB 4 trillion (around 11 percent of 2009 GDP) in the following two years for livelihood projects, infrastructure, ecological environment construction and post disaster reconstruction.	The government will increase investment by around RMB 2.5 trillion (2.5 percent of 2019 GDP) in the field of new types of infrastructure, next-generation information networks and new types of urbanization etc.
	cuts in taxes	In December 2008, the central government proposed "implementing structural tax reduction", reducing the value-added tax rate of most industries, reducing the income tax rate of small and micro enterprises, and exempting the enterprise income tax of primary processing enterprises of agricultural products.	Further cut taxes and fees, as shown in Table 7.3.
		In 2009 and 2010, taxes and fees on real estate transactions were reduced.	
other policy	increase in export tax rebates	From 2008 to 2009, the export tax rebate was increased 7 times, involving more than 10,000 kinds of commodities.	none

Source: PBOC, Ministry of Finance of China, and compiled by the author.

the deposit RRR four times, releasing about RMB 800 billion of long-term base currency (Monetary Policy Analysis Group of the People's Bank of China, 2009). In the years before 2008, in order to offset the rising base money supply due to increasing foreign exchange reserves, the PBOC had to continuously increase the RRR as shown in Figure 7.7.

In Q4 of 2008, the expansionary monetary policy also showed that the PBOC strongly encouraged commercial banks to increase loans. In that quarter, RMB 1.27 trillion of new loans were issued, which was 3.4 times that of Q4 2007 (seasonally unadjusted). In 2009, the lending machines of financial institutions continued to operate at a high speed. Financial institutions issued new loans amounting to RMB 10.5 trillion, almost double that in 2008, accounting for about 30 percent of GDP in 2009 (Monetary Policy Analysis Group of the People's Bank of China, 2010). In the first three quarters of 2010, new loans also reached RMB 6.6 trillion. At the end of 2009, China's broad money M2 reached RMB 60.6 trillion, an increase of 27.7 percent year-on-year, while the real GDP of that year only increased by 9.4 percent.

In October 2010, China officially ended its expansionary economic policy. At this time, the base currency increased by RMB 4.4 trillion compared with that of two years earlier, and the total assets of the PBOC reached RMB 24.87 trillion, an increase of 22.6 percent compared with that of two years earlier (Monetary Policy Analysis Group of the People's Bank of China, 2011).

In contrast, in the first half of 2020, the balance sheet of the PBOC remained stable. The new issuing loans of China's financial institutions were only RMB 12.6 trillion, an increase of 28 percent year-on-year, accounting for 12.7

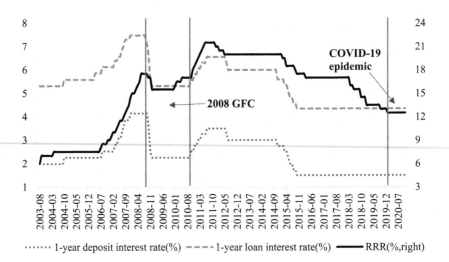

Figure 7.7 China's policy interest rates relating to deposits and loans and the RRR. Note: After October 2015, the interest rates of deposits and loans are no longer used as China's benchmark interest rates, and the PBOC no longer publishes interest rates standards relating to deposits and loans. Source: PBOC.

percent of GDP in 2019. At the end of November 2020, China's broad money M2 had increased by 10.7 percent year-on-year.

After the global financial crisis in 2008, the Chinese government also made great efforts to stimulate economic growth through fiscal policies In November 2008, the State Council issued ten measures to expand domestic demand, and determined to invest RMB 4 trillion (around 11 percent of 2009 GDP) in the following two years for livelihood projects, infrastructure, ecological environment construction, and post-earthquake-disaster reconstruction. On November 12, the central government announced an increase in tax rebates in respect of 3,770 categories of export products. By 2009, it had increased the export tax rebate seven times, involving more than ten thousand kinds of commodities. In December 2008, at the central economic work conference, central government proposed "implementing structural tax reduction", cutting the value-added tax rate of most industries, reducing the income tax rate of MSMEs, and exempting the enterprise income tax liability of primary processing enterprises of agricultural products(Yan Kun, and Yu ShuYi, 2011). In 2009 and 2010, the government also issued several policies to cut taxes and fees related to real estate transactions. It is estimated that the scale of public investment projects and taxes cuts adopted by the Chinese government was about RMB 4.5 trillion, accounting for 13 percent of GDP in 2009.

China's expansionary macroeconomic policy continued until the third quarter of 2010. As early as January 18, 2010, the PBOC began to raise the RRR again. In October 2010, the PBOC raised the benchmark interest rates of deposits and loans by 25 basis points (as shown in Figure 7.6). This marked Chinese government withdrawal from expansionary macroeconomic policy and the implementation of a tightening macroeconomic policy instead.

Affected by the COVID-19 epidemic, in first half of 2020, the fiscal expansion was unprecedented, and the target deficit-to-GDP ratio, new quotas of special government bonds and other important fiscal indicators were significantly increased. However, as the economy recovered better than expected after the second quarter, according to the fiscal expenditure data released by the Ministry of Finance, by November, the growth rate of fiscal expenditure was still 3.1 percentage points lower than in the fiscal budget, and the expenditure was about 4 percentage points slower than that of the same period the previous year. Compared with the proactive fiscal expenditure in the first half of 2020, with the gradual recovery of the economy, the general trend is that future fiscal stimulus will gradually return to normal levels following the special measures dealing with the epidemic.

Why did the Chinese government undertake a more comprehensive response to the global financial crisis in 2008? The reason was that, on the one hand, China's domestic demand was still small and its economic growth depended on external demand, so it was more affected by external shocks. On the other hand, in order to solve problems of domestic employment and income growth, it was necessary for China to maintain a high economic growth rate. However, the improvement of the economic situation in developed countries at that time was uncertain, so China could only maintain economic growth by increasing domestic investment.

In 2019, China's GDP had reached RMB 98.65 trillion, around US$ 14.3 trillion; the economic growth rate has continued to decline in recent years, the interest rate and the RRR have also been continuously cut, and the debt leverage ratio of enterprises and the government is at a high level. All these factors limited the room for the implementation of China's monetary and fiscal policies. Therefore, if the spread of the epidemic is effectively controlled and the economy returns to normal, there is no need for expansionary monetary and fiscal policies.

7.7 The overall assessment and outlook for China's monetary and fiscal policies

China's financial system and economic development are characterized by government control. The macro policies of the PBOC and the Ministry of Finance are the important factors affecting the development of the financial system and the real economy.

A series of monetary and fiscal policies adopted by China during the epidemic have stabilized market expectations, ensured basic production and employment, and increased residents' income. Social life has basically returned to normal, economic growth has been better than expected, and the money supply has remained stable. The stock market index has risen by about 28 percent from its low point at the end of March. On the whole, these policies have been effective.

Generally speaking, the objectives of the monetary policy of the PBOC have "3+1" component parts, including economic growth (and promoting full employment with economic growth), price stability, balance of payments maintenance, and reasonable fluctuation of the RMB exchange rate. The first three objectives are mainly related to the real economy, and the last one is mainly related to financial market stability, including the reform and development of the financial system, as well as macro-prudential regulation and the prevention of financial risks.

On November 26, the PBOC released the *China monetary policy report 2020 Q3*(Monetary Policy Analysis Group of the People's Bank of China, 2020c). According to the report, the economic situation is better than expected and can achieve positive growth rate in 2020. On the whole, monetary policy is returning from its loose status when coping with the COVID-19 epidemic to a stable neutral orientation in the post-epidemic era.

At the central economic work conference held by the Political Bureau of the CPC Central Committee in mid-December, it was proposed that sound monetary policy should be flexible, targeted, reasonable and moderate for the following year, so that the growth rate of money supply and aggregate financing to the real economy should basically match the nominal economic growth rate, and keep the macro debt leverage ratio basically stable.

In early August, China's Ministry of Finance released the *Report on the implementation of China's fiscal policies in the first half of 2020* (Research Group of Ministry of Finance of the People s Republic of China, 2020), which disclosed that in the first half of 2020, enterprises and residents taxes and fees had actually been reduced by more than RMB 1.5 trillion. According to the report, the implementation of fiscal policies in the future should be more proactive and effective, should guarantee construction funds for major projects, and pay attention to quality and efficiency. Specifically, the use of financial funds includes funds for stabilizing and ensuring employment, continuously improving people's livelihoods, continuing to implement tax reduction and fee reduction policies, ensuring the operation of market entities, ensuring food and energy security, and ensuring the normal functioning of primary-level governments.

At the central economic work conference, it was proposed that China continue to implement proactive fiscal policies in 2021 and maintain the necessary support for economic recovery, but proactive fiscal policies should be improved in terms of quality, efficiency, and sustainability. With the epidemic under control, we expect that China's fiscal policy will return to normal in 2021, that the fiscal deficit rate will remain stable or even decline slightly, and that further taxes and fees reductions for enterprises and residents will continue to be implemented.

On December 7, 2020, the General Administration of Customs of China released import and export trade data. In US dollar terms, China's exports in November exceeded expectations, with a growth rate of 21.1 percent year-on-year, and a trade surplus of US $75.43 billion. In the first 11 months of 2020, exports increased by 2.5 percent year-on-year, and the trade surplus reached US $459.92 billion, an increase of 23.0 percent year-on-year. The main reason is that after the arrival of winter, the number of new COVID-19 cases in foreign countries accelerated again, and the demand for medical supplies and online office supplies has increased significantly, while China's production and supply system is the first to recover in the world, and its ability to meet the demand is strong. From this point of view, China has adopted a series of effective fiscal and monetary policies.

As mentioned in section 3, monetary policy during COVID-19 epidemic mainly focuses on dealing with short-term and medium-term adverse impacts. In the long run, fiscal policy, such as a series of taxes and fees reduction, may be more conducive to China's long-term steady economic growth.

References

Guo ShuQing, Regional Financial Reform and Opening-up Will Be First Implemented in Shanghai Free Trade Zone: Speech at the Opening Ceremony of the 12th Lujiazui Forum[J]. *Chinese Industry & Economy*, 2020(14):21–24.

International Monetary Fund, *World Economic Outlook: A Long and Difficult Ascent*. Washington, DC, October 2020.

Li KeQiang, *Government Work Report-Delivered at the third Session of the 13th National People's Congress on May 22, 2020[M]*. Beijing: People's Publishing House, May 2020.

Monetary Policy Analysis Group of the People's Bank of China, *China Monetary Policy Report Q4 2008[R]*. Beijing: The People's Bank of China, 2009:1–57.

Monetary Policy Analysis Group of the People's Bank of China, *China Monetary Policy Report Q4 2009[R]*. Beijing: The People's Bank of China, 2010:1–54.

Monetary Policy Analysis Group of the People's Bank of China, *China Monetary Policy Report Q4 2010[R]*. Beijing: The People's Bank of China, 2011:1–54.

Monetary Policy Analysis Group of the People's Bank of China, *China Monetary Policy Report Q1 2020a[R]*. Beijing: The People's Bank of China, 2020:1–61.

Monetary Policy Analysis Group of the People's Bank of China, *China Monetary Policy Report Q2 2020b[R]*. Beijing: The People's Bank of China, 2020:1–59.

Monetary Policy Analysis Group of the People's Bank of China, *China Monetary Policy Report Q3 2020c[R]*. Beijing: The People's Bank of China, 2020:1–73.

Research Group of Ministry of Finance of the People's Republic of China, *Report on the China's Fiscal Policy implementation in the First Half of 2020 [R]*. Beijing: Ministry of Finance of the People's Republic of China, August 6, 2020:1–12.

Yan Kun, and Yu ShuYi. Structural Tax Reduction in China under the Fight against the Global Financial Crisis [J]. *Taxation Research*, 2011(01):13–20.

Yi Gang, China's Monetary Liquidity in the Banking System Will be Adequate at a Reasonable Level: Speech at the Opening Ceremony of the 12th Lujiazui Forum[J]. *Chinese Industry & Economy*, 2020(13):30–32.

8 The case of Japan

Eiji Ogawa[1]

8.1 Introduction: COVID-19 in Japan and its economic impacts

The COVID-19 pandemic has spread throughout the world since February 2020 after it started in Wuhan, China at the end of 2019. It has affected people and economies worldwide. The number of people suffering from the virus has also been increasing in Japan since the first positive diagnosis on January 16, 2020. It has reached 233 thousand positive cases as of the end of 2020.

Two surges in COVID-19 had occurred in Japan by October 2020. In November Japan faced a third surge larger than the previous two (Figure 8.1). There were about 1,600 positive cases per day at peak-Covid in August. The number of daily positive cases marked an all-time high record high at 4,322 on December 31, 2020.

The pandemic has had a tremendous impact on both domestic economies and international markets. The global economy is facing its worst crisis since World War II. The global economy is facing a more severe economic slump than during the global financial crisis (GFC). Similarly, the Japanese economy is extremely depressed by the impacts of COVID-19 (IMF 2020).

This chapter describes Japan's fiscal and monetary policy responses to COVID-19 in comparison to its response to the GFC. Section 2 overviews the public health policy implemented by the Japanese government. Section 3 explains the economic impact of COVID-19 on the Japanese economy in comparison with the effects of the 2008 GFC. Section 4 overviews the fiscal policy response of the Japanese government in respect of COVID-19 from the beginning of the pandemic in February 2020 to December 2020. Section 5 provides an overview of how the Bank of Japan has conducted monetary policy during the same period. In sections 4 and 5, we review how the Japanese government and the Bank of Japan conducted their fiscal and monetary policies in respect of the GFC in comparison with their response to COVID-19. Section 6 provides an

1 Professor, Faculty of Economics, Tokyo Keizai University. e-mail: eogawa@tku.ac.jp.

DOI: 10.4324/9781003153603-8

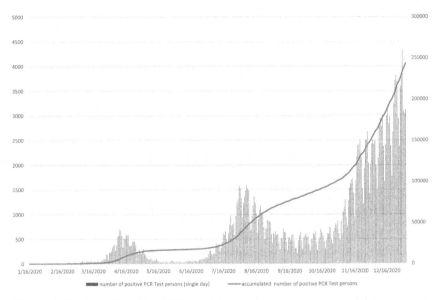

Figure 8.1 Number of positive PCR tests (per day) and total number of positive tests (Data: Ministry of Health, Labor and Welfare).

overview assessment of the policy responses by the Japanese government and the Bank of Japan to COVID-19.

8.2 Public health policy

The Japanese government recognized the importance of stopping the spread of COVID-19 from the perspective of the economy. In order to protect people's lives and health, first of all, it invested resources particularly in strengthening measures to prevent the spread of the disease. With regard to masks, disinfectant solutions etc., where demand greatly exceeded the norm due to the effects COVID-19, it secured sufficient supply volumes and ensured their distribution to medical institutions and other necessary facilities.

The Japanese government has declared only one State of Emergency in respect of COVID-19 (Cabinet Secretariat, 2020) so far (before November 30, 2020), which did not include any lockdown. When the infection rates of COVID-19 spread in Japan in the first surge, the Japanese government declared a State of Emergency under Article 32, paragraph 1 of the Act on Special Measures for Pandemic Influenza and New Infectious Diseases Preparedness and Response. The duration of the emergency was 29 days from April 7 to May 6, 2020. The locations covered by the emergency measures were Saitama, Chiba, Tokyo, Kanagawa, Osaka, Hyogo, and Fukuoka Prefectures. However, because infections of COVID-19 spread all over Japan, the targeted areas were expanded to all 47 prefectures of Japan on April 16. The duration of this expanded emergency was from April 16 to May 6.

Thereafter, the number of newly reported cases showed a downward trend. However, there were still areas where the delivery of medical care by the health system continued to be stretched, so measures to reduce new infections were enforced. On May 4, 2020, the period during which emergency measures were enforced was extended until May 31, 2020, continuing to target all 47 prefectures. Subsequently, as the infection rates were found to have slowed down, a comprehensive decision was made to reduce the targeted areas where emergency measures were enforced to seven prefectures (Hokkaido, Saitama, Chiba, Tokyo, Kanagawa, Kyoto, Osaka, and Hyogo) on May 14, 2020 and then to five prefectures (Hokkaido, Saitama, Chiba, Tokyo, and Kanagawa) on May 21, 2020. Eventually, on May 25, 2020, the Japanese government declared the lifting of the State of Emergency as it deemed that the emergency measures were no longer necessary.

The Japanese government tried to ensure an effective testing system was in place as a response to the spread of the disease. In addition, it requested public cooperation to prevent the spread of the disease by avoiding closed spaces, crowded spaces, and close contacts (the three Cs). It fundamentally strengthened counter-cluster measures to break the chain of the infection.

At the same time, it promptly built medical treatment structures focused on medical care for patients with severe symptoms in preparation for a further sudden increase in the number of infected people. An "Emergency Comprehensive Support Grant for COVID-19" was set up for these measures to prevent the spread of the disease and the development of medical treatment structures. Thus, each prefecture could flexibly and dynamically implement measures required according to the epidemiological situations in their regions.

The Japanese government has accelerated the research and development of therapeutic medicines and vaccines as the highest priority. It has tried increasing the capacity to accept returnees to Japan, strengthening information dissemination, and promoting international cooperation with other infected countries in order to minimize the risk of the spread of the disease.

The Japanese government included allocations required for these measures in the supplementary budget for FY2020. Included in the supplementary budget, the Japanese government has made provisions for measures to prevent the spread of the infection, build medical treatment structures, and develop pharmaceuticals.

First, the government has supported investments by firms that produce masks, disinfectants etc. in their production facilities to increase supply. It has ensured that their supply exceeds normal annual demand. It has distributed masks to long-term care and other facilities. Moreover, it has distributed two cloth masks per household to more than 50 million households nationwide. Second, the government is supporting the introduction of test equipment for PCR tests to promote quick testing at testing institutions and

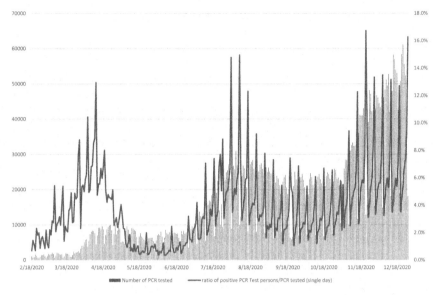

Figure 8.2 Number of PCR tests and ratio of positive PCR tests/total PCR tests. Data: Ministry of Health, Labor and Welfare.

medical institutions and to enhance testing capabilities as shown in Figure 8.2. It promotes the early identification of group infections, so-called clusters, and strives for the early detection of confirmed cases and the prevention of the aggravation of the symptoms under the cooperation of the national and local governments. Third, in preparation for a further surge in the number of infections, the government quickly built medical treatment structures focusing on the medical treatment for patients with severe symptoms. It significantly strengthened medical treatment structures from the perspective of both human resources and facilities. Fourth, the government accelerated the development and dissemination of effective pharmaceuticals and vaccines in order to fundamentally solve the spread of COVID-19. At the same time, it ensured the early use of pharmaceuticals and vaccines whose safety and effectiveness were confirmed.

Public health policy has contributed to suppressing an explosive increase in the number of infected persons in 2020. Figure 8.3 shows the changing numbers of total deaths after the first reported death from COVID-19. The death toll drastically increased in the first and second surges while it has not accelerated in the current third surge. On one hand, the number of deaths in terms of the accumulated number of positive PCR tests increased in the first surge. Thereafter, the number of deaths to positive tests ratio drastically decreased in June and July as the daily number of positive PCR tests increased. The death ratio has been gradually decreasing since the second surge.

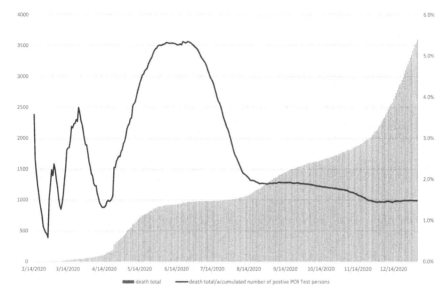

Figure 8.3 Total deaths and ratio of total deaths/cumulated number of positive PCR tests. Data: Ministry of Health, Labor and Welfare.

8.3 Economic impact of COVID-19: comparison with the 2008 global financial crisis

The rate of change in real GDP in Japan (annualized rate of changes from previous quarters) recorded a decrease of 28.8 percent in the second quarter of 2020 as shown in Figure 8.4. It recorded a positive 21.4 percent growth rate of GDP in the third quarter of 2020. However, real GDP (2011 base) has made only a partial recovery. Figure 8.4 shows that the real GDP of Japan dropped from 527 trillion yen in the first quarter of 2020 to 484 trillion yen in the second quarter of 2020. It increased to 508 trillion yen in the third quarter of 2020. The third quarter recovery amounted to roughly half of the decrease (43 trillion yen) in the second quarter.

Figure 8.5 shows movements in levels and rates of change from the same month of the previous year of the seasonally adjusted index of industrial production. In May 2020, the index of industrial production and the rate of change of industrial production was at 78.7 (compared with 100 in 2015) and down 12.2 percent respectively. However, the industrial production index increased to 91.5 in September 2020 which means a 50 percent recovery compared with the decrease from 99.8 in January 2020 to 78.7 in May 2020.

The impact has been more severe on the service industries which rely on face-to-face interactions, compared with industrial production in Japan as shown in Figure 8.6. In May 2020, sales in the services industries decreased to 23.4 trillion yen. It recorded a decrease of 22.9 percent compared with

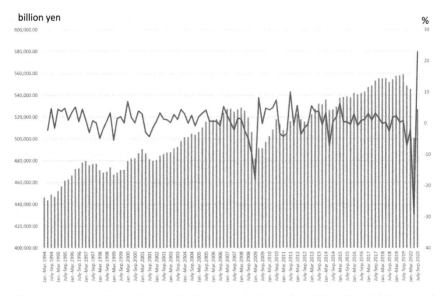

Figure 8.4 Level and growth rate of real gross domestic product. Data: Statistics Bureau of Japan.

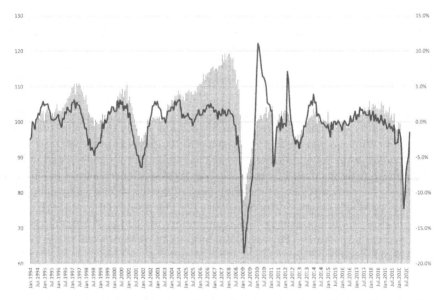

Figure 8.5 Level and rate of change of seasonally adjusted indices of industrial production (2015 base). Data: Statistics Bureau of Japan.

6 José Alonso Ortiz, Adam Smith's translator

A new interpretation

Jesús Astigarraga

Alonso's Valladolid

When José Alonso Ortiz, author of the first practically complete Spanish translation of *The Wealth of Nations* (WN), arrived in the Castilian city of Valladolid in 1781, he was a young lawyer aged twenty-five with few professional achievements.[1] Originally from Granada, where he had been born in 1755, he was leaving behind his formative years at the university in his hometown, having been awarded degrees in theology in 1774 and in civil and canon law four years later. These had enabled him to become an articled clerk and to work intermittently as a teacher of civil law at the university. Once settled in Valladolid, he completed his legal training and qualified as a lawyer in 1782. In the years that followed Alonso practised law and was briefly an advisor to the Valladolid *Corregimiento* and *Intendencia*—Chancery and Municipality. He began working as a translator in 1786, and one of his works was a translation of the WN, which was published in 1794 and reissued in 1805–1806 by Casa Santander, one of the most prestigious publishers in the city.

Although Alonso's main steps through life are well known, little research has been done on his time in Valladolid. However, it is essential to reconstruct this period if his versions of the WN are to properly understood, as it was during the fifteen or so years that Alonso lived there before settling in Madrid in 1795 that he became a renowned translator. Valladolid was then a town of about 20,000 inhabitants.[2] It was a major economic hub in the interior of Castile, with activity typical of a region that focused on grains, vines and livestock, while also being an important regional centre for services (Almuiña 1974, 18; Enciso 1980, 65). Valladolid was also the seat of the bishop, the Inquisition and the Chancery, as well as housing one of the three major universities in Spain together with Salamanca and Alcalá de Henares; the Colegio of Santa Cruz (1484–1793), one of the seven main colleges in the Spanish university structure, was attached to it. Valladolid had once been home to the Court of Castile, and these institutions were now the mainstay of the city's cultural activity. Alonso was the witness in the emergence of a network of new institutions that channelled the Enlightenment culture's arrival in the city and endowed it with a thriving cultural activity for a provincial capital (Almuiña 1974, 33–54). This

DOI: 10.4324/9781003152804-7

network was forged around the Academia geográfico-histórica (1764)—the Academy of Geography and History—which aimed to educate local nobility in these two disciplines and in physics and geometry; the Real Academia de Matemáticas y Nobles Artes (1779)—the Royal Academy of Mathematics and Noble Arts—which specialised in mathematics, drawing and architecture; the Real Academia de San Carlos de Jurisprudencia Nacional (1784)—the Royal Academy of San Carlos of National Jurisprudence—oriented to spreading legal culture and linked to the powerful Chancery; and, finally, the Real Sociedad Económica de Valladolid (1783)—the Valladolid Economic Society—where the Real Academia de Medicina y Cirugía (1785)—the Royal Academy of Medicine and Surgery—was created.

These institutions were born by local initiative, although they generally followed Court directives. Such was the case of the Sociedad Económica, the only body that explored economic issues. Although little is known about the society's history due to the scarcity of sources (Demerson 1969; Enciso 1975; 2010, 319–48), it is another example of the importance of these patriotic institutions in local elites' involvement in Enlightenment ideas and social practices. It was founded in September 1783 by distinguished members of the Valladolid municipal authorities and nobility and was approved by the Council of Castile within a year because the statutes drawn up in Valladolid followed the pattern established by the Madrid Society, which it resembled in terms of internal organisation and activities. The Sociedad Económica was not particularly active in spreading economic ideas, but it did create a drive for socioeconomic reform in the city, using subsidies and prizes to promote activities for agricultural and industrial development, modernising the charity network and encouraging educational efforts through the creation of "patriotic schools" for teaching literacy and crafts. Like the Matritense, it set up a Ladies' Board and undertook advisory work for the Council of Castile with Floridablanca's guidance. Despite experiencing the usual problems facing such institutions, including a hostile environment (Enciso 1975, 155–78), it had eight dozen members drawn from four social groups: the nobility, the clergy, legal experts linked to the Chancery and university teachers (Demerson 1969, 34–38).

At the heart of this society and the other institutions named were the movers and shakers in Valladolid's Enlightenment culture, such as jurist and historian Floranes; Hernández de Larrea, bishop of Valladolid, who had previously been extremely active in Zaragoza as founder of the Aragon Society and its Chair of Civil Economy (1784); Santiváñez, who settled in the city in 1787 after teaching at the University of Valencia and the Seminary of Vergara, and various writers and magistrates such as Silvela and Del Plano. Valladolid was also the temporary residence of magistrate Mon y Velarde, during his time at the Chancery (1786–1781), and poet Meléndez Valdés (1791–1798). Some of them reinforced the reformist tendencies of these institutions and they also created other informal cultural activities and bodies, such as the meetings on Spanish law set up by Floranes, the gatherings organised by Meléndez Valdés, Santiváñez's teaching academy and the Casa Santander publishing house, a genuine *machine de guerre* in

Notes

1　This is a brief summary of the biographical information to be found in the following works: Schwartz (1990; 2000), Perdices and Reeder (2003), Fuentes and Perdices (1996) and Menudo (2013).

2　Described by one commentator as "the only serious one we have in Spanish of Carthon and Lothmon" (Alonso 1920, 15).

3　There are various illustrations of this dynamism in Garriga et al. (2019) and Pinilla and Lépinette (2016).

4　Since only Alonso's first translation (1794) is analysed here, citations refer to the first edition published in 1794, specifying the volume (I, II, III and IV) followed by the page numbers in the original.

5　"se hallarán a veces en la traducción algunos términos que mirados por la escrupulosidad del diccionario podrían parecer algo bárbaros; pero que atendida la materia se deberán tener por facultativos y propios: reflexionando sobre todo que si los términos logran explicar bien los conceptos solo por esto cumplen con el oficio de voces significativas" (Smith 1794, I, "El traductor").

6　The expressions from Alonso's translation to be analysed are in italics.

7　Although the aim here is not to compare the two editions of Alonso's translation (the first in 1794 and the second in 1805–1806, "much corrected and improved" as the title page indicates), it is interesting to note that the system notes has been modified from one edition to the other. The second edition contains fewer notes and seems to retain only those that are deemed in this section to be contextualising and ideological, while the purely technical ones are omitted.

8　Whole numbers have been obtained by rounding down from 0.1–0.5 and up from 0.6–0.9.

9　The change in the system of notes between the first edition of the *Riqueza* (1794) and the second edition in 1805–1806 is exemplified by the fact that chapter 7 contains fewer notes: in the second edition there are only nine.

10　"(★) La diferencia del aligador y el cocodrilo, animales que suelen llamarse indiferentemente caimanes, puede verse en Mr. la Harpe, en su *Compendio de los viajes*, tratando de México."

11　The following is an example of this procedure: "When, on his return from his first voyage, Columbus entered this court as if in triumph (+)", footnote: "(+) At that time the king and queen were in Barcelona" (Smith 1794, III, 124).

12　"(★) Esta es en el día con poca diferencia la política de España."

13　"(★) El autor escribía todo esto por los años de 1775, en que principiaron los grandes debates del Parlamento inglés con las Asambleas de sus Colonias: no se trataba en la Gran-Bretaña de otra cosa que de esta famosa contestación; cada uno proponía los medios que creía más oportunos para la consolidación de la paz: y Adam Smith fue uno de los que reprobaban la conducta que observaba el gobierno con aquellos establecimientos: en efecto por las consecuencias que se siguieron de las medidas que tomó la Gran-Bretaña, se ve patentemente el acierto con que discurría nuestro autor, y su profunda penetración política. De aquella época pues deben entenderse todos los párrafos que hablan de la materia en este capítulo."

14　"(+) Es muy verosímil, que si la Gran-Bretaña hubiera abrazado los medios de reunión que aquí propone el autor, al principio de la revolución de sus colonias, ni se hubiera derramado tanta sangre, ni acaso se hubiera verificado su total independencia."

15 "me pareció muy conducente añadir en algunas advertencias marginales lo que en aquellos casos encontré de particular en España, para que el lector pudiese con más oportunidad aplicar sus reglas generales a las circunstancias del país en que vive: o bien sirviesen de noticias curiosas que ilustrasen algún tanto la materia. No he pretendido con ellas entrar en una formal discusión de lo acertado, o errado de las máximas del autor."

16 "bien que suprimiendo algunas particularidades, pero muy pocas, o por absolutamente impertinentes a nuestra nación, o por ser poco conformes a la santa religión que profesamos, protestando con ingenuidad que quitadas, en nada se adultera el fondo de la obra, y no expurgadas nada añaden a su perfección y complemento, como puede con facilidad desengañarse cualquiera que consulte con imparcialidad el original."

17 "Las continuadas guerras, y la serie de los sucesos de los siglos quince y diez y seis no permitieron […] como confiesan tanto sus naturales, como los extranjeros, […] por derechos de toneladas, San Telmo &c. extinguidos ya en el día."

18 "y otras disposiciones a que obligaron las fatales circunstancias de aquellos tiempos tan contrarias a los intereses de todos sus naturales, como ruinosas para el comercio y para la industria."

19 One could also try to estimate this calculation as a percentage, by saying that 19% is altered, taking each intervention as an abstract reference and assuming that each deliberate intervention changes the meaning of one page. However, this means of calculating seems difficult to justify because the value 1 intervention = 1 modified page can not immediately be assumed. In many cases the translator's intervention only affects one sentence, and in others, a mere adjective.

the Enlightenment cause. There must have been an intensely enlightened atmosphere in Valladolid in the 1780s when Foronda chose the Academia geográfico-histórica as the setting to read his "*Disertación sobre la libertad de escribir,*" the starting point of the struggle for freedom of expression in Enlightenment Spain, and Miguel de Lardizábal read his distinguished "*Apología de agotes de Navarra y chuetas de Mallorca.*" In short, this was the milieu in which Alonso must have matured as a translator, although there is only indirect evidence to corroborate this assumption.

Beristain and the *Diario Pinciano*

The first piece of evidence concerns Beristain, the true architect of Valladolid's cultural effervescence in the 1780s.[3] Born in Mexico, he obtained a degree in philosophy and travelled to Valencia at a very young age, where he studied theology and Holy Scriptures at the university and worked as a substitute lecturer. He arrived in Valladolid in October 1782, having acquired extraordinary credentials: during his period in Valencia he had been given "lessons in literature and good taste" by Mayans (Millares 1972, 4–5), had republished Montegón's *Odas de Filopatro* (1782) and joined the Sociedad Bascongada. It is hardly surprising that in March 1783 he was professor of theology at the University of Valladolid, and that during his six-year stay in the city he became the epicentre of its cultural activity. A member of the Academia Geográfico-Histórica and the Academia de Matemáticas, this scholar and bibliographer was also the founder and Censor of the Economic Society and created its Academia de Medicina. His leading role was underpinned by the network of contacts he wove during his frequent visits to court seats, especially with Floridablanca in whose service he worked cataloguing the manuscripts in the library at El Escorial (Almuiña 1978, 25–30).

The clearest proof of Beristain's key role in the Valladolid of the Enlightenment was his *Diario Pinciano* (DP; Alonso 1933; Guinard 1973, 357–64; Almuiña 1978). The city's first newspaper, once Floridablanca's permission to publish was obtained at the end of 1786, it appeared every week for a year and a half, was circulated by subscription and was open to outside contributors.[4] Its aim was to put the fledgling provincial press, of which the DP was a true emblem,[5] at the service of the official policy against the anti-Spanish currents of the European Enlightenment. Indeed, according to Beristain, "newspapers" should also bloom in the provinces and stimulate the creation of "opinion" so that Europe would have a true idea of "our Enlightenment."[6] The DP plan pointed the finger at Masson de Morvilliers and several paragraphs from his controversial article *Espagne* were copied for the *Encyclopédie Méthodique.*[7] The five sections—"historical, literary, legal, political and economic"—were designed to outline the history of Valladolid and its municipal politics, on the one hand, and the activity of different local institutions including the university and the Sociedad Económica, on the other. The fact that the newspaper appeared weekly and was densely packed with news suggests that Beristain had outside contributors, at least from time to time, among which Alonso has been cited (Almuiña 1974, 85; Enciso 1980, 121ff.). The DP carried accounts of academic discussions on luxury and entailed estates; it repeatedly criticised university teaching methods; it rang with echoes of Mirabeau, Rousseau, Marmotel, Vattel, Heinetius and other Enlightenment writers, and reported Santiváñez's founding of an academy to revitalise university teaching,[8] as well as lectures by Floranes, and others given by Antonio de Ulloa and Carlos Le Maur, who were in the city temporarily. The DP also carried reviews of locally published works, among which the two longest were those devoted to the Santiváñez's translations of Marmotel and Alonso's of Macpherson. In short, the paper was a kind of unofficial mouthpiece for the enlightened sectors at the head of cultural activity in Valladolid.

Not unsurprisingly, the DP was a controversial newspaper, which came of age in a climate of "aggressive pettiness" that was expressed in the form of pamphlets, anonymous letters and public mockery originating with the city council and the university (Almuiña 1978, 63–68). More serious was the fact that in 1786 Beristain was punished by the Inquisition and forced to reapply for his professorship, and that two years later several proposals in the DP were censored (Almuiña 1978, 57–61; Prado 1996, 216). Far from hiding this persecution from his readers, Beristain enlisted the help of people like Santiváñez to use the DP to attack the "buzzing drones" who branded him "impertinent" and "unfit to be a clergyman,"[9] and who he exposed for hiding behind anonymity, claiming the "freedom to print anything" that respected religion and decency.[10] However, the intense hostility towards the DP was one of the reasons for its premature closure in May 1787, which was also linked to financial trouble difficulties and its editor's problems with the Inquisition; having obtained a canonry in Vitoria in 1788, he put an end to his Valladolid sojourn.

Casa Santander

The second piece of evidence confirming Alonso's involvement in Valladolid's enlightened circles is his relationship with Casa Santander, which published his translations between 1786 and 1794. This was one of the city's most famous family bookshops and printing houses in the eighteenth century.[11] It owed its success to its founder, Tomás Santander, who worked as a bookseller, book dealer and paper manufacturer until his death in 1782. His widow and two sons—Raimundo and Mariano—with whom Alonso must have established a close relationship, kept the business open under various names until it closed in 1837. Thanks to Tomás's immense shrewdness, Casa Santander became an integral part of Valladolid cultural life. In 1777 he bought the printing press and much of the library of the suppressed Society of Jesus. At that time, Tomás shared his work in his printing house with various posts at the university— bursar and treasurer—for which he was also the printer. His company also worked for the city council, the hospice and the economic society, and was the DP's first publisher, also offering its premises as a meeting place for its readers.

Casa Santander was not only a printing house, but was also a prominent book dealer. Its market covered peninsular Spain and the colonies and included newspapers and banned books with dangerous regularity. The owners were in constant contact with France and supplied these publications to elites in an area that extended far beyond the city of Valladolid: according to Floranes, Casa Santander bookshop was one of the "best-served in Castile," while according to an anonymous contemporary it was responsible for "a good part of the Enlightenment that we enjoy today in Castile" (Palomares 1974, 51). Casa Santander also enjoyed close relations with other bookshops that were also known for selling banned books in Cádiz, Madrid, Valencia and Salamanca. It is therefore not surprising that his centrally-located establishment was a hub in the social network of Enlightenment life in Valladolid.

The Santander family's boldness is well illustrated by its three generations' permanent conflicts with the Inquisition. In a setting in which circulating banned books was commonplace, their persecution was one of the "most important of all those carried out by the Valladolid court during the eighteenth century" (Prado 1996, 202). Tomás was tried in 1777 but the chief victims were his two sons, against whom twenty-four cases were brought between 1792 and 1799, mainly related to the distribution of banned publications: in fact, according to witnesses at the time, "more than three parts" of the works in their bookshop had been banned (Prado 1996, 216–17).[12] They were also accused of slandering the Inquisition and of desiring its abolition. The inquisitors' statements singled out their shop as the epicentre of the forbidden books trade and of the "most revolutionary spirits" (Larriba 2013, 149). They also highlighted the two booksellers' insolence when it came to obeying the Inquisition: they served harsh sentences until 1799, which left their bookshop in a delicate financial situation.

During Alonso's years in Valladolid Casa Santander established itself as a thriving printing house. It was one of the main private printers in the country and the most successful in Valladolid (Cruz 2014, 320–21). Like all printers (Escolar 1993, 392–629), its output focused on religious themes in a range of formats and satisfied local demand,[13] which mainly centred on such subject matter (Matos 2012, 294–95); however, they are also an example of how the publishing world was gradually opening up to other topics. In 1797, the Casa Santander published Meléndez Valdés's complete poems, following these with Mably's translation in the nineteenth century. It was around this time that Valladolid libraries began to stock books that were committed to the Bourbon reform (Matos 2012, 746–50) and also to the changes that these advocated at university level. As was generally the case, these reforms reaped only meagre rewards in Valladolid.[14] The main effect of the 1771 decree had been to increase enrolment: in 1779 Valladolid was the second university in Spain in terms of student numbers, after Salamanca (Torremocha 1991, 57–61). This growth was particularly significant in the Faculty of Law, the university's largest most prestigious; together with Salamanca, it was the training ground for the Bourbon bureaucracy (Torremocha 1986, 49–50). With its services for printing handbooks and university textbooks, Casa Santander aimed to respond to this growing university clientele, which was more open to new Enlightenment publications than the rigid academic structure allowed.

It is against this backdrop that Casa Santander's gradual opening up to economic culture prior to publishing the translation of the WN in 1794 needs to be viewed. In addition to several merchants' handbooks, it published two texts: the first was Ruiz de Zelada's *Estado de la bolsa de Valladolid* (1777), a short-run production funded by the city council and covering municipal policy and supplies, while the second, *Memoria político-económica sobre el pan cocido* (1789), was more important and requires closer attention. Published anonymously in May 1789, it advocated improvements in grain milling and bread-making, a particularly pressing issue when it was written, at the height of the 1789–1790 agricultural crisis (Anonymous 1789). The delicate issue of the grain trade was addressed from the perspective of defending the liberalising line taken by the 1764 *Pragmática*, a veritable "masterful *coup d'état*" against the obstacles then hindering agricultural progress. The *Memoria*, however, contained a number of Physiocratic overtones and may have been inspired by Condillac's *Le commerce et le gouvernement* (1776), which had been translated into Spanish in 1781. The *Memoria* stressed the beneficial effects of private enterprise, which had restored farmers' "natural freedom." The freedom to store was the best antidote to monopolies and their excess profits. The text also evoked the advantages of "large-scale cultivation" and "well-off" landowners, who were spurred on by their "own interests" and ability to raise capital. In the background stood the example of successful British reforms, which Spain had accepted via the official free grain trade scheme. However, two caveats remained. The first was the land tax, which offered British landowners a system of guarantees and incentives that the Spanish tax structure lacked (Anonymous 1789, 32). The second was the price of grain. The author advocated setting an "average price" to reconcile "the just returns due to farmers with the reward and interest of merchants" (Anonymous 1789, 44). This meant going against "popular opinion," which was fuelled by the agricultural crisis, and defending a "just and moderate" increase in the price of bread (Anonymous 1789, 85–87). While wages rose in geometric proportion, prices rose in arithmetical proportion, and the proposed solution would thus benefit both sides of the market: the surplus in the hands of producers and consumers would increase at the same time, once the price had been paid. Moreover, this unusual *bon prix* would attract capital and new manufacturers, so "the largest population will always be found where bread is expensive." The *Memoria* thus laid bare Casa Santander's desire to intervene in support of Bourbon reformism, and there is no doubt that the writer was close to Beristain's DP. The *Memoria* censured Masson for his criticism of "proud" Spaniards, and dismissed his calculations of the population growth that would potentially be driven by improving Spanish agriculture, as there was no "less suspect witness" to the possibility of this improvement (Anonymous 1789, 20–30). In short, the "Valladolid son," anonymous author of the *Memoria*, came from the Beristain and Casa Santander circle in which Alonso moved.

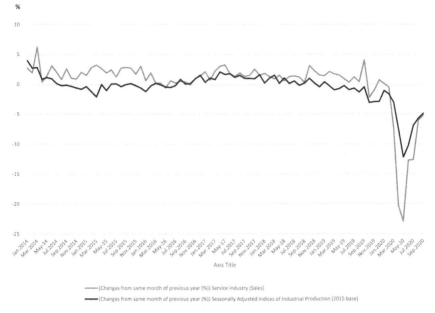

Figure 8.6 Rate of changes in sales in services sectors and the index of industrial production in Japan (changes from the same month of previous year (%)). Data: Statistics Bureau of Japan.

the same month of the previous year (30.5 trillion yen). It made a 50 percent recovery to 27.6 trillion yen in June 2020 but has remained at the lower level.

The GFC occurred, with the Lehman Brothers bankruptcy (Lehman shock) as a trigger, in September 2008. The GFC worsened the global economy in terms of international trade as well as international finance. Every country in the world faced depression although the degree varied from country to country. Among them, the United States, which was at the epicenter of the crisis, experienced a severe economic slump. At the same time, some European countries faced similar financial crises related to the subprime mortgage problem as the United States. On the other hand, the Japanese economy was affected by the depressed global economy in terms of international trade and finance, although it experienced a not so severe financial and banking crisis compared with those in the United States and some European countries.

Figure 8.7 shows the reduced exports as well as imports arising from the big contraction of international trade in the global economy after the GFC. Exports by Japan reduced from 7.1 trillion yen in September 2008 to 3.3 trillion yen in January, a decrease of 54 percent. In contrast, exports reduced from 6.3 trillion yen in February 2020 to 4.2 trillion yen in May 2020, a decrease of 34 percent. The reduction in exports arising from the GFC was much larger than that during the COVID-19 crisis.

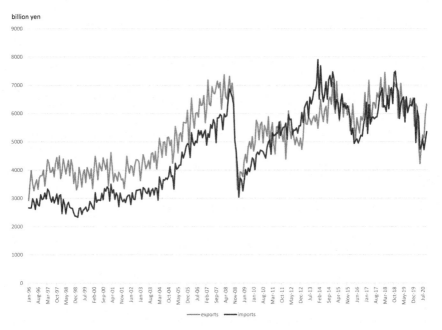

billion yen

Figure 8.7 Exports and Imports of Japan. Data: Bank of Japan.

As shown in Figure 8.4, the rate of change in real GDP (annualized rate of change from previous quarters) recorded a decrease of 17.8 percent in the first quarter of 2009. The reduction (minus 28.8 percent) of real GDP in the second quarter of 2020 was larger than that during the GFC. The economy recorded an increased 8.6 percent growth rate of GDP in the second quarter of 2009. When we look at movements in real GDP level in Figure 8.4, we find that the real GDP of Japan dropped from 507 trillion yen in the first quarter of 2008 to 463 trillion yen in the first quarter of 2009. The GFC decreased the real GDP of Japan by 44 trillion yen, which was almost the same amount as the decrease (43 trillion yen) occurring during the COVID-19 crisis, from the first quarter of 2020 to the second quarter of 2020.

The industrial production index decreased to 78.0 (compared with 100 in 2015) in February 2009 as shown in Figure 8.5. It recorded an 18.5 percent reduction from 119.4 in February 2008 to 78.0 in February 2009. The reduction was much larger than the 12.2 percent reduction during the COVID-19 crisis. The industrial production index increased from 78.0 in February 2009 to 100.7 in February 2010. The industrial production index eventually increased but remained at 100 which was about 20 percent smaller than the level before the GFC.

The Bank of Japan (BOJ) has compared the impacts on firms' sales during the COVID-19 crisis with those of the GFC in its *Financial System Report* (Bank of Japan, 2020f). The comparison is shown in Table 8.1. The rate of changes

Table 8.1 Simulated sales reduction in the COVID-19 crisis and actual reduction in the global financial crisis

| | Year-on-year change, % | | | |
| | COVID-19 Crisis | | Global financial crisis | |
	Large firms	SMEs	Large firms	SMEs
All industries	−8.8	−22.0	−19.7	−11.9
Basic materials manufacturing	−11.2	−21.3	−23.2	−18.3
Processing and assembly manufacturing	−11.3	−22.2	−23.8	−15.9
Construction	−6.4	−21.1	−6.5	−5.9
Real estate	−2.8	−21.6	1.1	−11.1
Wholesale	−6.6	−21.1	−27.0	−13.2
Retail	−3.6	−13.1	−3.4	−10.9
Transportation and communications	−6.2	−15.7	−8.0	−12.1
Food, accommodation, and consumer services	−16.5	−47.0	1.3	−6.2
Other non-manufacturing	−6.4	−23.1	−8.0	−10.2
All firms	−14.4		−16.2	

The rate of changes in sales during the GFC was computed from the rate of change in sales of each sector for the one-year period from October 2008 to September 2009. The rate of changes in sales during the COVID-19 crisis were simulated in each sector. For the simulation, the assumptions regarding the sales declines in fiscal 2020 are as follows. For large firms, the forecasts for individual listed firms are used, while for SMEs, the industry-level forecasts from the Tankan (Short-Term Economic Survey of Enterprises in Japan), adjusted by private-sector forecasts for real GDP growth, are used.
Source: Development Bank of Japan; Nikkei Inc., "NEEDS-Financial QUEST"; S&P Global Market Intelligence; Published accounts of each firm; BOJ.
Citation from BOJ, Financial System Report, October 2020.

in sales during the GFC was computed from the rate of change in sales of each industry for the one-year period from October 2008 to September 2009. On the one hand, the rate of changes in sales during COVID-19 were simulated in respect of each industry. The data source is the actual sales of large listed firms and the industry-level values of the Tankan (Short-Term Economic Survey of Enterprises in Japan) for small and medium-sized enterprises (SMEs). For the simulation, the assumptions regarding sales declines in fiscal 2020 are as follows. For large firms, the forecasts for individual listed firms are used, while for SMEs, the industry-level forecasts from the Tankan, adjusted by private-sector forecasts for real GDP growth, are used.

The Report pointed out that the key features of the firms' sales since the outbreak of COVID-19 are as follows: (1) the percentage decline for SMEs is much larger than that for large firms, meaning that the shock to SMEs is more severe; and (2) among SMEs, those in food, accommodation, and consumer services, have been most severely affected by measures to prevent the spread of infections, but also those in manufacturing industry are expected to see a large fall in sales. Compared to the expected rate of decline in sales, by firm size, amid the current COVID-19 crisis, the GFC was worse for large firms than for SMEs, since it was a shock that was triggered by a sharp fall in exports due to external factors. Meanwhile, by sector, while manufacturing saw a large drop in sales, the decline in food, accommodation, and consumer services has been relatively small during the GFC, indicating that the nature of the shock was quite different from COVID-19.

8.4 Fiscal policy

8.4.1 Fiscal policy against the global financial crisis

The first G-20 Summit (Summit on Financial Markets and the World Economy) was held in Washington D.C. in November 2008 immediately after the Lehman shock. The governments of the G-20 member states discussed adopting coordinated large-scale fiscal stimuli to boost the global economy. In accordance with international coordination in fiscal policy, the Japanese government adopted large-scale fiscal policy measures to boost the domestic economy.

The first fiscal 2008 supplementary budget by the Japanese government was passed in October 2008 entitled "Comprehensive Emergency Measures to Bring about Peace of Mind". It amounted to 1.8 trillion yen in the general account and 11.5 trillion yen in the overall project scale. Subsequently, the second fiscal 2008 supplementary budget was passed in January 2009 to implement "Measures to Counter Difficulties in People's Daily Lives" having been announced on December 19, 2008. It amounted to 4.7 trillion yen in the general account and 26.9 trillion yen in the overall project scale.

Moreover, the Japanese government passed the fiscal 2009 budget to implement "Emergency Measures to Defend People's Daily Lives and Japan's Economy" which amounted to 37 trillion yen in the overall project scale. In addition, the first supplementary budget for FY2009 was approved in May 2009. It amounted to 14.7 trillion yen in the general account as "Countermeasures to Address the Economic Crisis", and amounted to 57 trillion yen in the overall project scale. The second supplementary budget for FY2009 was approved in January 2010 to implement "Emergency Economic Countermeasures for Future Growth and Security" having been announced on December 8, 2009. It amounted to 7.2 trillion yen in the general account and 24.4 trillion yen in the overall project scale.

Thus, the Japanese government conducted the above-mentioned fiscal policy which in total amounted to 12 trillion yen (2 percent of GDP) in fiscal measures and 75 trillion yen in the overall project scale from the first and second 2008 and the 2009 supplementary budgets. The fiscal measures included (1) employment measures, (2) measures to facilitate SMEs financing (the Financial Services Agency (FSA) requested financial institutions to facilitate financing for SMEs), and (3) measures to revive local areas. The government has tried to implement the latest emergency economic package, aimed at ensuring safety and security, under the basic fiscal policy of not relying on the issuance of deficit-covering government bonds.

Specifically, the above-mentioned "Emergency Measures to Defend People's Daily Lives and Japan's Economy" had two aspects of policy response measures. The first measures were fiscal response measures. They included countermeasures for employment, support for housing and daily life (fixed-sum stipend (2 trillion yen)), increasing the amount of national tax revenues allocated to local governments to implement job-creating businesses and other policies (1 trillion yen), a reserve budget for emergency economic responses, and tax cuts for housing and capital investment. The second response measures were financial responses. They included increasing the maximum level of the government's total equity participation in financial institutions based on the Act of Special Measures for Strengthening Financial Functions (10 trillion yen added to the existing limit), and conducting and increasing "emergency response operations" that make use of government finance (emergency credit limit (6 trillion yen), an emergency lending limit for government-affiliated financial institutions (3 trillion yen), and an emergency credit guarantee and lending limits (30 trillion yen).

8.4.2 Emergency Economic Measures to Cope with COVID-19

The Japanese government made use of several active fiscal measures in response to COVID-19. At first, the government used the limited reserve fund of its budget of FY2019 to take about 446 billion yen of fiscal measures (2.1 trillion yen in terms of the project size) in February and March 2020. Immediately after the decision, the Japanese government made the decision to implement Emergency Economic Measures to Cope with COVID-19 in the first and second supplementary budgets in FY2020. Its project scale was 304 trillion yen (19.8 trillion yen for Comprehensive Economic Measures to Create a Future with Security and Growth,[2] 2.1 trillion yen for the first and second round of emergency measures,[3] 95.2 trillion yen for the first supplementary budget, 113 trillion yen for the second supplementary budget, and 73.6 trillion yen for the third supplementary budget). The total budget amounts in the national general account were 75.6 trillion yen (27.5 trillion yen (general account 25.6 trillion yen and special account 1.9 trillion yen) for the first supplementary

---

2 This refers to matters that are expected to have an effect in the future among "Comprehensive Economic Measures to Create a Future with Security and Growth" that was approved by Cabinet on December 5, 2019).

3 This refers to matters pertaining to the first round (approved by the Novel Coronavirus Response Headquarters on February 13, 2020) and the second round (approved by the Novel Coronavirus Response Headquarters on March 10, 2020) of "Emergency Measures for Novel Coronavirus Infection".

budget, 31.8 trillion yen for the second supplementary budget, and 19.2 trillion yen for the third supplementary budget).

The government used both the reserve fund in the national budget and unimplemented budget expenditures in FY2019 (Cabinet Office, 2019) to make the two Emergency Response Packages against COVID-19. The first package of 15.3 billion yen was decided on February 13. It included livelihood supports for workplace returnees and the acceleration of R&D into vaccines. The second package of 430.8 billion yen was decided on March 10. It included expansion of the special measures on employment adjustment subsidies.

The Emergency Economic Measures to Cope with COVID-19 were decided on as the first supplementary budget of FY 2020 on April 7, partly revised on April 20 and passed on April 30. Its total amount was 25.6 trillion yen. The Emergency Economic Measures were increased as the second supplementary budget of FY 2020 on May 27 and passed on June 12. Its total amount was 31.8 trillion yen. The additional fiscal stimulus in the third supplementary budget was announced by the Japanese government on December 8, 2020. Its total amount is 19.2 trillion yen in terms of the national general account for the third supplementary budget.

The Emergency Economic Measures to Cope with COVID-19 included emergency support for households and SMEs, securing employment, and financial measures to support firms in respect of cash management (Cabinet Office, 2020). Table 8.2 summarizes the cash payments, tax measures, and financial measures that the Japanese government has implemented for corporate financing during the COVID-19 crisis.

Regarding emergency support for households, the government made cash payments to all residents for the purpose of fostering national solidarity against COVID-19. It promptly and appropriately supported households through a simple mechanism, and uniformly paid out 100,000 yen per person to all residents. This measure is important for the government to provide a kind of safety net for lower income individuals who lose their jobs due to COVID-19. However, the amount is not large enough to enable them to maintain their living standards. It would be more effective if the government focused on lower income individuals rather than all residents in Japan. On the other hand, the cost of the program was not low and amounted to 12.9 trillion yen in government expenditure.

Next, the government supported business continuity of SMEs and sole proprietors and set up a new grant system that can serve as a source of recovery assistance and can be widely used by the entire business community. It makes a cash payment of 2 million yen to corporations and 1 million yen to sole proprietors, whose revenue falls by more than 50 percent in any month of 2020 compared to the previous year. The scheme amounts to 2.3 trillion yen.

Thirdly, regarding securing employment, the government enhanced the employment adjustment subsidies providing financial assistance to employees to take temporary leave from work and thus avoid dismissal. It raised the subsidy rate to four-fifths of income for small and medium enterprises and two-thirds for large enterprises during the emergency response period. In addition,

Table 8.2 Contents of major measures to support corporate financing

Major measures to support corporate financing		Overview of measures	Fiscal expenses and total size of measures	
			First supplementary budget	*Second supplementary budget*
Cash payments	Subsidies for sustaining businesses	Cash payments for SMEs and sole proprietors (up to 2 mil. yen)	2.3 trillion yen	1.9 trillion yen
	Rent assistance subsidy	Cash payments for supporting rent payments (up to 6 mil. yen)	–	2.0 trillion yen
	Expansion of employment adjustment subsidies program, etc.	Subsidy rates increased for leave allowance (up to 100% for SMEs and up to 75% for large firms)	0.8 trillion yen	1.3 trillion yen
Tax measures	Special tax measures, such as tax payment moratorium	National and local taxes and/or social insurance contributions possibly deferred for one year	26 trillion yen	–
Financial measures	Effectively interest-free loans by government-affiliated financial institutions	Interest subsidies provided to government-affiliated financial institutions	Approx. 15 trillion yen	Approx. 33 trillion yen
	Effectively interest-free loans by private financial institutions	Interest subsidies provided to private financial institutions through local governments' loan programs	Approx. 24 trillion yen	Approx. 28 trillion yen
	Crisis response loans to medium-sized and large firms by government-affiliated financial institutions	Long-term loans with preferential interest rates through government-affiliated financial institutions	Approx. 5 trillion yen	Approx. 5 trillion yen
	Equity support by government-affiliated financial institutions and funds	Equity support mainly through subordinated loans and capital injections	–	Approx. 12 trillion yen

Source: Cabinet Office; Ministry of Finance.
Citation from BOJ, Financial System Report (2020).

the employment adjustment subsidy was expanded to include non-regular workers who are not covered by employment insurance. It amounted to 0.5 trillion yen in total.

Fourthly, the government gave financial support for cash management to small-sized enterprises as well as medium-sized and large companies. It offered concessional loans, which are effectively interest-free without collateral combined with interest subsidies for small-sized enterprises through private financial institutions, as well as though government-affiliated financial institutions. It offered medium-sized and large companies financial support by using the Crisis Response Loans of the Development Bank of Japan and the Shoko Chukin Bank. These amount to 15.5 trillion yen (3.8 trillion yen in the first supplementary budget and 11.6 trillion yen in the second supplementary budget.

8.4.3 Increase in fiscal deficit and accumulating outstanding JGBs

The above-mentioned large fiscal stimulus has caused a deterioration in the Japanese government's accounts (Ministry of Finance, 2020). Government finances had a stable trend in expenditure and an upward trend in tax revenues in 2010s. However, government expenditure had a sudden increase in 2020 due to the first and second supplementary budgets of FY 2020 for the Emergency Economic Measures to Cope with COVID-19. It faces a larger fiscal deficit in 2020 as shown in Figure 8.8. The value of outstanding Japanese

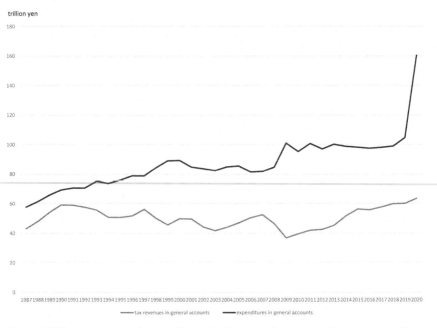

Figure 8.8 Tax revenues and expenditures in the general accounts of government. Data: MOF.

Government Bonds (JGB) has been accumulating constantly over time. For the same reason the ratio of outstanding JGBs to GDP has been increasing.

The JGBs are classified into special deficit financing bonds, construction bonds, and reconstruction bonds. Between them, the special deficit financing bonds have been accumulating the fastest. In 2020, their outstanding valuation increased by the size of the huge fiscal deficit caused by the fiscal measures for COVID-19. The outstanding costs of the special deficit financing bonds increased from 618 to 671 trillion yen. The ratio of total outstanding JGBs to GDP increases from 160.8 percent to169.0 percent as shown in Figure 8.9.

The increased fiscal deficit in 2020 accumulates the amount of outstanding JGBs and, in turn, increases interest payments or the interest burden of the Japanese government, even though the interest rate is kept at a quite low level as shown in Figure 8.10. The BOJ's monetary policy has contributed to the quite low interest rate on the JGBs. The BOJ has been conducting a yield curve control in which it controls short- and long-term interest rates to remain at negative and around 0 percent, respectively, as explained in the next section.

Thus, the fiscal response policy against COVID-19 is increasing the fiscal deficit and accumulating outstanding JGB debt. The Japanese government has no choice but to conduct fiscal policy to mitigate the adverse effects of the COVID-19 crisis on the Japanese economy for the moment. However, the Japanese government should stabilize outstanding JGB debt from the viewpoint of long-run sustainability of government debt. For this purpose, it needs to increase taxes, such as consumption tax (Japanese version of value-added

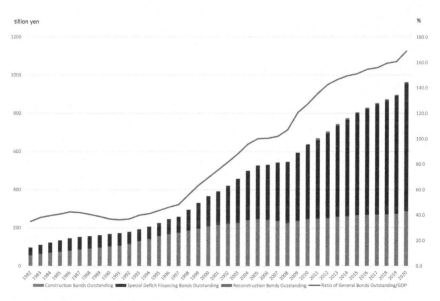

Figure 8.9 Value of Japanese Government Bonds outstanding and its ratio to GDP. Data: MOF.

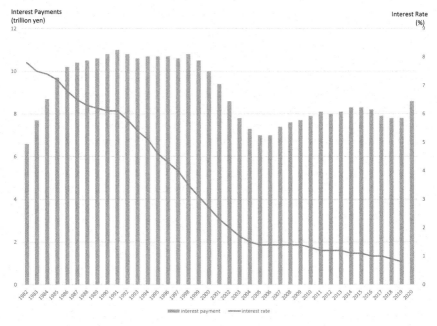

Figure 8.10 Interest payments and interest rate. Data: MOF.

tax) after it achieves economic recovery from the current economic slump caused by the COVID-19 crisis. In addition, creeping inflation (for example, 2 percent inflation that is the inflation target of the BOJ) would contribute to the gradual reduction in the real burden of government debt without dislocating the economy.

8.5 Monetary policy

8.5.1 Monetary policy response against the global financial crisis

In addition to coordinated fiscal stimuli, central banks in developed countries simultaneously began to conduct quantitative easing monetary policies with zero interest rates as shown in Figures 8.11 and 8.12. Moreover, the Federal Reserve Board (FRB) facilitated international coordination in providing US dollar liquidity to financial markets in the global economy. They developed currency swap arrangements among central banks so that the FRB could provide US dollar liquidity to other central banks in exchange for their home currencies. In these circumstances, the coordinated monetary policies provided abundant money, which moved around the world governed by increased financial globalization.

The BOJ reduced policy interest rates and further increased the flexibility of money market operations to maintain accommodative financial conditions.

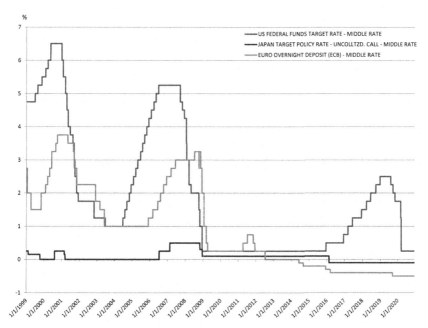

Figure 8.11 Policy interest rates of the Bank of Japan, the FRB, and the ECB. Data: Datastream.

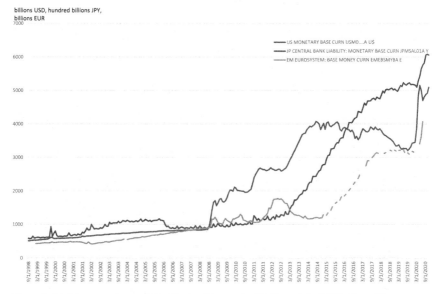

Figure 8.12 Monetary bases of the Bank of Japan, the FRB, and the ECB. Data: Datastream.

First, the BOJ lowered its target for the uncollateralized overnight call rate from 0.5 percent to 0.3 percent on October 31, 2008, from 0.3 percent to 0.1 percent on December 19, 2008, and to 0–0.1 percent on October 5, 2010. Second, the BOJ introduced the Complementary Deposit Facility (0.1 percent interest rate) in order to further facilitate the provisioning of sufficient liquidity and ensure stability in money markets on October 31, 2008.

The BOJ decided to take the following three measures to further facilitate corporate financing in addition to measures regarding outright purchases of JGBs on December 19, 2008. First, the BOJ increased outright purchases of JGBs. The amount of outright purchases of JGBs was increased from 14.4 trillion yen per year (1.2 trillion yen per month) to 16.8 trillion yen per year (1.4 trillion yen per month). On March 18, 2009, the amount of outright purchases of JGBs was increased to 21.6 trillion yen (1.8 trillion yen per month).

Secondly, the BOJ introduced three measures to facilitate corporate financing on February 19, 2009, which were abolished on March 31, 2010. The BOJ implemented (a) "Special Funds-Supplying Operations to Facilitate Corporate Financing", (b) outright purchases of CP, and (c) outright purchases of corporate bonds amounting to 35.7 trillion yen, 2.5 trillion yen, and 0.3 trillion yen, respectively, to the corporate sector during the period February 2009 to March 2010. It amounted to 38.5 trillion yen in total in the year.

Thirdly, the BOJ introduced an Asset Purchase Program in order to encourage a decline in longer-term interest rates and various risk premiums to further enhance monetary easing on October 28, 2010. The total amount of the Program was about 35 trillion yen. Purchases of assets amounted to about 5 trillion yen. The fixed-rate funds-supplying operation against pooled collateral amounted to about 30 trillion yen. The maximum outstanding amount for JGBs and treasury discount bills (T-bills), CP, corporate bonds, ETFs, and J-REITs was about 3.5 trillion yen (of which about 1.5 trillion yen was for JGBs), about 0.5 trillion yen, about 0.45 trillion yen (conditional on obtaining authorization), and about 0.05 trillion yen (conditional on obtaining authorization), respectively.

The FRB introduced a currency swap arrangement with the European Central Bank (ECB) and the Swiss National Bank (SNB) in order that each of them should provide broad access to US dollar liquidity and funding to financial institutions in December 2007. Also, the FRB concluded similar arrangements with the BOJ on September 18, 2008 immediately after the Lehman shock. On September 29, the FRB expanded and extended this from the end of January 2009 to the end of April 2009. In October, the BOJ introduced measures to improve liquidity in short-term US dollar funding markets in concert with the Bank of England (BOE), the ECB, the FRB, and the SNB (Bank of Japan, 2008). The central banks conducted tenders of US dollar funding with 7-day, 28-day, and 84-day maturities at fixed interest rates for full allotment. Funds were provided at a fixed interest rate, set in advance of each operation. Counterparties in these operations were able to borrow any amount they wished against the appropriate collateral in each jurisdiction. Accordingly, the sizes of the reciprocal currency arrangements (swap lines) between the Federal Reserve and the other central banks were increased to accommodate whatever quantity of US dollar funding was demanded.

8.5.2 Quantitative and qualitative monetary easing (QQE) with yield curve control

The BOJ had continued with "Quantitative and Qualitative Monetary Easing (QQE) with Yield Curve Control" programs aiming to achieve the price stability target of 2 percent before the COVID-19 pandemic in February 2020 (Bank of Japan, 2020a). The BOJ has made a change in monetary policy in respect of the QQE since Mr. Haruhiko Kuroda became the governor of the BOJ in 2013. The BOJ has been continuing expanding the monetary base until the year-on-year rate of increase in the observed consumer price index (CPI, all items less fresh food) exceeds 2 percent and stays above this target in a stable manner although it has actually been smaller than the target figure as shown in Figure 8.13.

The BOJ conducted a yield curve control policy in which it controls short- and long-term interest rates so that they remain at negative and at around 0 percent respectively. The BOJ sets guidelines for market operations for both

Figure 8.13 CPI inflation rates. Data: Statistics Bureau of Japan.

Figure 8.14 Short- and long-term interest rates. Data: Statistics Bureau of Japan.

short-term policy interest rates and the long-term interest rates. It has applied a negative interest rate of minus 0.1 percent to the Policy-Rate Balances in current accounts held by financial institutions at the BOJ. At the same time, the BOJ has conducted purchases of JGBs in a flexible manner so that their amounts outstanding increase at an annual pace of about 80 trillion yen. Uncollateralized overnight call rates have remained negative while newly issued 10-year government bond yields have moved around zero interest rate, as shown in Figure 8.14.

Moreover, the BOJ set a guideline regarding asset purchases other than the JGB purchases to increase the monetary base. The monetary base movements are shown in Figure 8.12. It has purchased Exchange-Traded Funds (ETFs) and Japan Real Estate Investment Trusts (J-REITs) so that their amounts outstanding increase at annual paces of about 6 trillion yen and about 90 billion yen, respectively. Also, it has maintained their amounts outstanding in respect of CP and corporate bonds at about 2.2 trillion yen and about 3.2 trillion yen, respectively.

8.5.3 BOJ's measures in response to COVID-19

The BOJ has taken some measures in response to COVID-19. It has enhanced monetary easing through the following measures (Bank of Japan, 2020c, 2020d). The first measures are measures to facilitate corporate financing including the introduction of new operations. The BOJ has increased the upper limit in respect of CP and corporate bonds purchases by 20 trillion yen in total. In addition, the maximum amounts outstanding of a single issuer's CP and corporate bonds purchases are raised substantially, and the maximum remaining maturity of corporate bonds purchases is extended to five years. The 20 trillion yen increase in the upper limit of CP and corporate bonds purchases is much larger than the 2.8 trillion yen of implemented outright purchases of CP and corporate bonds during the period from February 2009 to March 2010.

The BOJ introduced a new operation (the "Special Funds-Supplying Operations to Facilitate Financing in Response to the COVID-19") to provide loans against corporate debt (of about 25 trillion yen as of end-April 2020) as collateral at an interest rate of 0 percent with maturity up to one year. Twice as much as the amount outstanding of the loans is included in the Macro Add-on Balances in current accounts held by financial institutions at the BOJ.

Moreover, the BOJ introduced a New Fund-Provisioning Measure to Support Financing Mainly of Small and Medium-Sized Firms on May 22, 2020 (Bank of Japan, 2020e). It is a fund-provisioning against eligible loans, such as interest-free and unsecured loans made by eligible counterparties based on the government's Emergency Economic Measures to Cope with COVID-19. It includes also loans to small- and medium-sized firms affected by COVID-19 which are equivalent to the above eligible loans. It amounts to about 30 trillion yen in total. The BOJ provides funds to eligible counterparties against pooled collateral for up to 1 year at a loan rate of 0 percent with the maximum amounts outstanding of eligible loans reported by those counterparties. Regarding the Macro Add-on Balances, twice as much as the amounts outstanding of the loans are included in the Macro Add-on Balances in current accounts held by financial institutions at the BOJ. Moreover, a positive interest rate of 0.1 percent is applied to the outstanding balances of current accounts held by financial institutions at the BOJ, corresponding to the amounts of outstanding loans provided through this measure.

The BOJ provides ample more yen funds by making active purchases of JGBs and T-Bills with a view to maintaining stability in the bond market and stabilizing the entire yield curve at a low level. It is supposed that the increase in the amount of issuance of JGBs and T-Bills in response to the government's Emergency Economic Measures will have an impact on the market. BOJ purchases the necessary amount of JGBs without setting an upper limit so that the ten-year JGB yield will remain at around 0 percent. The BOJ actively purchases ETFs and J-REITs for the time being so that their amounts outstanding increase at annual paces with the upper limits of about 12 trillion yen and about 180 billion yen, respectively.

The BOJ conducts coordinated actions to enhance the provision of US dollar liquidity via the standing US dollar liquidity swap line arrangements with the Bank of Canada (BOC), the Bank of England, the European Central Bank, the FRB, and the Swiss National Bank (Bank of Japan (2020b)). The central banks lower the pricing on the standing US dollar liquidity swap arrangements by 0.25 percent. They offer US dollars weekly with an 84-day maturity, in addition to the 1-week maturity operations currently offered.

8.6 Conclusion

This chapter focused on Japan's monetary and fiscal policy responses to the COVID-19 crisis. Japan has experienced a third Covid-19 surge since November 2020. The number of infected people has rapidly increased especially in urban areas which include Tokyo and Osaka. There were over four thousand positive PCR test persons per day in December 2020. However, the development of COVID-19 in Japan has not been as severe compared with other countries. The measures that have been taken by the government may have contributed to the less severe development of COVID-19, although there have not been any lockdowns in Japan.

The Japanese economy has been facing a depression which is the equal to or worse than that during the GFC. The rate of change in real GDP in Japan (annualized rate of changes from previous quarters) recorded minus 28.8 percent in the second quarter of 2020, which was a larger reduction compared with minus 17.8 percent in the first quarter of 2009 during the GFC. The impact has been more severe on the services sectors which rely on face-to-face type interactions, compared with industrial production in Japan. In addition, the impact of the COVID-19 crisis on SMEs is more severe than on large firms.

The Japanese government has undertaken active fiscal measures in response to COVID-19 under the Emergency Economic Measures to Cope with COVID-19 since April 2020. It is likely to take time for the positive effects of these measures on the Japanese economy to become apparent. On the other hand, the large government expenditure increases the amount of outstanding special deficit financing bonds from 618 to 671 trillion yen. The ratio of total outstanding JGBs to GDP has increased from 160.8 percent to169.0 percent. The increased fiscal deficits and the accumulating outstanding JGBs might have adverse effects on JGB markets in the future, although the BOJ has been conducting a kind of accommodating monetary policy against the accumulation of government bonds in order to keep the long-term interest rate at zero percentage.

The BOJ has been conducting responses to COVID-19 to enhance monetary easing through measures to facilitate corporate financing including the introduction of the new operations. At the same time, it has been making both ample provision of yen funds available by conducting active purchases of JGBs and ample provision of US dollar liquidity through coordinated central bank action. For the moment, the BOJ's monetary policy measures have been contributing to keeping financial markets stable as well as long-term interest rates at a lower level in Japan. However, corporate financing may get more severe in the coming years as well as in 2020 because companies could face continuing net cash outflows in a worst-case situation where COVID-19 has adverse effects on their sales and profits.

References

Bank of Japan (2008), *Further Measures to Improve Liquidity in Short-Term U.S. Dollar Funding Markets*, October 13, 2008.

Bank of Japan (2020a) *Statement of Monetary Policy*, January 21, 2020, May 22, 2020, June 16, 2020, July 15, 2020, and September 17, 2020.

Bank of Japan (2020b) *Coordinated Central Bank Action to Enhance the Provision of Global U.S. Dollar Liquidity*, March 15, 2020.

Bank of Japan (2020c) *Enhancement of Monetary Easing in Light of the Impact of the Outbreak of the Novel Coronavirus (COVID-19)*, March 16, 2020.

Bank of Japan (2020d) *Enhancement of Monetary Easing*, April 27, 2020.

Bank of Japan (2020e) *Introduction of a New Fund-Provisioning Measure to Support Financing Mainly of Small and Medium-Sized Firms*, May 22, 2020.

Bank of Japan (2020f) *Financial System Report*, October 2020.

Cabinet Office (2019) *Comprehensive Economic Measures to Create a Future with Security and Growth*, December 2019. www5.cao.go.jp/keizai1/keizaitaisaku/2019/20191205_econ omic_measures_all.pdf

Cabinet Office (2020) *Emergency Economic Measures to Cope with the Novel Coronavirus (COVID-19)*, April 2020.www5.cao.go.jp/keizai1/keizaitaisaku/2020/20200420_econ omic_measures_all.pdf

Cabinet Secretariat (2020) *Basic Policies for Novel Coronavirus Disease Control*, March 28, 2020, revised on May 25, 2020. https://corona.go.jp/en/news/pdf/basic_policy_2020 0531.pdf

International Monetary Fund (2020) *Policy Responses to COVID-19: Japan, 2020*. www.imf .org/en/Topics/imf-and-covid19/Policy-Responses-to-COVID-19#J.

Ministry of Finance (2020) *Debt Management Report 2020: The Government Debt Management and the State of Public Debts, 2020*. www.mof.go.jp/english/jgbs/publication/debt_m anagement_report/2020/esaimu2020.pdf

9 The case of Korea

Woosik Moon and Wook Sohn

9.1 Introduction

After its initial outbreak in China, Covid-19 quickly spread to Korea, and then to European countries and the US. The spread of Covid-19 was so unexpected that it brought about drastic responses to stem its spread, leading many countries to introduce lockdowns. The economic impact was very serious, in comparison to the potential economic meltdown during the 2008 global financial crisis.

As highlighted in the title of the book edited by Baldwin and di Mauro (2020), "Mitigating the COVID economic crisis: Act Fast and Do Whatever It Takes", the first immediate policy response requirement perception was to react as quickly and on as large a scale as possible. Similarly, the IMF (2020a) considered the Great Lockdown as the worst economic downturn since the Great Depression. The initial solution proposed was the same as in the 2008 global financial crisis.

It now seems clear that the Covid-19 crisis could not be rapidly overcome over a short timescale. The resolution of the crisis will take much longer than initially anticipated and the cohabitation of the economy and Covid-19 will continue until the wide immunization of people has taken place. More importantly, the economic crisis did not originate from the financial sector but from the social distancing and non-interacting brought about by the public health crisis. Therefore, the goal of the fiscal and monetary policy responses should not be to preemptively stem the financial crisis but to mitigate the impact of the public health crisis and alleviate the impact on the economy. Notwithstanding this, the actions taken by many governments and central banks were, with few exceptions, rapid and large-scale responses, probably reinforced by the successful experiences of handling the 2008 global financial crisis. But, if two crises are different, so should the reactions to them be.

Against this backdrop, this chapter tries to assess whether or not the fiscal and monetary policy responses taken by the Korean government and Bank of Korea are appropriate for the Korean economy. As with other major economies hit hard by Covid-19, Korea reacted through rapid and large-scale accommodation policies, emphasizing that these would be preemptive actions as in the

DOI: 10.4324/9781003153603-9

2008 global financial crisis. But Korea had no lockdown. Although economic recovery was delayed due to the social distancing regulations, the impact of Covid-19 remained rather limited. This suggests that, unlike in the case of the 2008 global financial crisis, the more appropriate response may be a gradual response over a longer time frame to mitigate its economic impact, which should be taken in tandem with the evolution of Covid-19. Furthermore, given the enormous costs ensuing from the misallocation of financial resources linked to the large-scale accommodation policies, responses targeting vulnerable sectors and groups may be more suitable for the goal of alleviating the impact on the Korean economy. A gradual and targeted approach in place of a rapid and undiscriminating response may be the right approach.

The organization of this chapter is as follows. Section 2 begins by looking at the economic impact of the Covid-19 pandemic on the Korean economy. Section 3 examines and assesses the fiscal policy responses taken by the Korean government. Section 4 assesses the monetary policy responses taken by the Bank of Korea. Finally, section 5 summarizes the conclusions of this chapter.

9.2 Economic impact of the Covid-19 pandemic on the Korean economy

9.2.1 Development of Covid-19 in Korea

Initially the Korean government mismanaged the control of Covid-19. This ended up with disastrous consequences. By late February 2020, Korea was the country with the second highest number of Covid-19 cases after China. Although its Asian neighbors were all successful in blocking the spread of Covid-19, Korea failed in the early blocking of the spread of the pandemic. This disastrous outcome was even more disappointing because, unlike its Asian neighbors, Korea had suffered an outbreak of Middle East Respiratory Syndrome (MERS) in 2015, which encouraged Korea to reform its public health policies, particularly regarding the handling of infectious diseases. For instance, the Korean government granted greater authority and autonomy to the Korea Centers for Disease Control and Prevention (KCDC) as the control tower for the containment of infectious diseases. Laws were also amended to promote public–private medical partnerships, authorizing emergency use of testing kits and treatments, and to enable health authorities to collect data needed for the contact-tracing of infected individuals. These reforms were supposed to help contain the spread of Covid-19. But, unlike its Asian neighbors e.g. Taiwan and Singapore, the Korean government underestimated and misjudged the risk of contagion from Covid-19, and was extremely reluctant to introduce any travel restrictions on foreign entrants, particularly Chinese entrants, to Korea even when almost all other countries decided to do so. Thus, only with the outbreak of a Covid-19 cluster in Daegu, a Southeastern region, did the Korean government become more perceptive about the risks from the virus. Despite its belated initial response to the spread of Covid-19, however, the Korean government managed to contain the spread of the virus, thereby avoiding a serious lockdown. At the core of this successful response lies the Korean health authorities' strategy of robust and preemptive "Testing, Tracing, and Treatment (the 3Ts)" and Korea's robust public health infrastructure and advanced information and tracing technology. Moreover, the Korean public continued to voluntarily participate in wearing face masks and in maintaining social distancing. This allowed the Korean government to "flatten the curve" without resorting to massive lockdowns.

As of the end of 2020, new waves of contagion continued to take place. Particularly alarmingly, the number of new cases reached 1,000 per day in December 2020. Broadly speaking, however, it seems that Korea was successful in containing Covid-19. As of the end of 2020, the performance of Korea looks outstanding compared to the US and European countries that suffered lockdowns, although it is mediocre compared to its Asian neighboring countries such as Taiwan, Hong Kong, and Singapore. Figure 9.1 shows that at the end of 2020, Korea had a grand total of around 20 thousand cases and three-digit daily cases.

Until vaccination is widely diffused, the Covid-19 pandemic is likely to subsist. In particular, given the delayed acquisition of the necessary vaccine by the Korean government, social distancing and restrictions on mobility will continue to prevail until the end of 2021 and the normalization of international travel will be delayed. This is likely to have a lingering impact on the economy.

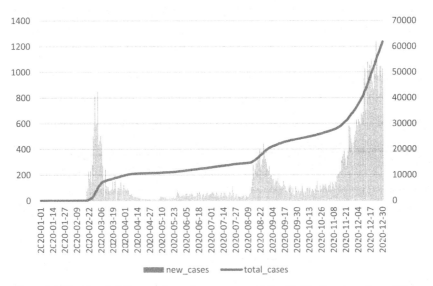

Figure 9.1 Total and daily number of new cases of Covid-19. Sources: Korea Disease Control and Prevention Agency, Our World in Data (https://ourworldindata .org/covid-cases).

9.2.2 Economic impact of Covid-19

In 1997, when Korea was for the first time hit by a currency crisis triggered by a sudden outflow of capital, the origin of the shock was completely domestic, but its impact was bigger than any other financial crisis Korea ever had. In 2008, the crisis triggered by the US subprime mortgage market meltdown developed into a global financial crisis but its spillover to the Korean economy turned out to be relatively limited. In 2020, the outbreak of the Covid-19 pandemic had both domestic and global impacts on the Korean economy. Concerning the domestic impact, the spread of the Covid-19 brought about a sharp fall in domestic demand, in particular in the services sector requiring face-to-face interactions (e.g., food & accommodation, wholesale & retail, and educational services) and in domestic output, as the impact of Covid-19 began to fully materialize. At the same time, Covid-19 affected the global economy as well as the Korean economy, which, through the drop in export demand, would further decelerate economic growth in Korea.

Hit by the domestic and global spread of Covid-19, economic growth in Korea shrank significantly. In the first and second quarters of 2020, real GDP declined by 1.3% and y 3.3% quarter-on-quarter respectively. From the third quarter, however, the Korean economy rebounded. In the third and fourth quarters, GDP grew by 2.1% and 1.1% respectively, quarter-on-quarter. Over the whole year of 2020, GDP contracted only by 1%.

Figure 9.2 shows the trajectory of real GDP for the past three economic crises. It seems that the extent of the impact of the Covid-19 crisis will be similar to that of the 2008 global financial crisis, although it will be definitely inferior to that of the 1997 currency crisis. Given the current on-going spread

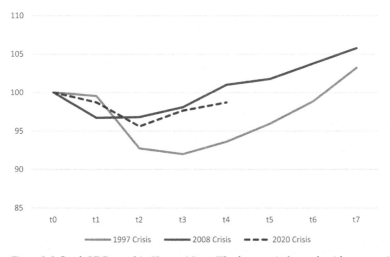

Figure 9.2 Real GDP trend in Korea. Note: The base periods are the 4th quarter 1997, 3rd quarter 2008, and 4th quarter 2019. Source: ECOS, Bank of Korea.

of Covid-19 in Korea and around the world, it is difficult to predict exactly how long it will last. But clearly it will not be over even in 2021. One important question in this regard is to know what the government and central bank should do if the recovery continues to be delayed. Korea managed to avoid a complete lockdown and therefore economic activity went on with only limited social distancing, which would necessitate small, targeted but lasting policy measures to support the sluggish economy and labor market, but not big and undiscriminating stimulus packages.

Following the trend in output, the unemployment rate increased in the second quarter of 2020 as the impact of Covid-19 began to fully materialize. For instance, it went up to 4.3% in May from 3.4% in January, reflecting the loss of jobs mainly in the services sector. However, it soon went down to 3.4% in November. The unemployment rate has not deteriorated very much during the course of the pandemic. This is, at least in the short-run, because of the relative success in the containment of Covid-19, but more importantly due to the rigidity of the labor market in Korea. Figure 9.3 illustrates the unemployment rate trends in Korea during the three crises periods. It is expected that the current employment recovery will take a longer time than that of the 2008 global financial crisis, which took around five quarters.

Furthermore, a drop in aggregate demand and a plunge in international oil prices after the spread of Covid-19 brought down consumer price inflation to around 0%. Unless supported by strong economic recovery, inflation is expected to remain very low in the near future (See Bank of Korea, 2020). Unlike in the case of the previous crises, however, asset markets quickly recovered after Covid-19 arrival. Stock prices bounced back quickly after an initial drop. In the meantime, the rise in housing prices, particularly in Seoul, continued even

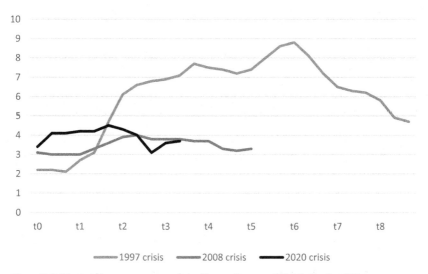

Figure 9.3 Unemployment rate trends in Korea. Source: ECOS, Bank of Korea.

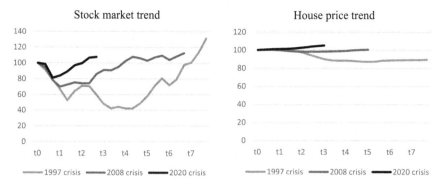

Figure 9.4 Stock and real estate market trends in Korea. Source: ECOS, Bank of Korea.

amid the Covid-19 pandemic. It seems that under the extremely low interest rates prevailing in Korea, the main transmission channel of the monetary policy would work through asset price rises. Figure 9.4 shows that Covid-19 had little negative impact on the asset market, particularly the real asset market. Rather, the impact was positive, given the unprecedented expansionary fiscal and monetary policy responses taken by the government and the Bank of Korea.

Besides its impact on public health, the economic damage brought about by the Covid-19 pandemic seems rather mitigated in Korea, at least until the end of 2020. This may be due to the unprecedently accommodative macroeconomic policies implemented by the Korean government and the Bank of Korea as well as successful containment of Covid-19.

9.3 Fiscal policy responses to the Covid-19 crisis

9.3.1 Budgetary policy

Unlike many other advanced economies, budgetary policy in Korea had been rarely countercyclical for stabilizing the economy. The Korean government prioritized budgetary consolidation and sound fiscal principles ever since it implemented fiscal reform in the early 1980s. Most fiscal expenditures were for long-term economic and development projects and an increase in the fiscal deficit was always regarded as harmful to the long run competitiveness of the Korean economy. Korean government officials were historically more Classical than Keynesian in this respect. A countercyclical fiscal policy, however, gained prominence in the aftermath of the 1997 currency crisis. Given a weak social safety net, the Korean government had to increase its social expenditure. During the 2008 global financial crisis, the Korean government also took active steps to counter the economic slowdown by drawing up a large-scale supplementary budget and front-loading its fiscal expenditures. Nonetheless, the long-rooted policy stance favoring fiscal soundness changed little.

This fiscal stance came to be challenged under the current government of President Moon Jae-in. Even before Covid-19 hit the Korean economy, the government set its policy priority on lessening income and wealth inequalities, and on strengthening the social safety net and expanding expenditure on social protection and security. Against this backdrop, the government launched the so-called income-led growth campaign, putting in place a series of measures reinforcing social policies and income redistribution, which ended up with turning budget balances into deficits amidst the slowdown of the economy.

With the outbreak of Covid-19, the budgetary laxity of the Korean government deepened. The government reacted to the negative pandemic economic shock by a massive and swift increase in fiscal spending, although the damage caused by the Covid-19 crisis was milder in Korea than in other advanced economies (See IMF 2020b). As shown in Table 9.1, the budgetary support provided has also been much larger than the budgetary response to the 2008 global financial crisis. The newly prepared supplementary budget amounted to a total of KRW 66.9 trillion in 2020 compared to 28.4 trillion in 2009. Therefore, the government deficit ballooned to 3.7% of GDP while the national debt would increase by 6.3% of GDP resulting in a debt to GDP ratio of 44% in 2020, up from 37.7% in 2019. In contrast, the budget deficit was just 1.7% of GDP and government debt increased by 3.0% in 2009.

As of the end of 2020, the Korean government had drawn up four supplementary budgets in the calendar year. The first and second supplementary budgets of KRW 11.7 trillion (0.6% of GDP) and KRW 12.2 trillion were approved in March and April respectively against the backdrop of National Assembly elections. Subsequently, the third supplementary budget of KRW 35.1 trillion (1.8% of GDP) and fourth supplementary budget of KRW 7.8 trillion ensued in July and September.

Of these supplementary budgets, the second budget was particularly controversial. Not alone did they incorporate programs for epidemic prevention and public health maintenance to cope with the Covid-19 pandemic, they it also included diverse programs to support employment and low-income families and to provide liquidity to SMEs, strategic companies hit by Covid-19, and to digital and local industries. These programs were clearly necessary to strengthen social protection and were a countercyclical reaction by the government. Amid the approaching National Assembly elections, however, the Korean government quickly set up a cash transfer[1] program entitled Emergency Disaster Relief, probably prompted by the enactment of the Coronavirus Aid, Relief, and Economic Security (CARES) Act in the US. The second budget was just to fund this program, which was initially designed to target only the

---

1 The payment is in effect made in the form of cash or consumption coupons depending on the recipient's income level. Given that consumption coupons are considered to be almost the same as cash, there is no need to distinguish between them in this study.

Table 9.1 Budgetary measures during the 2008 GFC and 2020 Covid-19

	2008 GFC	*2020 Covid-19*
Total supplementary Budget (Trillion KRW)	KRW 28.4 tn (2009)	KRW 66.9 tn[1] (2020)
Main programs (Trillion KRW)	*Support for employment and low-income families*	*Support for employment and low-income families*
	Job maintenance support KRW 2.8 tn	Job maintenance support KRW 8.9 tn
	Low-income family support KRW 4.1 tn	Low-income family support KRW 3.5 tn
	Support for companies and industries	*Support for companies and industries*
	Support for SMEs, exporters, and self-employed: KRW 4.5 tn	Support for SMEs, self-employed, and companies KRW 4.3 tn
	Green growth and future economy support KRW 2.3 tn	Liquidity support for industries hit by Covid-19 (airlines, etc.) KRW 3.1 tn
	Local economy support KRW 3 tn	Digital and green growth support KRW 5.1 tn
		Local industry support KRW 3.7 tn
		Emergency disaster relief support:
		First program KRW 12.2 tn
		Second program KRW 7.8 tn
		Epidemic prevention support KRW 4.8 tn
	Tax cuts and waivers	*Tax cuts and waivers KRW*
Consolidated fiscal deficit (% of GDP)	−3.1 %	
Government debt Increase (% of GDP) (2)	26.8% ->29.8% (2009)	37.7% −> 44% (2020)

Sources: Compiled by the authors based on the data from Ministry of Economy and Finance and Bank of Korea.
Note 1: Sum of four consecutive supplementary budgets KRW 11.7 tn (1st) + KRW 12.2 tn (2nd) + KRW 35.1 tn (3rd)) + KRW 7.8 tn (4th)

bottom 70% of families by income level. Ultimately, the government decided to make an universal cash transfer to all Korean families, irrespective of their income levels and by the end of August, the government had completed the payment of KRW 1 million to families with four or more members, KRW 0.8 million to three-person families, KRW 0.6 million to two-person families and KRW 0.4 million to single-person families. Around 21 million Korean families benefited from this one-off payment. It will be very hard to calculate the exact impact of this cash transfer program on the Korean economy and politics. But at least it has raised important economic questions regarding the rationale behind the program and the scope of its beneficiaries. Although the economic impact of the pandemic was relatively mild, Korea was one of only three countries that adopted universal transfer programs among the OECD member countries (OECD, 2020). Furthermore, the effectiveness of government transfers as a means to stimulate the economy has been questioned (Bayer et al. 2020 and Park et al. 2020). For instance, Park et al. (2020) show that the fiscal multiplier for government transfers is estimated to be the lowest compared to those for government consumption or investment.

As the number of Covid-19 cases increased and the restrictions on mobility strengthened in September 2020, the government decided to again conduct an emergency disaster relief program and prepared the fourth supplementary budget. This second program, however, unlike the first emergency disaster relief program, was not directed at all Korean families but discriminately targeted vulnerable people and sectors hit directly by Covid19. This time, the support centered on SMEs (KRW 3.8 trillion), employment support (KRW 1.4 trillion), support for low-income families (KRW 0.4 trillion), and daycare support (KRW 2.2 trillion).

The execution of four consecutive supplementary budgets was unprecedented in the economic history of Korea. Regarding the fiscal policy response to Covid-19, it seems that the dominant view was for the government to spend big and rapidly to boost the economy and jobs (Baldwin and Mauro, 2020; IMF, 2020a). But there is no guarantee that the Emergency Disaster Relief Program with a cash transfer to all families can efficiently produce the desired effect. To say the least, there is a need to support vulnerable sectors and groups hardest hit by the Covid-19 pandemic, but it does not justify unnecessarily large government spending, which reflects political interests under the guise of economic necessity. What is serious is that this type of spending can become permanent, not temporary. As M. Friedman once said, "Nothing is so permanent as a temporary government program" (Friedman, 1984).

9.3.2 Off-budget liquidity support

In addition to its budgetary policy, the Korean government also provided an off-budget liquidity support package amounting to KRW 175 trillion, which was expanded several times amid the deepening Covid-19 crisis.

The liquidity support package amounting to KRW 50 trillion was launched in March 2020 when the Korean government held the first "Emergency Economic Council Meeting". The goal was to support small merchants and SMEs affected by Covid-19 and to help stabilize financial markets such as the corporate bond market and stock market. The size of the financial support package was soon expanded to KRW 100 trillion, incorporating support for large companies. Of this amount KRW 58.3 trillion was used to directly support households and companies through specialized state banks and KRW

41.8 trillion was allocated to stabilize financial markets. To expand financial safety nets for vulnerable debtors including the provision of micro-loans and assistance for debt restructurings, a further KRW 35 trillion was added to the existing package of KRW 100 trillion. Furthermore, to address companies' temporary liquidity problems and prevent job losses in key industries such as the airline, shipping, shipbuilding, and automobile industries, a KRW 40 trillion fund for key industries was established in April 2020. This support was provided on condition that the supported companies maintained employment and that profits generated would be shared with the government if business was normalized.

In the meanwhile, the Korean government, represented by the Financial Services Commission (FSC), introduced a set of temporary deregulatory measures on the capital adequacy, liquidity and asset quality requirements of financial institutions to help boost their funding capacity amid the Covid-19 crisis.

9.4 Bank of Korea monetary and financial responses

9.4.1 Monetary policy

To cope with the decline in real activity, the Bank of Korea usually relies on two instruments, base rate cuts and adjustments to the Intermediated Lending Support Facility (ILSF). While base rate changes affect the economy indiscriminately across the whole sectors, the ILSF allows the Bank of Korea to conduct targeted monetary policy by ensuring the allocation of funds to selected sectors, such as SMEs. To this end, the Bank of Korea provides low-interest rate funds within the given ceilings to the commercial banks (Bank of Korea, 2017).

Amid the 2020 Covid-19 crisis, the Bank of Korea provided similarly speedy monetary responses. First, along with the implementation of an expansionary budgetary policy, the Bank of Korea cut its base rate in March by 50 basis points, from 1.25% to 0.75%. In May, the Bank of Korea again cut the base rate by 25 basis points to a historic low of 0.50%. These decisions reflected the large downward adjustment in the outlook for GDP and inflation, given the expectations that the economic effects of the Covid-19 pandemic would last longer. But it seems that they had only a limited stimulus effect on the Korean economy because, as Figure 9.5 shows, long-term interest rates did not drop significantly despite a rather big cut in the short-term interest rates.

Second, to support in particular the SMEs affected by Covid-19, the Bank of Korea raised the ceiling on the ILSF by KRW 10 trillion won, from KRW 25 trillion to KRW 43 trillion, to encourage commercial banks to increase their loans to SME companies. In addition, the Bank of Korea lowered the interest rate on support programs under the ILSF from 0.50–0.75% to 0.25% in order to strengthen the incentives for banks to lend to SMEs, alleviate the interest burden of SMEs, and improve their financial conditions.

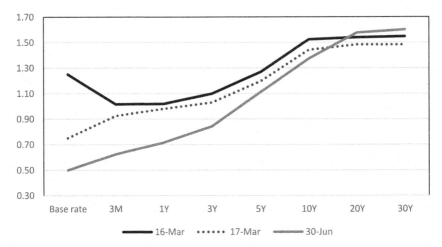

Figure 9.5 Movements in the yield curve. Source: ECOS, Bank of Korea. Note: The bold
   Blue line indicates the yield curve one day before the interest cut, the dotted line
   the yield curve after the cut by 0.5% and the grey line the yield curve 30 days
   after the cut by 0.75%.

It is now clear that the consequences of the Covid-19 crisis will have a
longer duration than foreseen when the BOK decided to cut its base rates.
Monetary policy will not be effective unless the Covid-19 pandemic is also
addressed. The goal of monetary policy is no longer to stem recession by
preemptive and brave monetary actions but to lessen the burden and hardships
of borrowers suffering from the Covid-19 pandemic. The easing of monetary
policy seems better when gradually implemented in tandem with the evolution
of social distancing and mobility restrictions. Furthermore, quantitative measures may be more effective by extending access to cheap credits to vulnerable
groups and sectors. The more aggressive extension of the ILSF seems more
desirable than base rate cuts.

9.4.2 Financial market stabilization policy

Apart from conducting monetary policy, central banks perform a vital role as
lenders of last resort (LOLR), providing liquidity support to individual institutions and financial markets, to ensure financial stability. In the wake of the
2008 global financial crisis, the LOLR function was strengthened, ending up
with the revision of the Bank of Korea Act that added financial stability as
another mandate of the Bank of Korea. In tandem with the Covid-19 crisis,
this function was further strengthened. Table 9.2 summarizes the measures
taken by the Bank of Korea to stabilize financial markets during the global
financial crisis and the Covid-19 crisis.

Table 9.2 Supply of liquidity for financial stability during the global financial crisis and Covid-19 crisis (unit: trillion KRW)

	2008 global financial crisis	*2020 Covid-19*
Liquidity provisions		
• RP Purchases	KRW 16.8 tn	KRW 19.4 tn
• Outright purchase of TBs	KRW 1.7 tn	KRW 11.0 tn
• RP purchases from non-bank financial companies		KRW 3.5 tn
Enhancing OMO Capacity	Expansion of the eligible collateral and institutions for the OMOs	Expansion of the eligible collateral and institutions for the OMOs
Contribution to Bond Market Stabilization Fund	KRW 2.1 tn (out of KRW 5 tn)	
Contribution to Bank Recapitalization Fund	KRW 3.3 tn (out of KRW 20 tn)	
Temporary Corporate Bond Backed Loan Facility		Up to KRW 10 tn (scheduled to be abolished in February 2021)
SPV Loans (to purchase lower-rated corporate bonds and CPs)		KRW 3.5 tn (out of total KRW 8 tn)
FX swap arrangement	$30 billion	$60 billion

Source: Compiled by the authors based on the Bank of Korea homepage (www.bok.or.kr).
Note: The figures in parenthesis indicate the ceilings committed to by the Bank of Korea

During the global financial crisis, the main instruments of the Bank of Korea to provide market liquidity and thus secure the stability of the financial system as a whole were the open market operations (OMO). The Bank of Korea (BOK) provided total liquidity of KRW 16.8 trillion through the programs of regular and periodic RP and KRW 1.7 trillion through the outright purchase of government bonds. Furthermore, it widened the scope of the collateral eligible for its open market operations, and greatly increased the number of counterpart securities firms for its RP transactions (provision of liquidity through OMOs could be useful to avoid the so-called stigma effect). This was the first time that the BOK fulfilled its LOLR function through extending its regular monetary policy operational framework. In collaboration with the government, the BOK also supplied KRW 2.1 trillion to financial institutions that subscribed to the Bond Market Stabilization Fund. Against a ceiling of KRW 5 trillion, the BOK committed to provide the necessary liquidity to the subscribed financial companies by purchasing government bonds and Monetary Stabilization bonds from them. However, the BOK had no direct link with the Fund, which was completely under the control of the Financial

Services Committee. Furthermore, in March 2009, the BOK provided KRW 3.3 trillion to the Bank Recapitalization Fund to increase banks' equity capital to facilitate the expansion of credit supply and the smooth implementation of corporate restructuring. More importantly, the Bank of Korea concluded a swap arrangement with the US Federal Reserve, amounting to $ 30 billion. This contributed enormously to stabilizing foreign exchange markets because there were always capital outflows behind the financial crises in Korea.

During the Covid-19 crisis, the Bank of Korea followed the previous measures adopted in 2008 by expanding the supply of Korean won through open market operations to secure the stability of financial and foreign exchange markets. Against this backdrop, the Bank of Korea strengthened the OMOs with the introduction of unlimited RP transactions. For instance, the Bank of Korea provided total liquidity KRW 19.4 trillion through the unlimited RP transactions and KRW 11 trillion through the outright purchase of government bonds. The Bank of Korea also supported non-bank financial companies, which was a newly introduced support tool. Financial markets which have grown larger, more complex and interconnected than ever before, require bolder and more comprehensive interventions to stabilize financial markets. These interventions were to a great extent due to the revision of the BOK Act in 2011 that added financial stability as an additional BOK mandate to its price stability mandate.

The unprecedented Covid-19 crisis required policy measures geared both towards supply as well as demand shocks. Korean companies were hit hard amid concerns of reduced corporate profits and credit rating downgrades. In particular, the shortage of liquidity was serious for companies in sectors such as the airline and travel sectors. The corporate bond credit spread widened significantly. For example, the spread between the government bonds and higher-rated corporate bonds (AA rated bonds), which remained at around 40 bp until the proliferation of Covid-19, increased to almost 80 bp, reflecting the increased bankruptcy risk in the corporate sectors (Bank of Korea, 2020).

Although the Korean banks are largely immune to the pandemic, the bankruptcies of these above-mentioned companies will have a negative spillover effect in the financial sector, threatening financial stability, which requires government and the Bank of Korea support for these companies as well. Thus, to specifically address this problem, the Bank of Korea introduced two new facilities, benchmarking the two facilities introduced by the Federal Reserve System in the US, the Primary Market Corporate Credit Facility and the Secondary Market Corporate Credit Facility.

The first facility was called the Corporate Bond-Backed Lending Facility (CBBLF). The CBBLF was designed to serve as a safety net for companies, banks, and non-bank financial institutions facing severe difficulties in raising funds due to the prolonged impact of Covid-19. It operates as a standing lending facility providing banks and non-bank financial institutions, including securities companies and insurance companies, with ready access to credit from the Bank of Korea when they post eligible corporate bonds as collateral. Article

80 (Credit to For-profit Enterprises) of the Bank of Korea Act, which provides for loans to non-bank financial institutions, was invoked for the second time since the 1997 currency crisis when loans were made to the Korea Securities Finance Corporation and Credit Management Fund. The ceiling for the facility is 10 trillion won. The interest rate is 0.85 percentage points over the yield on Korean Monetary Stabilization Bonds (182 days). The CBBLF is expected to contribute to stabilizing the corporate bond market and to improving funding conditions for financial institutions

Second, along with the Korean government, the Bank of Korea launched an SPV loan scheme to purchase lower-rated corporate bonds and commercial papers. This was to address the strong credit risk aversion in the financial markets with high credit spreads and ongoing financial difficulties for lower-credit-rating companies in the wake of the Covid-19 pandemic. It seems that this would substitute for the role of the Bond Market Stabilization Fund used in 2008. Thus, to ensure financial market stability, a total of KRW 10 trillion was directly invested in the SPV set up by government without any intermediation by banks. Purchases of corporate bonds and commercial paper are financed through the Bank of Korea's primary loans, while the Korea Development Bank, the government's bank, takes charge of subordinated loans. In particular, lower-rated corporate bonds and commercial paper were also included in the instruments to be purchased to ease credit risk aversion towards non-prime bonds and to ensure stability in the credit and securities markets. Figure 9.6 illustrates the detailed operation of this new instrument.

In general, these measures have been assessed as pertinent and successful, contributing to the mitigation of the impact on the financial markets of the Covid-19 pandemic. It is, however, noteworthy that if the difficulties of companies continue in circumstances where Covid-19 lasts for a long time, the problem of bad loans can become another big risk.

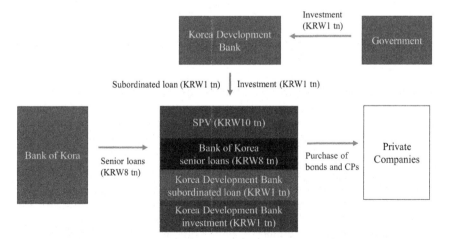

Figure 9.6 Financial structure of the SPV. Source: Bank of Korea (2020).

Third, like in the 2008 global financial crisis, the Bank of Korea has expanded the supply of foreign currency liquidity to secure the stability of foreign exchange markets during the pandemic crisis. In this regard, the Bank of Korea established a temporary bilateral currency swap arrangement (swap line) for the provision of US dollar liquidity in March 2020. It signed a $60 billion bilateral currency swap arrangement with the Federal Reserve System amid surging demand for US dollars in the global financial markets. This was double the amount of the swap it concluded with the Federal Reserve System during the 2008 global financial crisis, and it immediately stabilized the foreign exchange market. The Bank of Korea also raised the ceilings on the FX derivatives positions of commercial banks by 25% and lowered the FX liquidity coverage ratio by 10 percentage points. In addition, it temporarily lifted the levy on banks' non-deposit FX liabilities.

9.5 Conclusion

The Covid-19 pandemic certainly had a big impact on many countries, especially the US and European countries when they had to lockdown their economies. The pandemic has brought about the worst global economic recession since the Great Depression, exceeding the impact of the 2008 global financial crisis. In contrast, however, its impact on the Korean economy has turned out to be rather limited compared to the lockdown countries as there was no lockdown in Korea, even though there were restrictions on mobility and social distancing requirements. As long as the pandemic is contained and short-lived, it cannot be said that its economic impact will be greater than that of the 2008 global financial crisis.

No doubt, there is a strong need to respond against the pandemic, but it does not automatically justify the same policy response being taken by the Korean government and the Bank of Korea as during the global financial crisis. Preemptive and massively accommodative monetary policy has always been the international recommended norm in times of economic crisis. However, the pandemic economic experiences of the US and many European countries are different to those of Korea. Given these circumstances, the stimulation package provided for in Korea may not be optimal. As full economic recovery is difficult to expect until the defeat of the disease by vaccine, an excessively large and preemptive response to boost the economy does not seem urgent, at least for the Korean economy. The goal of fiscal and monetary policy should be focused more on alleviating and curing the social and economic losses and pains than on boosting the economy. At the end of 2020, there was a serious resurgence of cases in Korea, highlighting again the need to alleviate these economic and social pains.

From this perspective, the current fiscal and monetary responses of the Korean government and the Bank of Korea seem disproportionate in their size and content. On the budgetary policy side, in particular, the emergency disaster relief program targeting all Korean families should not have been an urgent policy. The Korean government has spent excessively, never questioning its role as savior of first resort rather than as savior of last resort, irrespective of the nature of the crisis occurring. As the Covid-19 pandemic has different consequences on different groups and sectors, a more targeted fiscal policy response would have been desirable. On the monetary policy side, the case is not that much different. A gradual easing of the money supply might have been better as the excessive asset market boom testifies. The accessibility and availability of funds is much more important than the cost of funds. Furthermore, financial firms were hardly affected compared to industrial sectors, particularly SMEs, the service sector, and airline companies hit directly by the Covid-19 pandemic. This requires more target-oriented monetary policy responses.

References

Baldwin and di Mauro (2020), Mitigating the COVID Economic Crisis: Act Fast and Do Whatever It Takes, March, Available at https://voxeu.org/content/mitigating-covid-economic-crisis-act-fast-and-do-whatever-it-takes

Bayer, C., B. Born, R. Luetticke, and G. J. Müller (2020), The Coronavirus Stimulus Package: How Large is the Transfer Multiplier? CEPR, DP14600, June.

Bank of Korea (2017), Monetary Policy in Korea.

Bank of Korea (2020), Monetary Policy Report, June, Available at www.bok.or.kr/eng/bbs/E0000628/list.do?menuNo=400215

Friedman, M. (1984), "Tyranny of the Status Quo." In David J. Theroux eds. *Politics and Tyranny: Lessons in Pursuit of Freedom*, Available at miltonfriedman.hoover.org/friedman_images/Collections/2016c21/1984Tyranny.pdf

IMF (2020a) World Economic Outlook: The Great Lockdown, April, Available at www.imf.org/en/Publications/WEO/Issues/2020/04/14/weo-april-2020

IMF (2020b), Fiscal Monitor: Policies for the Recovery, October, Available at www.imf.org/en/Publications/FM/Issues/2020/09/30/october-2020-fiscal-monitor

OECD (2020), Tax and Fiscal Policy in Response to the Coronavirus Crisis: Strengthening Confidence and Resilience, May, Available at www.oecd.org/coronavirus/policy-responses/tax-and-fiscal-policy-in-response-to-the-coronavirus-crisis-strengthening-confidence-and-resilience-60f640a8/

Park et al. (2020), "Results of Bank of Korea Macro-econometric Model (BOK20) Construction", Monthly Bulletin, Bank of Korea (In Korean).

10 The case of Singapore

Hwee Kwan Chow and Kong Weng Ho

10.1 Introduction

Singapore is a small densely populated island city-state with a population of 5.7 million and a total land area of 724.2 square kilometers. The country is also a global travel hub, and thus is susceptible to infectious disease outbreaks. Indeed, in 2003, the severe acute respiratory syndrome (SARS) infected 238 people and killed 33 over three months in Singapore. The SARS episode had an impact on Singapore's collective psychology, as the community experienced both the health and economic costs of the crisis. This resulted in a better appreciation of the threat from infections which led to the cohesive public response to the preventive measures minimizing virus transmissions during the Covid-19 outbreak.

Notable infection preparedness efforts were made post SARS (Lin et al., 2020). These included augmenting the infrastructure for outbreak management, such as stockpiling personal protective equipment, critical medications, and vaccines for up to six months supply requirements, as well as boosting intensive care and patient isolation facilities. For instance, a new 330-bed isolation building called the National Centre for Infectious Diseases was built at one of the major hospitals. Regular scenario-based simulation exercises are conducted and evaluated at public hospitals to train professional manpower in outbreak response. The government also adopted the Disease Outbreak Response System Condition (DORSCON), a color-coded framework to guide the extent of the public health response to different severity levels of threat.

While these preparations were critical in supporting Singapore's management of the Covid-19 outbreak, new lessons have emerged during the course of the pandemic and policy responses have been adjusted to the evolving situation. The following section traces the course of the Covid-19 pandemic crisis in Singapore and the attendant public health policy responses. This is followed by an assessment of the economic impact of the pandemic crisis on the Singapore economy in comparison to the impact of the global financial crisis (GFC). The monetary policy responses, the financial policies implemented by the central bank to ensure financial stability, as well as unprecedented fiscal policy responses taken by the government are then discussed. A summary

DOI: 10.4324/9781003153603-10

assessment of the effectiveness of these policies is provided in the conclusion section.

10.2 The Covid-19 outbreak and public health policy responses

The first case of Covid-19 disease in Singapore was diagnosed on 23 January 2020. Cognizant of the need to combat the Covid-19 crisis on multiple fronts, a multi-ministry taskforce was swiftly convened that provided recommendations in respect of government-wide coordinated responses as well as clear and consistent public communication on the disease. Information on anonymous Covid-19 positive cases was shared publicly through the Ministry of Health website while misinformation was quickly dispelled to prevent public anxiety and speculation. Public engagement with daily updates on the Covid-19 situation using social media, as well as the credibility of the specialists involved in the public information campaign, helped foster an environment of trust.

In early February 2020, the government raised the DORSCON risk assessment from yellow to orange which signaled that the virus threat was severe but that there was not widespread transmission. Measures to reduce the risk of infection were quickly adopted including travel restrictions, widespread testing, and quick quarantine/isolation policies. Patients with confirmed Covid-19 underwent detailed interviews and digital footprints were used to construct 14-day activity contact maps. Digital technology was effectively deployed for systemic and exhaustive contact tracing and isolation. The early intervention measures and cohesive public responses successfully controlled the community spread of the coronavirus in Singapore.

Nonetheless, there were Covid-19 outbreaks at several foreign workers dormitories by end March 2020. This was a consequence of the migrant worker population being initially overlooked by public health officials and this group provided the overwhelming majority of Covid-19 cases in Singapore. The epidemic curve in Figure 10.1 records the number of daily confirmed cases in Singapore with a breakdown into three categories, namely imported cases, dormitory resident cases, and community cases. On 20 April, a daily high of 1,426 cases was recorded among migrant workers. To contain the spread of the virus, mandatory quarantine was imposed and thorough testing was carried out. With the exception of healthy personnel in essential services, all foreign workers living in dormitories were told to stop work. The government created community health facilities for those who were at low risk, while those at higher risk were admitted to hospital.

Singapore was placed on "Circuit Breaker" measures that included stay-at-home orders and a *cordon sanitaire* from 7 April 2020 to 1 June 2020. In response to a significant decline in community infection rates, a three-phased approach to the safe resumption of activities was implemented from 2 June 2020. In phase one, only businesses that did not pose a high risk of transmission re-opened and individuals could leave home only for essential activities.

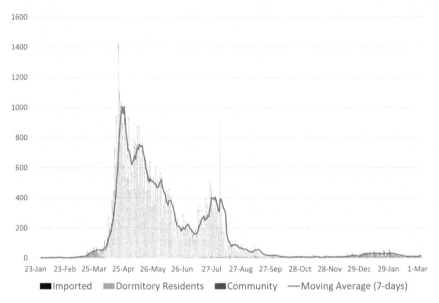

Figure 10.1 Epidemic curve: daily number of cases. Source: https://covidsitrep.moh.gov.sg/.

As the number of community transmission cases had remained low and stable, phase two started on 19 June 2020, with more businesses as well as sports and recreation facilities re-opening with safe management measures. All students fully returned to school in phase two. The migrant workers situation was turned around by 19 August when all dormitories were declared free of the virus.

To enable further easing of restrictions and the resumption of more activities and events, rapid antigen tests and better digital contact tracing tools were developed. By the end of 2020, Singapore is expected to have entered phase three whereby gatherings and events could resume with limited crowd sizes. As of 26 November 2020, there were approximately 58,102 confirmed cases out of a population of 5.7 million, with 28 fatalities (see https://covidsitrep .moh.gov.sg/).

10.3 Impact of Covid-19 pandemic on the Singapore economy

The small and very open nature of the Singapore economy means it is highly susceptible to a fallout in the global economy. Due to the pandemic crisis, real GDP in Singapore contracted on a year-on-year basis by 0.3 percent 13.2 percent and 5.8 percent in quarters one to three of 2020 respectively. In comparison during the GFC, Singapore posted flat growth of −0.1 percent in 2008Q3 and then contracted by 3.4 percent, 7.7 percent, and 1.2 percent in

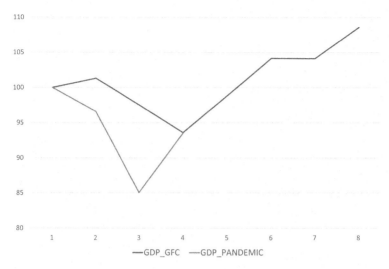

—GDP_GFC   —GDP_PANDEMIC

Figure 10.2 Comparison of Singapore's GDP index across the two crises. Source: Author's computation; data from the Department of Statistics, Singapore.

the following three quarters respectively before posting positive year-on-year growth again. Figure 10.2 is a plot of Singapore's GDP indexed to its value just before the onset of the GFC and the pandemic crisis, in 2008Q2 and 2019Q4 respectively.

We observe that the contraction in Singapore's economic output resulting from the pandemic crisis is more severe when compared to the impact from the global financial crisis. After all, domestic efforts to contain the coronavirus outbreak have led to both demand and supply side shocks to the economy.[1] It is also likely that the pandemic crisis will be more protracted than the GFC in view of the unfortunate resurgences in the number of Covid-19 cases experienced by various countries.

We next examine the performance of the major sectors of the Singapore economy during the Covid-19 crisis and the GFC. Table 10.1 records the three quarters changes in output associated with the two crises, i.e. we compare the changes in real GDP output between the first three quarters of 2020 and those of 2019 as well as the changes between 2008Q4–2009Q2 and 2007Q4–2008Q2. Two of the sectors that were severely affected by the pandemic crisis were (i) accommodation and food services and (ii) transportation and storage. These two sectors which shrank by 29.7 percent and 25.6 percent respectively, include the tourism-related and air transport industries that were

---

1 The implementation of circuit breaker measures requiring the closure of most physical workplace premises from 7 April to 1 June in order to safeguard public health, was initially estimated to lower Singapore's annual GDP by 2.2 percent (MTI, 2020).

Table 10.1 Performance of major economic sectors: year-on-year 3 quarters changes (%)

Industry (output change)	Pandemic	GFC
Overall GDP	−6.5	−4.1
Manufacturing	5.7	−12.2
Construction	−35.4	27.3
Wholesale & Retail Trade	−5.5	−7.5
Transportation & Storage	−25.6	−10.6
Accommodation & Food Services	−29.7	−5.5
Information & Communications	1.3	8.1
Finance & Insurance	4.7	−6.9
Business Services	−13.1	3.9

Source: Author's computation; data from the Department of Statistics, Singapore and the CEIC database.

hit by international travel restrictions. Hence, these sectors shrank by a much greater magnitude than during the GFC whose corresponding decreases were 5.5 percent and 10.6 percent respectively.

The construction industry is typically used for pump priming purposes during downturns so that that it can lend support to the economy, as was the case during the GFC when the sector expanded by 27.3 percent in output terms. However, the pandemic crisis dealt a severe blow to the construction industry, shrinking it by 35.4 percent due to manpower disruptions brought about by containment measures in response to the coronavirus outbreaks in the foreign worker dormitories. Meanwhile, the customer-facing retail trade and business services sector were badly affected by the closures of shops and physical workplaces. For instance, output in the business services sector fell by 13.1 percent during the pandemic but grew by 3.9 percent during the GFC.

While the financial services sector was unsurprisingly one of the poorer performing sectors during the GFC, shrinking by 6.9 percent, it served as a bright spot in the economy during the pandemic crisis. Indeed, the finance and insurance industry sector grew by 4.7 percent during the Covid-19 pandemic crisis helped by the ability to carry out financial activities remotely. This was facilitated by the central bank's push toward the adoption of digital technologies in finance, and the ongoing digital transformation in local banks that started long before the onset of the pandemic crisis. Likewise, the manufacturing sector expanded during the pandemic crisis but shrank during the GFC. The impact from the pandemic crisis is varied across different manufacturing industries, in part because exemptions were granted to those critical to local and global supply chains, such as to firms in the electronics and biomedical industries.

Turning to the labor market, total employment which stood at around 3.7 million at the end of 2019 shrank by 171,000 in the first three quarters of

2020.[2] This could be attributed to containment measures for curbing disease transmissions and was a much sharper adjustment in the labor market compared to the GFC. The economy experienced only a slowdown in job expansion in 2008Q4, with net job losses of 13,900 in the first half of 2009 and an expansion of the job market in the second half of 2009. Across industries, it is the services sector that has borne the brunt of job losses during the pandemic crisis, shedding 107,200 jobs in the first three quarters of 2020 with the main drag coming from the accommodation and food services industry. This is compounded by the 36,600 and 26,900 job losses over the same period in the construction and manufacturing sectors respectively. By contrast, in the three quarters from 2008Q4 to 2009Q2, employment grew in the services and construction sectors by 30,700 and 23,000 respectively, offsetting the 45,500 job losses in the manufacturing sector during the GFC.

10.4 Easing the monetary policy stance

Singapore uses the exchange rate instead of the usual benchmark interest rate as a monetary policy operating instrument. This is a reflection of the openness of the Singapore economy to trade and capital flows. Hence, monetary policy implementation involves the management of the Singapore Dollar against an undisclosed trade-weighted basket of currencies denoted as S$NEER (Chow, 2007). Adjustments to the monetary policy stance could take the form of a single or a combination of changes to the level of the S$NEER, the slope of its appreciation path and the width of the policy band. For instance, the Monetary Authority of Singapore (MAS) could ease the monetary policy stance by lowering the level at which the policy band is centered and/or reducing the slope of the appreciation path of the policy band. The width of the band can be widened when there is excessive volatility in the international foreign exchange markets.

MAS typically issues its monetary policy statements in April and October each year in its half-yearly monetary policy cycle. Meanwhile, interest rates in Singapore are endogenous and follow global interest rates. Figures 10.2a and 10.2b provide the time plots of the S$NEER around the pandemic crisis and the GFC periods, i.e., from 3 May 2019 to 30 October 2020 and 4 January 2008 to 26 June 2009 respectively. The S$NEER is a weekly average series, indexed at 100 to the average for the week ending 8th January 1999. The three vertical lines in each figure mark the two monetary policy cycles immediately before and after the onset of the relevant crisis.

We observe from Figure 10.3a that the S$NEER started to plunge in late January 2020 with news of the outbreak of coronavirus in Wuhan, China. The S$NEER fell by about 2 percent over February and March but has stabilized

---

2 The employment data in this paragraph are extracted from the Singapore Department of Statistics website.

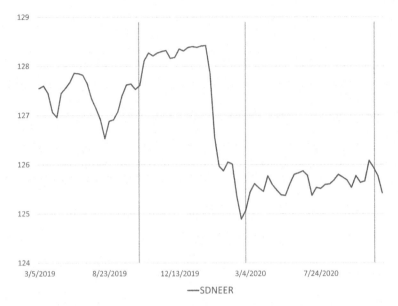

Figure 10.3a Covid19 pandemic crisis

since then. In its end–March 2020 monetary policy statement, MAS announced a re-centering of the policy band to the then-prevailing lower level as well as a reduction in the slope of the appreciation path to 0 percent. However, the width of the band was kept the same. This is the first time that both the level and slope of the policy band were adjusted downward simultaneously.

The accommodative monetary policy stance was maintained in the subsequent policy cycle. As announced in the 14 October 2020 monetary policy statement, there was no change to the level, slope, and width of the policy band.[3] This stance reflects the expectations of weak growth momentum and low core inflation going forward. Following a fall in the US$ LIBOR, the domestic three-month interbank rate (S$ SIBOR) declined from 1.8 percent in October 2019 to about 1.0 percent as of late March 2020; and fell further to 0.4 percent in October 2020.

We see from Figure 10.3b that the S$NEER also weakened in the second half of 2008. In comparison to the pandemic crisis, the depreciation was of a slightly smaller magnitude and spread more gradually over more than three months. As announced in the October 2008 monetary policy statement, MAS reduced the slope of the appreciation path to 0 percent but there was no re-centering of the policy band. It was only in the subsequent monetary

---

3 Net purchase of foreign exchange from intervention operations was US$44.4 billion from 1 January 2020 to 30 June 2020, higher than the US$29.9 billion from 1 July 2019 to 31 December 2019 (see www.mas.gov.sg/statistics/reserve-statistics/foreign-exchange-operations).

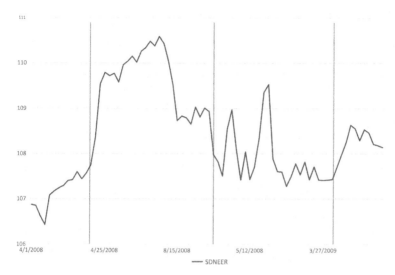

Figure 10.3b Global financial crisis. Data source: www.mas.gov.sg/statistics/exchange-rates.

policy statement in April 2009 that the S$NEER was re-centered at the then-prevailing lower level while the slope of the policy band was unchanged. No adjustments were made to the width of the band in both cycles. Meanwhile, the S$ SIBOR rate fell from 1.9 percent in September 2008 to 0.7 percent in March 2009 in tandem with the easing of global interest rates.

As the speed of the weakening of the S$NEER is faster in the pandemic crisis vis-à-vis the GFC, a stronger monetary policy response during the pandemic crisis was called for. Hence, both the level and slope of the policy band were adjusted downward simultaneously. Nonetheless, as explicitly stated in the April 2020 monetary policy statement,[4] "This stable monetary policy stance also reflects the primary role of fiscal policy in mitigating the economic impact of COVID-19". By contrast, reliance on a fiscal response to the global financial crisis was not mentioned in the corresponding monetary policy statements.

10.5 Central Bank's financial policies

While the global financial crisis can be characterized as a financial shock that adversely affected the real sector, the pandemic crisis is a shock that directly hits the real sector, from which the authorities try to insulate the financial sector. As detailed on its website (MAS, 2020a), MAS offered the following slew of support measures in response to the Covid-19 pandemic crisis.

---

4 See the April 2020 monetary policy statement, paragraph 17, available at www.mas.gov.sg/news/monetary-policy-statements/2020/mas-monetary-policy-statement-30mar20.

10.5.1 Reinforcing financial stability

The central bank conducted money market operations to provide ample liquidity in the banking system to ensure the funding markets functioned smoothly.[5] A new MAS SGD Term Facility was established on 28 September 2020 to complement the existing overnight MAS Standing Facility and to serve as a liquidity backstop. This new facility offers SGD funds in 1-month and 3-month tenors and accepts more forms of collateral. The broadened collateral pool includes cash and investment-grade (BBB-grade and above) debt securities issued by governments, central banks, public sector entities, and non-financial corporations, denominated in SGD and G10 currencies. Furthermore, residential property loans are accepted as collateral for domestic systemically important banks. MAS raised the asset encumbrance limit imposed on locally incorporated banks from then-current 4 percent to 10 percent, so that they can have greater leeway in pledging residential property loans as collateral to access funding.

In March 2020, MAS entered into a USD 60 billion swap line arrangement with the US Federal Reserve until 30 September 2020. This was later extended to expire on 31 March 2021. The new MAS USD facility provided US dollar liquidity to financial institutions. The eligible collateral pool at this facility was expanded to a wider range of cash and debt securities including investment-grade securities in SGD and major currencies.

10.5.2 Helping individuals reduce debt obligation

MAS has partnered with financial institutions to provide a package of relief measures that support individuals facing financial difficulties due to the coronavirus pandemic. These measures included deferring or extending repayment of loans; lowering interest rates on personal unsecured credit; easier refinancing of investment property loans; and waiving fall-below bank service fees. In October 2020, these measures were extended so that individuals with difficulties resuming full repayments of property loans can apply to reduce installment payments to 60 percent of their monthly installments. These measures were well-received: for instance, the deferment of residential property loans by individuals amounted to nearly S$20 billion by end August 2020 (MAS, 2020b).

10.5.3 Easing business cashflow constraints

The central bank also worked with the financial industry to offer a package of measures to ease the financial strain on small and medium enterprises (SMEs) facing temporary cashflow constraints. The package included lower short-term repayment obligations for secured loans; and assistance with insurance

---

5 See Chow and Wong (2020) for a discussion on the determinants of the amount of liquidity required in the Singapore banking system.

premium payments. The support measures were extended in October to provide eligible SMEs with the option of deferring 80 percent of principal payments on secured loans.

In addition, MAS established a new Singapore dollar facility with the aim of lowering the cost of loans to SMEs. The facility offered low-cost funding at 0.1 percent p.a. for a 2-year tenor until 30 September 2021 to participating finance institutions, in order to support their lending under *Enterprise Singapore* (ESG)'s Enhanced Enterprise Financing Scheme comprising the SME Working Capital Loan and Temporary Bridging Loan Program. As stated in the MAS 12 October 2020 media release:[6]

> Since its introduction in April 2020, the Facility has disbursed a total of S$5.7 billion to eligible financial institutions in support of their lending to companies under the ESG Loan Schemes. Taken together, the Government's risk sharing through the ESG Loan Schemes and MAS' lower-cost funding through the Facility have helped to lower borrowing costs for local enterprises to a range of 1.5% to 3.0% per annum under the TBLP, from 6% or more for other unsecured working capital loans.

10.5.4 Enabling financial institutions to face pandemic challenges

The central bank made adjustments to regulatory and supervisory protocols to focus the financial sector on the pandemic priorities. These included adjusting capital and liquidity requirements for banks; setting accounting loan loss allowances; and extending report timelines etc. MAS encouraged banks and finance companies incorporated in Singapore to have an upper limit on their total dividends per share for FY2020 at 60 percent of 2019 levels. Furthermore, these financial institutions were urged to provide shareholders with the option of receiving the dividends in scrip in lieu of cash. Such "pre-emptive" measures were aimed at boosting the financial institutions' ability to support the credit needs of firms and individuals should the Covid-19 crisis be prolonged. In addition, MAS issued guidance and advice on operational, technological and cyber risks to safeguard the management and operational resilience of the financial sector.

10.5.5 Enabling financial and Fintech sectors to build long-term capabilities

Apart from short-term measures to face pandemic challenges, MAS offered a S$125 million support package to financial institutions and Fintech firms to enhance long-term skills and capability building. Apart from supporting employee training and manpower costs, this included a digital acceleration

---

6 See media release dated 12 October 2020, paragraph 3, available at www.mas.gov.sg/news/media -releases/2020/mas-extends-facility-to-support-lending-by-banks-and-finance-companies-to-smes.

grant for the adoption of digital solutions by smaller financial institutions and Fintech firms, as well as supporting Fintech firms' access to digital tools. Another S$35 million productivity solutions grant was provided to the financial services sector that co-funds the adoption of digital solutions by smaller financial institutions for regulatory reporting.

In view of the differing nature of the crisis, financial policies in response to the GFC were more focused on confidence building measures. For instance, MAS announced in October 2008 a blanket guarantee (until end 2010) on deposits of individuals and non-bank customers in financial institutions holding MAS licenses (Sharma, 2013). The assurance given by MAS on deposits during the GFC was to ensure the stability of banks and to eschew bank runs. To ensure businesses had access to credit, the government also took on a significant share of bank lending risks through the Special Risk-Sharing Initiative. There were also similar measures undertaken in both crises. For instance, MAS maintained a higher level of liquidity in the banking system through its money market operations during the GFC, when there was a heightening of frictional liquidity demand. In response to the global USD funding pressure, MAS also opened a swap facility with the US Federal Reserve to facilitate USD funding for financial institutions but in the lower amount of USD 30 billion (MAS, 2009).

10.6 Government fiscal policies

Covid-19 was an unexpected public health crisis with severe economic consequences, which were also partly the consequence of policy responses, such as the circuit breaker in Singapore from 7 April to 1 June 2020, effectively a partial lockdown allowing only essential services to operate. The government has responded with fiscal support corresponding to the increasing impact of the pandemic, initially focusing on immediate assistance in respect of jobs, businesses, and households, and later refined to providing more sector-specific assistance as the situation evolved with more detailed information available, and to preparing for post-pandemic recovery and growth, as outlined in the four unprecedented consecutive Budgets and two Ministerial Statements by the Minister of Finance from February to October 2020. The outline of the key fiscal responses in the four Budgets and two Ministerial Statements are as follows.

10.6.1 Unity Budget

The Unity Budget (Heng, 2020a) was delivered on 18 February 2020 when the Covid-19 outbreak started to impact Singapore, especially the aviation and tourism industries, as well as disrupting supply chains. A total of S$6.4b was allocated to tackle the immediate challenges: S$800m to support the frontline agencies in fighting and containing the outbreak, a Stabilization and Support Package, amounting to S$4b, to assist workers and businesses, and a Care and Support Package, amounting to S$1.6b, to support households.

The Jobs Support Scheme (JSS) was introduced, offsetting 8 percent of the wages of 1.9m citizen and permanent resident employees, up to a maximum S$3,600 monthly wage cap for three months, amounting to S$1.3b. The Wage Credit Scheme was enhanced to support wage increases for Singaporean workers, with a higher wage ceiling at S$5,000, and higher co-funding levels, amounting to S$1.1b, benefiting 700,000 Singaporean employees. A 25 percent Corporate Income Tax Rebate was granted for the financial year 2020, capped at S$15,000 per company, at a cost of about S$400m.

Sector-Specific Assistance was introduced for sectors affected more severely: 30 percent property tax rebate for licensed hotels, serviced apartments, and Meetings, Incentives, Conventions and Exhibitions (MICE) venues; 15 percent property tax rebate for Changi Airport; one month rental waiver to stallholders in hawker centers and markets; half-month rental wavier to commercial tenants of Other Government Agencies, such as the Housing Development Board (HDB). The planned Goods and Services Tax (GST) rate increase will not take effect in 2021, to alleviate concerns of businesses and households over operating costs and the cost of living.

Apart from the immediate fiscal responses to deal with the outbreak, the Transformation and Growth programs are focused on the long-term economic and human capital development of Singapore, amounting to S$8.3b over the next three years. This is to enable stronger partnerships globally and in Singapore, to deepen enterprise capabilities via innovation, digitalization, and overseas ventures, and to develop people via tertiary education before employment, upskilling during working years, mid-career support, and life-long learning.

10.6.2 Resilience Budget

As the outbreak escalated further after the Unity Budget Statement, further fiscal responses were needed as public health measures to contain the outbreak caused further economic hardship impacting severely the aviation and tourism sectors, even globally, and the Resilience Budget (Heng, 2020b) was delivered on 26 March 2020, to enhance and extend the schemes introduced in the Unity Budget, with an additional outlay of S$48.4b, and the in-principle support from the President to draw up to S$17b from Singapore's reserves.

The JSS was enhanced to increase the co-funding of wages from 8 percent to 25 percent for most sectors, with higher levels of 50 percent for the food services sector, and 75 percent for the aviation and tourism sectors. The monthly qualifying wage ceiling was raised from S$3,600 to S$4,600. The JSS was extended until the end of 2020. With these enhancements and extensions, a total of S$15.1b was available to benefit the 1.9 million citizen and permanent resident employees under the JSS. The Wage Credit Scheme (WCS) will be enhanced with additional S$500m funding, from September to end-June 2021.

The self-employed were supported: the Self-Employed Person Training Support Scheme saw the training allowance raised from S$7.50 to S$10 per hour, and extended to December 2020, costing a total of S$48m. The Self-Employed Person Income Relief Scheme (SIRS) provides S$1,000 a month for a period of nine months for eligible self-employed, amounting to a total of S$1.2b. For lower-income workers, the Workfare Special Payment was enhanced to S$3,000 in cash for each eligible worker. The SGUnited Traineeships and SGUnited Jobs programs were introduced to create 8,000 traineeships and 10,000 jobs.

The unemployed will be supported by allowing more flexibility in their applications for ComCare assistance, and a Temporary Relief Fund will be set up in April 2021 to provide them with immediate financial assistance. Furthermore, the Covid-19 Support Grant was introduced, from May to September, to help workers who become unemployed due to the pandemic, all amounting to a total of S$145m in support for the unemployed.

The Care and Support Package announced in the Unity Budget will be enhanced, amounting to a total of S$4.6b: increased cash payouts to adult Singaporeans, ranging from S$300 to S$900; additional cash payouts to each Singaporean parent with at least one young Singaporean child, from S$100 to S$300; grocery vouchers tripled and given to needy Singaporeans amounting to S$300 in 2020 and S$100 in 2021; grants given to Self-Help Groups to be doubled to S$20m over two years and increased additional grants given to Community Development Councils (CDCs) amounting to S$75m.

Greater flexibility on fees and loans will be exercised by the government: freezing all government fees and charges from 1 April 2020 to 31 March 2021; suspending all loan repayment and interest charges of student loans for 1 year, from 1 June 2020 to 31 May 2021. There will be an automatic deferment of income tax payments for companies and the self-employed, for three months. The Property Tax Rebate will be enhanced: qualifying commercial properties hit badly by Covid-19 will pay no Property Tax for 2020; other non-residential properties affected by Covid-19 will enjoy a Property Tax Rebate of 30 percent for 2020.

The Enterprise Financing Scheme (EFS) – SME Working Capital Loan program will be enhanced, and the Temporary Bridging Loan program (TBLP) was introduced: the enhanced EFS-Trade Loans program will see the maximum loan quantum increased from S$5m to S$10m and the government's risk-share increased from 70 percent to 80 percent; the subsidy for Loan Insurance Schemes will be increased from 50 percent to 80 percent; the TBLP will be expanded to all sectors, with the maximum support loan increased from S$1m to S$5m; additional support beyond TBLP via EFS-SME Working Capital Loans will be made available, with the maximum loan quantum increased from S$600k to S$1m; the government will work with Participating Financial Institutions to defer capital payments for one year on the EFS-Working Capital Loans and the TBLP loans when businesses make such requests. A loan capital of S$20b will be set aside in the Resilience Budget.

Sector-Specific Support will be enhanced: an additional S$350m will enhance the aviation support package to fund rebates, and rental relief;

S$90m will be set aside to assist the tourism sector; a Point-to-Point Support Package for taxi and private hire car (PHC) drivers will be enhanced and extended, at a cost of S$95m; eligible drivers will continue to receive the Special Relief Fund payments of S$300 per vehicle per month until end-September; a one-year road tax rebate and a six-month waiver of parking charges at government-managed parking facilities for private bus owners will be introduced, at a cost of S$23m; the arts and culture sector will receive an additional $55m support package in respect of job retention, upskilling & digitalization.

The following schemes will help build economic resilience: the SG Together Enhancing Enterprise Resilience (STEER) program where for every S$2 raised by Trade Associations and Chambers (TACs) or business groups for qualifying initiatives, the government will provide S$1, a doubling of the previous matching rate; the SMEs Go Digital program, the Productivity Solutions Grant (PSG) and the Enterprise Development Grant (EDG) programs have been enhanced and extended until Dec 2020; higher course fee subsidies and absentee payroll up to 90 percent for the aviation, tourism, food services, and retail trade sectors, until June 2020; enhanced training support will be extended to the arts and culture and land transport sectors, starting from 1 April 2020; the 90 percent absentee payroll rates will be extended to all employers, to provide additional cash flow relief when they send their workers for training, from 1 May 2020; the duration of enhancements to cover eligible courses will be extended, starting before 1 January 2021; and Singaporeans may use the base S$500 Skills Future Credit Top-up for courses, starting from 1 April 2020, ahead of the initial date in October 2020.

10.6.3 Solidarity Budget

By the first week of April 2020, the outbreak became a pandemic, and local transmissions in Singapore had increased, triggering a circuit breaker, which was a partial lockdown, allowing only essential services to continue, starting 7 April 200 for four weeks, but it was extended subsequently to 1 June 2020. With heightened public health measures and more restricted economic activities, the Solidarity Budget (Heng, 2020c) was delivered on 6 April 2020 to save jobs and protect livelihoods, to help businesses preserve their capacity and capabilities, and to help households tide over during the circuit breaker, with a total fiscal outlay of S$5.1b.

The Jobs Support Scheme will be further enhanced: there will be higher subsidy rates for all firms: 75 percent of gross monthly wages, for the first S$4,600 of wages paid in April; the first JSS payout was brought forward from May to April 2020. The Foreign Worker Levy was waived for the month of April, and a Foreign Worker Levy Rebate of $750 for each work permit or S pass holder, based on previous levies paid in 2020, will be provided to employers. The rental waiver for industrial, office and agricultural tenants of government agencies will be increased from 0.5 month to 1 month.

The government's risk share of loans made under the Temporary Bridging Loan, the Enterprise Financing Scheme – SME Working Capital Loan, and the Enterprise Financing Scheme – Trade Loan programs will be increased from 80 percent to 90 percent for loans initiated from 8 April 2020 until 31 March 2021. The SIRS will be extended automatically to also include the self-employed who earn a small income from employment, and the current Annual Value threshold will be raised from S$13,000 to S$21,000 so that more self-employed may benefit from the scheme. Households will receive a Solidarity Payment of S$600, increased from S$300 under the Care and Support Package, to be paid starting the middle of April; other cash payouts under the Care and Support Package were brought forward to June instead of August.

10.6.4 Fortitude Budget

The pandemic continued to drag down the global economy, affecting Singapore adversely with a rising unemployment rate amid the circuit breaker, and the Fortitude Budget (Heng, 2020d) was delivered on 26 May 2020 to focus on job protection and business transformation, with additional supports for households, the community, and frontline agencies to combat the evolving health crisis, amounting to a total fiscal outlay of S$33b. Together with the earlier Unity Budget, Resilience Budget, and Solidarity Budget, the four budgets had allocations totaling S$92.9b, close to 20 percent of Singapore's GDP, to support businesses and the people of Singapore. The Fortitude Budget will be funded out of reserves, with in-principle support from the President, for a further draw of S$31 billion. In the earlier Resilience and Solidarity Budgets, the President gave approval to draw S$21 billion from reserves.

Focusing on jobs, the Fortitude Budget extended the JSS from a seven-month support scheme by a further month, with the additional support to be paid in October 2020, continued the wage subsidy rate at 75 percent until August 2020 for firms which could not resume operations after the end of circuit breaker (from 7 April to 1 June), refined the classification of some firms in different JSS tiers so that they would receive increased support from 25 percent to either 50 percent or 75 percent. In total, these JSS enhancements will cost S$2.9b, and the JSS in total will provide supports amounting to S$23.5b for ten months.

The Foreign Worker Levy Waiver was extended for up to two months, with a 100 percent waiver in June, and 50 percent in July. The Foreign Worker Levy Rebate was S$750 in June, and S$375 in July. The planned hike in CPF contribution rates for senior workers was deferred by one year, from 1 January 2021 to 1 January 2022. To assist SMEs, a cash grant will be provided to offset the rental costs of SME tenants, to be disbursed automatically from end-July through the property owner. This cash grant for SMEs will cost about S$2b. Commercial tenants and hawkers using government properties will receive four months of rental waivers, increased from two months; industrial, office, and agricultural tenants of government agencies will receive two months of rental waivers, an increase of one month.

To support promising start-ups, the Fortitude Budget will set aside S$285 million to catalyze and crowd in at least a matching sum of S$285 million from private investments, additional to the S$300m under the Unity Budget for deep-tech start-ups under the Startup SG Equity program. More than $500 million will be allocated to support businesses in respect of digital transformation: bonuses of S$300 per month over five months to encourage stallholders in hawker centers, wet markets, coffee shops, and industrial canteens to use e-payments; Digital Resilience Bonuses of up to S$5,000 for eligible firms adopting PayNow Corporate and e-invoicing, as well as for business processes or e-commerce solutions, and other advanced solutions.

The SGUnited Jobs and Skills Package was expanded, creating more than 40,000 job opportunities (15,000 from the public sector and 25,000 from businesses), and about 25,000 traineeship positions in 2020 (21,000 from the SGUnited Traineeships program, 4,000 places under a new SGUnited Mid-Career Traineeships scheme). A new SGUnited Skills program, progressively rolled out in July 2020, expanded training capacity for about 30,000 job seekers in 2020, giving them a training allowance of S$1,200 per month during the course of their training. Employers will receive incentives to hire citizen and permanent resident workers who complete eligible traineeship and training schemes: for eligible workers aged 40 and above, a doubling of the incentive to cover 40 percent of their salary over six months, capped at S$12,000 in total; for eligible workers under 40, this incentive will cover 20 percent of their monthly salary over six months, capped at S$6,000 in total. In total, the SGUnited Jobs and Skills Package will account for S$2 billion in 2020.

The Fortitude Budget will set aside another S$800 million for the Covid-19 Support Grant program for those who lost their jobs, or were placed on no-pay leave, due to Covid-19. The U-Save rebates will be doubled through a one-off GST Voucher – U-Save Special Payment, for eligible HDB households. A one-off S$100 Solidarity Utilities Credit will be given to each household with at least one Singapore citizen, to be credited in the July or August utilities bill.

10.6.5 Two Ministerial Statements

By the middle of August 2020, Covid-19 in Singapore was under control, but the global economy remained weak, and two Ministerial Statements were delivered on 17 August 2020 and 5 October 2020 outlining schemes to support jobs (especially for sectors worse hit by the pandemic), to create jobs, and to prepare Singapore for post-pandemic growth.

The Ministerial Statement (Heng, 2020e) on 17 August extended the JSS for up to seven additional months from September 2020 to March 2021: 50 percent wage subsidy for the aerospace, aviation, and tourism sectors, for seven more months; 50 percent wage subsidy for the environmental building sector, for two more months, followed by a 30 percent wage subsidy for the subsequent five months; 30 percent wage subsidy for the arts and entertainment, food services, land transport, marine and offshore, and retail sectors for an additional seven months; for the large majority of the remaining sectors, 10 percent support for seven further months; for the biomedical sciences, financial services, and ICT sectors, 10 percent wage support for four additional months. This extension will provide most businesses with wage support ranging from 10 percent to 75 percent for 17 months.

The Jobs Growth Incentive (JGI) program was introduced in the Ministerial Statement (2020e) on 17 August, a S$1b program to support new hires of citizen and permanent resident workers over the following six months: 24 SGUnited Jobs and Skills Centers will be set up in the heartlands; the government will provide co-payments of 25 percent (50 percent for new hires aged 40 and above) of salaries for one year, subject to a cap. An additional S$187m will be used to extend support measures in the Enhanced Aviation Support Package up to March 2021. The government will set aside S$320 million for tourism credits called SingapoRediscovers Vouchers. The Startup SG Founder program will be enhanced, with an additional S$150m to enhance the program in phases, providing startup capital grants and mentorship.

In the second Ministerial Statement (Heng, 2020f) delivered on 5 October 2020, the Minister of Finance outlined the steps involved in the safe re-opening of the economy and social activities in terms of public health measures (securing safe and effective vaccines, enhancing Polymerase Chain Reaction (PCR) testing capability, enhancing contact tracing via the Trace Together app and tokens and the SafeEntry program, and enhancing the safe management of social activities) and outlining the envisioned roadmap for the future of Singapore (inclusive and resilient society, dynamic and growing economy).

The Enhanced Training Support Package (ETSP) will be extended for another six months, until 30 June 2021, to provide enhanced course fee subsidies for firms in the hardest-hit sectors. It will be extended to include the marine and offshore sector, and the absentee payroll rates will be lowered to 80 percent from January 2021, capped at S$7.50 per hour, in view of the gradual economic recovery. The JGI program will provide a higher tier (50 percent) of wage support to all Persons with Disabilities, applicable for new hires from September 2020 to February 2021. Various Capability Building grant programs will be enhanced or extended: the Market Readiness Assistance Grant, the Productivity Solutions Grant, the Enterprise Development Grant, and the PACT programs. The TBLP will be extended for six months, until September 2021, at reduced levels. On top of the Baby Bonus Cash Gift, there will be an additional one-off support for newborns, providing eligible parents with up to S$10,000 in benefits.

The measures announced in the two Ministerial Statements were partially funded by reallocations from the four earlier Budgets.

10.6.6 Immediate relief and long-term strategies

The four special Covid-19 Budgets and two Ministerial Statements programs are holistic and address not just the immediate needs of various sectors and households but also the long-term strategies of the nation, covering the community and families, workers and businesses, economic transformation and preparation for growth post-pandemic, and long-term security related to climate change, aging population, all backed up by Singapore's reserves – a hugely beneficial strategic asset. Close to S$100 billion or about 20 percent of Singapore's GDP has been committed to support Singaporeans, and the overall budget deficit for 2020 is S$74.2 billion; up to S$52 billion is planned to be draw from accumulated national reserves. In comparison, the total fiscal outlay in response to the GFC was S$20.5b, with S$4.9b drawn from national reserves.

The government has been quick and decisive in implementing public health measures, such as the circuit breaker, which was a partial lockdown allowing only essential services to operate, despite its negative impact on the economy. The moving of migrant workers to isolation centers with healthcare facilities away from hospitals, and border controls (such as compulsory Stay Home Notices and quarantine requirements for returning Singaporean residents and visitors) are critical measures to contain the spread of the virus in the community, contributing to a possible earlier economic recovery, which will be subject to the pace of the global recovery. Without effective containment measures, fiscal measures will be futile in the longer run with recurring subsequent waves of infection.

Fiscal responses were much focused on job protection at the height of the crisis, but the JSS started with only an 8 percent wage subsidy rate, which was quickly adjusted upward when the severe economic impact was felt, and further enhancements and extensions for specific sectors, such as aviation and tourism sectors were announced and implemented in a timely manner. The unprecedented and consecutive Budgets and Ministerial Statements programs demonstrated a timely assessment of the evolving situation, with the updating and fine-tuning of appropriate responses with the assistance of feedback from the community, businesses and the Labour Movement led by the National Trade Union Congress (NTUC), the efficient operation of government services, and perhaps most importantly, the sufficiency of national reserves available to combat the pandemic.

The pandemic revealed the urgent need for and hastened the technological transformation of the economy and society. When the Covid-19 began to stabilize in Singapore, the most recent Ministerial Statement (Heng, 2020f) envisioned a post-pandemic Singapore as an inclusive and resilient society, and as a Global-Asia node of technology, innovation, and enterprise; in other words, the post-pandemic or long-term fiscal strategies need to tackle potentially diverse or unequal recoveries of different groups and to connect with the growth engines in Southeast Asia.

10.6.7 Fiscal prudence and sustainability

The unprecedented fiscal outlay for immediate relief and the continued strategic preparation for the future are possible because of fiscal prudence, the availability and sufficiency of national reserves, without the need of borrowing heavily and passing on the financial debt burden to future generations. Fiscal prudence is built into the Constitution of the Republic of Singapore[7] which restricts governments in power from drawing upon reserves accumulated by previous governments, implying that deficits, if any, have to be balanced by surpluses accumulated by governments during their lifetime in government, which is typically a five-year term, unless altered with the consent of both the Parliament and the President, such as during the GFC and the current pandemic. As a result, together with economic growth, the fiscal rules in the Constitution are biased toward budget surpluses, which are accumulated as national reserves.

The national reserves of Singapore serve three objectives:[8] a buffer against crises, an investment income stream to finance part of the annual government budget, and as an asset with firepower capable of maintaining confidence in Singapore's exchange rate-centered monetary policy. The national reserves are managed by the Monetary Authority of Singapore, the Government of Singapore Investment Corporation (GIC), and Temasek Holdings, each investing in different funds. MAS manages the Official Foreign Reserves (OFR) and has been habitually accumulating foreign assets given the positive net savings of Singapore and persistent capital inflows. Being a central bank, MAS is the most conservative of the three investment arms, with a significant proportion of its portfolio invested in liquid financial market instruments.

GIC is a professional fund management organization that manages the government's foreign assets, with a globally diversified portfolio spread across various asset classes, mainly in public markets, with a smaller component in alternative investments, such as private equity and real estate. Its objective is to achieve good long-term returns to preserve and enhance the international purchasing power of the national reserves; GIC achieved an annualized 20-year real rate of return of 2.7 percent up to the year ended 31 March 2020.[9] Temasek Holdings, an investment company wholly owned by the government of Singapore, manages its investments on commercial principles and aims to maximize shareholder value over the long term, with a significant portion of its portfolio invested in Singapore (24 percent), and about 66 percent in Asia. Temasek Holdings has achieved an annualized shareholder return of 14 percent since its inception in 1974.[10]

It is crucial that the two investment agencies, namely GIC and Temasek Holdings, are managed by professional investors, making investment decisions independent of the government, and yielding good returns to the national

---

7 See Article 147, Article 148G, and Article 148I of the Constitution of the Republic of Singapore: retrieved from https://sso.agc.gov.sg/Act/CONS1963.
8 See Menon (2019).
9 See GIC (2020).
10 See Temasek (2020).

reserves. The total amount of the national reserves is not revealed as they are strategic assets to defend Singapore at times of crisis or speculative attacks on the Singapore Dollar. As of 31 March 2020, the OFR managed by MAS amounted to S$397 billion and the size of Temasek's portfolio was S$306 billion.[11] The GIC portfolio is valued significantly above US$100 billion but the exact figure is not disclosed. The net investment returns from MAS, GIC, and Temasek Holdings partially but significantly contribute to the annual budget of the government: the Constitution allows up to 50 percent of the expected long-term real returns from the net assets to become part of the budget revenues through the Net Investment Returns Contribution (NIRC).[12] The investment returns alleviate the pressure of raising taxes on the one hand and contribute to the further accumulation of reserves on the other hand.

At the same time, there are regular top-ups of various funds, such as the GST Voucher Fund (top-up of S$6b in the 2020 Budget), Coastal and Flood Protection Fund (top-up of S$5b), National Research Fund (top-up of S$2b), Skills Development Fund (top-up of S$2b), ElderCare Fund (top-up of S$750m), Special Employment Credit Fund (top-up of S$700m), and the Community Care Endowment Fund (top-up of S$500m) as preparations for key commitments in social spending and infrastructure investment for the future (Heng, 2020a). Furthermore, Singapore's national pension fund – the Central Provident Fund (CPF) – is a compulsory self-funding scheme for retirement, unlike pay-as-you-go schemes, relieving the strain on government budgets for social spending on retirees, which is important given Singapore's aging population. Special Singapore Government Securities are non-tradable bonds issued primarily to meet the investment needs of the CPF and the returns to the CPF are guaranteed by the government and are fair, being pegged to investments of comparable risk and duration in the market.

The prudent fiscal rules built into the Constitutions, the setting-up and regular top-ups of strategic funds for future use, including those for innovation and human capital development, the professional investment of national reserves yielding good returns, and the benefits of persistent economic growth have enabled the accumulation of a sizeable national reserve. The use of national reserves to counter the negative impact of crises, such as the current pandemic or the past GFC, requires the consent of the President of Singapore. During the GFC of 2008/9, President Nathan approved the drawing of S$4.9b from the national reserves for the first time. To combat the current pandemic, President Halimah has given in-principle support to drawing up to S$52b from the reserves. The sufficiency of national reserves relieves the government from borrowing and burdening future generations with debt financing. In fact, the Singapore Government currently issues domestic debt securities for reasons

11 See www.ifaq.gov.sg/MOF/apps/fcd_faqmain.aspx?FAQ=1567#FAQ_1567.
12 The NIRC contributed about 18.7 percent of revenue for financial year 2019. See www.mof.gov
   .sg/policies/fiscal.

unrelated to fiscal needs and under the Government Securities Act, the borrowing proceeds from the issuance of these securities cannot be spent and are invested.

In summary, the public finance system in Singapore has the following characteristics: fiscal responsibility, fiscal sustainability, and the building up of funds for future generations and longer-term challenges. The constitutional requirement of a balanced budget at the end of each government term sets the foundation of Singapore's fiscal prudence over the years, and together with sustained economic growth, government surpluses are accumulated, invested, and contribute to the national reserves which can be tapped strategically to combat the current pandemic.

10.7 Conclusion

Singapore seems to have managed the Covid-19 crisis well thus far. At the time of writing, there has apparently been no resurgence in cases and the number of fatalities has been kept very low, at around 30. In fact, community transmissions were curbed at low levels throughout the crisis accounting for only 2,271 cases out of the 58,102 total number of cases as of 27 November 2020. This can be attributed to pre-existing levels of preparation particularly due to the SARS experience in 2003. In particular, the enhanced infrastructure and strengthened capabilities for outbreak management greatly contributed to the authorities' highly competent handling of the Covid-19 pandemic crisis.

However, there was a societal blind spot which led to outbreaks at the foreign worker dormitories that contributed to the bulk of the Covid-19 cases in Singapore. Nonetheless, the swift corrective actions taken by the authorities that also paid close attention to the needs of foreign workers brought the situation under control, as well as preventing the spread of the virus to the local community. Overall, the concerted whole-of-government approach along with clear communication and the cohesive response of the public to intervention measures were key factors in the effective management of the crisis.

Compared to the GFC, the pandemic hit the Singapore economy much more severely, and it was primarily a public health crisis with an extensive impact on the economy and society. On a year-on-year basis, real GDP fell by 6.5 percent while total employment shrank by 171,000 in the first three quarters of 2020. MAS responded by lowering the level and reducing the slope of the S$NEER policy band simultaneously for the first time. The accommodative monetary policy stance was maintained during the following half-yearly policy cycle. Such stable monetary policy responses helped avoid inducing market volatility and economic uncertainty.

In addition, the provision of ample liquidity in the banking system as well as the establishment of a new MAS SGD Term Facility and a new USD facility, both with an expanded collateral pool helped to reinforce financial stability. In view of the healthy prevailing capital positions of financial institutions incorporated in Singapore, some of these measures were pre-emptive to ensure continuing credit support to firms and individuals should the crisis be prolonged. The central bank also worked with financial institutions to provide relief measures to individuals and SMEs facing financial difficulties. These measures were well received as they helped reduce debt obligations and lowered funding costs. The S$125 million support package offered by MAS to financial institutions will enhance long-term skills and build long-term capabilities, particularly the acceleration of digital transformation in the financial industry.

With supporting public health measures put in place to effectively contain the spread of the virus within the community, fiscal support seems to have been an appropriate and effective response to protect jobs and support businesses, especially with targeted measures for specific sectors most hit by the pandemic. The unprecedented huge amount of fiscal outlay to combat the pandemic, backed by sufficient national reserves, provided not just immediate reliefs, but also prepared the economy for transformation post-pandemic. Moreover, Singapore has accumulated sufficient reserves over the years, which are a strategic asset, enabling it to tackle the negative impact of the pandemic without incurring national debt, thanks to the fiscal prudence and sustainability put in place.

Indeed, the fiscal rules in the Constitution led to fiscal prudence and a bias toward budget surpluses, which are accumulated as national reserves, which in turn are well managed with good returns, contributing toward future budgets; this virtuous cycle, combined with a long-term fiscal strategy focusing on economic growth and transformation, contributes to the sufficiency of the national reserves as strategic assets to provide short-term relief in times of crises, such as the GFC and the current pandemic, and prepares Singapore for the future transformation of the economy.

Our assessment is that the monetary–fiscal policy mix applied to mitigate the economic impact of the Covid-19 crisis is an appropriate response. The stable yet accommodative monetary policy stance allowed fiscal policy to play a more prominent role in response to the crisis. The more direct fiscal measures targeted at individuals and businesses adversely affected by the pandemic are more effective than the broader and more indirect effects of monetary policy. Furthermore, the transformation of the economy called for by the pandemic shock is better facilitated by fiscal initiatives. Nevertheless, the eventual effectiveness of these policy measures for Singapore, a small and highly open economy, depend hugely on the global containment of the pandemic, the effectiveness and allocation of the vaccine, and the pace of global economic recovery.

References

Chow, H.K. (2007). "Singapore's Exchange Rate Policy: Some Implementation Issues," Singapore Economic Review Special Issue on *Exchange Rate Systems and Policies in East Asia*, 52(3), 445–458.

Chow, H.K. and Wong, F.C. (2020). "Monetary Policy Implementation in Singapore" In *Monetary Policy Execution in East Asia*, F. Rövekamp, M. Bälz, and H.G. Hilpert (eds.), Germany: Springer, Financial and Monetary Policy Studies.

GIC (2020). GIC Annual Report for the Year 2019/2020. [Online]. Available: https://report.gic.com.sg/index.html

Heng, S.K. (2020a). Unity Budget Statement, 18 February 2020. [Online]. Available: https://www.singaporebudget.gov.sg/budget_2020/budget-speech

Heng, S.K. (2020b). Resilience Budget Statement, 26 March 2020. [Online]. Available: https://www.singaporebudget.gov.sg/budget_2020/resilience-budget/supplementary-budget-statement

Heng, S.K. (2020c). Solidarity Budget Statement, 6 April 2020. [Online]. Available: https://www.singaporebudget.gov.sg/budget_2020/solidarity-budget/solidarity-budget-statement

Heng, S.K. (2020d). Fortitude Budget Statement, 26 May 2020. [Online]. Available: https://www.singaporebudget.gov.sg/budget_2020/fortitude-budget/fortitude-budget-statement

Heng, S.K. (2020e). Ministerial Statement-August 2020, 17 August 2020. [Online]. Available: https://www.singaporebudget.gov.sg/budget_2020/AugustStatement

Heng, S.K. (2020f). Ministerial Statement-October 2020, 5 October 2020. [Online]. Available: https://www.singaporebudget.gov.sg/budget_2020/ministerial-statement-oct-2020

Lin, R., T.H. Lee and D. Chien (2020). "From SARS to COVID-19: The Singapore Journey," *The Medical Journal of Australia*, 212(11), 497–503. Published online: 6 April 2020.

Menon, R. (2019). How Singapore Manages its Reserves, Keynote Speech at the National Asset-Liability Management Europe Conference, Singapore, 13 March 2019. [Online]. Available: https://www.bis.org/review/r190313b.htm

Monetary Authority of Singapore (2009). Financial Stability Review 2009. [Online]. Available: https://www.mas.gov.sg/publications/financial-stability-review/2009/financial-stability-review-2009

Monetary Authority of Singapore (2020a). MAS' Response to Covid-19. [Online]. Available: https://www.mas.gov.sg/regulation/covid-19

Monetary Authority of Singapore (2020b). Macroeconomic Review, October 2020. [Online]. Available: https://www.mas.gov.sg/publications/macroeconomic-review/2020/volume-xix-issue-2-oct-2020

Sharma, V. (2013). Global Financial Crisis: Impact on Singapore and Policy Measures Taken to Counter It. A Policy Brief. [Online]. Available: https://www.slideshare.net/VikasSharma128/singapore-gfc-vikasmar2013draft

Temasek (2020). Temasek Review 2020. [Online]. Available: https://www.temasekreview.com.sg/#home

Appendix

Chronicle of the macroeconomic responses in the US, Europe, and East Asia

Country	Monetary Policy	Fiscal Policy

US	• The Fed cut the FFR by 1.50%p
	  • (03/03) 1.50~1.75% → 1~1.25%
	  • (03/15) 1~1.25% → 0~0.25%
	• The Fed expanded the volume of RP transactions
	  • 1-day: 100 → 150 (3/9) → 175 billion USD (3/11)
	  • 14-day: 20 → 45 billion USD (3/9)
	• The Fed stabilized the financial market: expanded the additional volume of RP
	  • Limits: (3/12) 500 billion USD, (3/13) 1 trillion USD
	• The Fed purchased 700 billion USD worth of assets (3/15)
	  • US Treasury 500 billion USD, MBS 200 billion USD
	• The Fed reduced reserve requirement to 0.10% (3/15)
		• FIRST response to COVID-19 (Coronavirus Preparedness and Response Supplemental Appropriations Act) funding 8.3 billion USD (3/6)
		  • For "research and development of vaccines, as well as therapeutics and diagnostics"
		• Trump declared a national emergency and announced opening up access to up to $50 billion (3/13)
		  • Secured medical resources and crude oil for storage in the US Strategic Reserve, waived interest on federal student loans, etc.
		• SECOND response to COVID-19 (Families First Coronavirus Response Act) funding 192 billion USD (3/18)
		  • Paid sick leave, paid family medical leave
		• IRS extended the tax filing deadline to July 15 (3/20)
		• THIRD response to COVID-19 (Coronavirus Aid Relief and Economic Security Act, CARES Act) funding 2.2 trillion USD (3/27)

(Continued)

Country	Monetary Policy	Fiscal Policy
	• The Fed lowered pricing on standing US dollar liquidity swap arrangements with central banks of major countries (BOC, BOE, BOJ, ECB, SNB) by 25 basis points. The foreign banks agreed to begin offering US dollars weekly in each jurisdiction with an 84-day maturity. (3/15) • The Fed announced the establishment of a Commercial Paper Funding Facility (CPFF) for a year (3/17) • The Fed announced a Primary Dealer Credit Facility (PDCF) operating for at least for six months from March 20 (3/17) • The Fed broadened the program supporting the flow of credit to households and businesses by establishing a Money Market Mutual Fund Liquidity Facility (MMLF) (3/18) • The Fed announced the establishment of temporary US dollar liquidity arrangements (swap lines or bilateral currency swap arrangements) with the central banks of nine countries: South Korea, Australia, Singapore, Sweden, Brazil, Mexico, Norway, Denmark, and New Zealand. The arrangements were to be in place for at least six months. (3/19)	• Provided relief to individuals, such as one-time cash payments (approximately 300 billion USD) • Expanded unemployment benefits (approximately 250 billion USD) • Allocated up to 476 billion USD to programs such as the Paycheck Protection Program (PPP) for assistance to eligible businesses • Allocated up to 500 billion USD to the Economic Stabilization Fund to provide loans and make loan guarantees to states, municipalities, and eligible businesses (including backstopping the Federal Reserve 13(3) programs, 454 billion USD) • Support healthcare, medical, and hospital industries (more than 400 billion USD) • FOURTH response to COVID-19 (Paycheck Protection Program Flexibility Act of 2020, PPPF Act) funding approximately 484 billion USD (6/5) • Strengthened PPP with approximately 320 billion USD additional funding • 50 billion USD for Small Business Administration (SBA) disaster lending and 10 billion USD in SBA disaster grants • Provided funding for hospitals (approximately 75 billion USD) • Expanded capacity for COVID-19 testing (approximately 25 billion USD) • FIFTH response to COVID-19 (Health and Economic Recovery Omnibus Emergency Solutions Act, HEROES Act) funding 3 trillion USD • Intended to supplement the earlier CARES Act • The initial bill passed the House in May and the amended bill passed the House in October (US$2.2 trillion), then went to the Senate for consideration.

- The Fed expanded unlimited asset purchasing and supported the credit needs (3/23)
  ① PMCCF: Primary Market Corporate Credit Facility
  ② SMCCF: Secondary Market Corporate Credit Facility
  ③ TALF: Term Asset-Backed Securities Loan Facility
- The Fed announced the establishment of a temporary FIMA Repo Facility to support the smooth functioning of financial markets for at least six months from April 6 (3/31)
- The Fed announced a temporary reduction to its SLR (Supplementary Leverage Ratio, SLR) (4/1)
- The Fed announced another 2.3 trillion USD pump in the economy (4/9)
  • Expanded the size and scope of PMCCF and SMCCF: Planned to buy corporate bonds both at an investment-grade level as well as high-yield, or junk, bonds that had experienced lowered ratings since 3/22 (lowest assigned BB-)
  • Established Municipal Liquidity Facility[1]
  • Established MSNLF, MSELF[2]
  • Expanded the type of collateral accepted through TALF: CMBS and newly issued CLO

- Presidential Executive order issued to support further "Fighting the Spread of COVID-19" funding approximately 200 billion USD (8/8)
  • Extended enhanced unemployment benefits guaranteed by the federal government (at a reduced rate of 300 USD per week from 600 USD)
  • Extended the current moratorium on interest accrual and student loan repayments
  • Imposed a moratorium on eviction for certain renters subject to certain conditions

(Continued)

Country	Monetary Policy	Fiscal Policy
	• Expanded lending to small- and medium-sized businesses • Established Main Street Priority Loan Facility[3] (4/30) • Federal Reserve Board expanded the scope and eligibility for the Main Street Lending Program (4/30) and helped more small and medium-sized businesses receive support from the program through actions such as lowering the minimum loan amount and extending the repayment period (6/8) • Federal Reserve Board modified the Main Street Lending Program to provide greater access to credit for nonprofit organizations such as educational institutions, hospitals, and social service organizations (7/17) • The Fed required large banks to preserve capital by suspending share repurchases, capping dividend payments, and allowing dividends according to a formula based on recent income, during the third quarter (6/25)	

(Continued)

- The Fed announced an expansion of counterparties in the Term Asset-Backed Securities Loan Facility (TALF), Secondary Market Corporate Credit Facility (SMCCF), and Commercial Paper Funding Facility (CPFF) (7/23)
- The Fed announced an extension through December 31 of its lending facilities (PDCF, MMLF, PMCCF, SMCCF, TALF, MSLP, PPPLF) that were scheduled to expire on or around September 30 (7/28)
- Federal Reserve Board announces extensions of its temporary US dollar liquidity swap lines (with the central banks of nine countries) and the temporary repurchase agreement facility for foreign and international monetary authorities (FIMA repo facility) through March 31, 2021 (7/29)

EU
- A temporary envelope of additional net asset purchases of 120 billion EUR will be added until the end of the year (3/12)
  - 240 billion EUR → 360 billion EUR

- Parliament approved a €37 billion crisis response (3/13)
  - The EU also used 1 billion euros of EU money to guarantee up to 8 billion euros in loans to 100,000 virus-hit firms in tourism, retail, transport, and other ailing sectors.
- The European Commission decided to suspend EU fiscal rules to tackle the COVID-19 pandemic (3/23)

Country	Monetary Policy	Fiscal Policy
	• Announced easing of conditions for targeted longer-term refinancing operations (TLTRO III[4]) to provide immediate liquidity support to the euro area financial system (3/12) • Lowered the interest rate by 25 basis points below the average rate applied in the Eurosystem's main refinancing operations • Increased borrowing limit to 500 billion EUR • Decided on additional longer-term refinancing operations (LTROs) to provide immediate liquidity support to banks and to safeguard money market conditions (LTRO[5]) (3/12) • All of these mature on 24 June 2020 when the fourth operation of TLTRO III settles • The ECB announced the 750 billion EUR Pandemic Emergency Purchase Programme (PEPP[6]) (3/18) • Prepared detailed criteria such as raising the issue limit of 33% when buying bonds (3/25)	• EU finance ministers agreed on a 540 billion EUR package to support member states, companies, and workers through the coronavirus crisis (4/9) • About 2% of the eurozone's GDP (240 billion EUR) was made available to countries seeking assistance via the ESM (European Stability Mechanism) • Provided safety net for companies through the EIB (European Investment Bank) (200 billion EUR) and workers via the new instrument for temporary Support to mitigate Unemployment Risks in an Emergency (SURE) (100 billion EUR)

- Expanded the range of eligible assets under the corporate sector purchase program (CSPP) to non-financial commercial paper (3/19)
- Announced extension of the Additional Credit Claims (ACC[7]) framework, waiver to accept Greek sovereign debt instruments as collateral in Eurosystem credit operations, and adoption of a general reduction of collateral valuation haircuts (4/7)
- The ECB decided to reinforce the broader package of collateral easing measures adopted by the Governing Council on April 7, 2020 (4/22)
  - Marketable assets and issuers of these assets that met the minimum credit quality requirements for collateral eligibility on April 7, 2020 (BBB- for all assets, except asset-backed securities (ABSs)) will continue to be eligible in cases of rating downgrades

- The European Commission issued its proposal on a Recovery Fund, and the Multiannual Financial Framework was agreed upon by the European Parliament and the Council on April 23 (5/27)
  - Included 500 billion EUR in grants and 250 billion euros in loans to member states in support of healthcare systems, businesses, and jobs
- The Member States in the Council reached an agreement on the regulation establishing the SURE[9] (up to 100 billion EUR)
  - The Council approved a total of 87.9 billion EUR for financial support to 17 Member States (Italy 27.4 billion EUR, Spain 21.3 billion EUR, Belgium 7.8 billion EUR, Greece 2.7 billion EUR) (8/24)
  - Portugal 5.9 billion EUR (8/25)
  - Hungary (TBD)

(*Continued*)

Country	Monetary Policy	Fiscal Policy

	• The interest rate on all targeted longer-term refinancing operations (TLTRO III) reduced by 25 basis points to −0.5% from June 2020 to June 2021. The ECB also announced new PELTRO[8]. (4/30)
	• The ECB decided to increase the envelope for the pandemic emergency purchase program (PEPP) (6/4)
	  • The envelope for the PEPP set to be increased by €600 billion to a total of €1,350 billion (750 billion EUR → 1,350 billion EUR)
	  • The horizon for net purchases under the PEPP will be extended to at least the end of June 2021 from December 2020
	  • The maturing principal payments from securities purchased under the PEPP will be reinvested until at least the end of 2022
	• New Eurosystem repo facility (EUREP) to provide euro liquidity to non-euro area central banks (6/25)
	  • The Eurosystem will provide euro liquidity to a broad set of central banks outside the euro area against adequate collateral (available until the end of June 2021)	

UK

- The Bank of England cut the base rate by 0.65%p:
  - 0.5%p on March 11, 0.15%p on March 19
- Launched a new Term Funding Scheme with additional incentives for lending to SMEs (TFSME) (100 billion GBP)
- Reduced the UK countercyclical capital buffer rate of banks' exposures to UK borrowers to 0% (from 1%) with immediate effect
- Launched a COVID Corporate Financing Facility (CCFF) (3/17)
- Increased APF[10] asset purchasing
  - Increased Bank of England's holdings of UK government bonds and sterling non-financial investment-grade corporate bonds by 200 billion GBP to 645 billion GBP (3/19)
  - Additional 100 billion GPB increase to take the total target stock of asset purchases to 745 billion GPB (6/18, only for UK government bonds purchasing)

- Unveiled 30 billion GBP fiscal expansion plan (3/11)
  - 5 billion GBP for the NHS, 500 million GBP "hardship funding" to help vulnerable people, loans of up to 1.2 million GBP to small- and medium-sized businesses
- Budget to cut in corporation tax and scaled back a tax break for entrepreneurs (20 billion GBP)
- Announced a 330 billion GBP rescue package of loan guarantees to help UK businesses survive the economic fallout from the coronavirus pandemic (3/17)

- Announced the Corona Virus Job Retention Scheme (CRJS) (3/20), effective from 4/20)
  - Provided grants to employers to pay 80% of a staff wage each month, up to a total of 2,500 GBP per person per month for three months
  - Extended until the end of October and to eligible workers, including furloughed workers (5/12)

(*Continued*)

Country	Monetary Policy	Fiscal Policy
	• The MPC voted unanimously that the Bank of England should enlarge the TFSME (3/19, effective in April) • Central banks agreed to increase frequency of 7-day maturity operations from weekly to daily to improve swap lines' effectiveness in providing USD funding (3/20) • These daily operations will commence on Monday, March 23, 2020, and continue at least through the end of April • Activated the Contingent Term Repo Facility (CTRF[1]) (3/24) • On March 26 and April 2, the CTRF will lend reserves for three months with no limit (additional operations if necessary)	
France	• The general monetary policy measures that apply to France are those taken by the European Central Bank (Eurosystem) for the euro zone as a whole. • As of April 2020, the Banque de France has decided to modify its eligibility criteria for accepting additional private claims: • Loans to companies with a one-year probability of default of up to 1.5%, regardless of the rating system, and a maximum residual maturity of 30 years (compared to five years previously).	• Due to the economic and social consequences of the COVID-19 crisis in 2020, the French government has adopted four successive amending finance laws ("*Projets de Loi de Finance Rectificative*", PLFR) • PLFR 1: March 23. The first amending finance law for 2020 was adopted to deal with the COVID-19 epidemic. It follows the announcements made by the French President on March 12, 2020. • To overcome the economic crisis, it introduces a 300 billion euros State guarantee on loans given to companies by banks. This measure, implemented on March 16, lasted until the end of 2020, and aimed to help companies of all sizes. The State guarantee may represent of up to 90% of the loan and finance up to 25% of a company's annual turnover.

- Loans to companies benefiting from a State guarantee within the plan implemented to help banks finance companies that are facing the effects of the health crisis. In November 2020 these loans reached 128 billion EUR out of an overall amount of 1,187 billion EUR of loans to companies.

- PLFR 2: April 25. The aim is to strengthen the first amending finance law of March 23, 2020. The 45 billion EUR economic emergency plan adopted in March to support the economy and employment was extended by 110 billion EUR.
- PLFR 3, July 30: With the worsening economic situation due to the COVID-19 crisis, the emergency measures supporting employees and companies were extended. Their means were reinforced to reach a total of nearly 31 billion EUR for partial activity and 8 billion EUR for the solidarity fund for very small enterprises (VSE).
- September 3: The economic recovery plan reached a commitment of 100 billion EUR by 2022. In 2020, at least 15 billion EUR in credits were committed from all public administrations to the recovery, mostly coming from the PLFR 3. The finance bill for 2021 carries additional resources from the State budget to aid economic recovery.
- At the end of July 2020, 470 billion EUR had been spent to support companies, particularly VSE/SMEs, and to protect employees.
- PLFR 4, November 30: This fourth draft amending budget law for the year 2020 was also based on macroeconomic and public finance forecasts, which were more deteriorated than previous ones. Another 20 billion EUR was dedicated to help companies and small businesses, employees, and precarious households; this represented the cost of one month's lockdown (15 billion EUR) and a temporary extension of certain measures after the second lockdown.

(*Continued*)

Country	Monetary Policy	Fiscal Policy
Germany	• The general monetary policy measures that apply to France are those taken by the European Central Bank (Eurosystem) for the euro zone as a whole.	• Unveiled a plan to invest 12.4 billion EUR in easing Corona Virus impact, including public investment (3/8) • Upgraded the short-time working scheme: subsidies for short term working extended from 6 to up to 12 months (3/13) • Announced 756 billion EUR package to mitigate the damage of the Corona Virus outbreak (3/23), including • Established an economic stabilization fund (Wirtschaftsstabilisierungsfonds or WSF) to recapitalize corporates, and purchase equity stakes (100 billion EUR) and loan guarantees (400 billion EUR) • Additional 100 billion EUR in credit to public-sector development bank KfW for loans to struggling businesses • German coalition agreed to 10 billion EUR extension of coronavirus relief (4/23), including: • tax cuts for restaurants and unemployment benefits, etc. • German coalition agreed to 130 billion EUR stimulus package (6/3), including: • Value-added tax rate cut by 3% (20 billion EUR) • Other tax measures, including extended loss carryback, special depreciation schemes (8 billion EUR) • Support local communities (10 billion EUR) • Investment in new technologies, including climate-friendly technology (50 billion EUR) • Family support, 300 EUR per child (2 billion EUR)

- Agreed to contribute to the European Union recovery package: total 750 billion EUR, German share about 185 billion EUR (7/21)
- Extended the country's short-term working scheme to potentially 24 months, maximum until December 2021, funding approximately 10 billion EUR (8/25)
- Extended subsidies for self-employed people in arts, music, and other branches, granted aid to restaurants, fitness centers etc. affected by the second lockdown, funding approximately 30 billion EUR (11/25)

Italy

- The general monetary policy measures that apply to France are those taken by the European Central Bank (Eurosystem) for the euro zone as a whole.

- Introduced measures worth 3.6 billion EUR 36, including tax cuts and tax credits for companies (3/1)
- Approved a 25 billion stimulus package to support businesses and financial market stability (3/11)
- DL 18/2020 introduced a package of 24.8b. The major measures are 8.3b EUR for firms (tax holidays and loan collaterals), 10.5b EUR for unemployment measures, and 3.2b of EUR for the NHS. (03/17)
- Approved a new emergency decree offering more than 400 billion EUR worth of liquidity and bank loans to companies affected by the COVID-19 crisis (4/6)
- Approved a 55 billion economic stimulus package (5/13)
- DL34/2020 introduced a 57b EUR economic stimulus package to support businesses and households.
- Major measures included 23b EUR for firms (tax holidays refunds and grants), 5.1b EUR for the NHS, 24.3b EUR for unemployment benefits, and 6.4b EUR to support households and the welfare system. Included 44b EUR of guarantees for loans to the business sector. (05/19)
- DL104/2020 introduced a 24.9b of EUR economic stimulus package to support business and households. Major measures included 10b EUR for firms (tax holidays refunds and grants), 8.6b EUR for unemployment benefits, and 6.3b EUR to support households and the welfare system. (08/14)
- DL137/2020 introduced a 2.4b EUR economic stimulus package to refund firms that had to keep activities closed for COVID-19 containment measures.

(Continued)

Country	Monetary Policy	Fiscal Policy
		• Included 2.1b EUR for unemployment benefits. (10/29)
		• DL149/2020 introduced 2.2b EUR economic stimulus package to refund firms that had to keep activities closed for COVID-19 containment measures. Included 08.b EUR for minor measures. (11/09)
		• DL154/2020 introduced a 1.5b EUR economic stimulus package to refund firms that had to keep activities closed for COVID-19 containment measures.
		• Included 0.5b EUR for minor measures. (11/23)
		• DL157/2020 introduced 6b EUR of tax holidays for micro firms and professionals. Included 2b for monthly benefits for some atypical workers. (11/30)

Japan	• Purchased government bonds worth a total of 650 billion JPY over three purchases
	• Coordinated central bank action to enhance the provision of global U.S. dollar liquidity (3/15)
	• Facilitated corporate financing, 0% interest rate (3/16)
	• Increase in CP and corporate bonds: 1 trillion JPY of each asset (2 trillion JPY total)
	• Active purchases of ETFs and J-REITs: twice as much as the outstanding amount (4/27)
	• Further enhanced monetary easing (4/27)
	• Expanded the range of eligible collateral to private debt in general, including household debt from about 8 trillion JPY to about 23 trillion JPY as of the end of March 2020
		• 1st COVID-19 emergency response package (2/13)
		  • Secured 15.3 billion JPY in supporting the establishment of outpatient facilities and consultation centers for individuals returning to Japan
		• 2nd COVID-19 emergency response package (3/10)
		  • Established fiscal measures of a total of 430 billion JPY, including accelerating medical treatment structures, supporting temporary school closures, and protecting employment and business continuation
		  • Provided a total of 1.6 trillion JPY of liquidity support, including real interest-free unsecured loans, for small- and medium-sized business operators
		• 3rd emerging economic package (total scale of 108 trillion JPY) to stimulate the economy, including the first and second packages and a stimulus package (26 trillion JPY) from December 2019 (4/7)
		  • Emergency support households, including additional child allowance, employment, and business support for SMEs and sole proprietors such as no interest, no collateral loans for SMEs, etc.

- Increase in purchases of CP and corporate bonds: 7.5 trillion JPY of each asset

- Introduced a new fund-provisioning measure—the Special Program (total 75 trillion JPY) (5/22, effective from June 2020 to March 2021)
  - Purchases of CP and corporate bonds (maximum amount outstanding; about 20 trillion JPY)
  - The Special Funds-Supplying Operations to Facilitate Financing in Response to the Novel Coronavirus (COVID-19) (fund-provisioning against private debt pledged as collateral: about 25 trillion JPY as of the end of April)
  - A new fund-provisioning measure to be introduced (fund-provisioning against eligible loans such as interest-free and unsecured loans made by eligible counterparties based on the government's emergency economic measures: about 30 trillion yen)

- Updated the version of the economic emergency relief package as the first supplementary budget of FY 2020 (4/20)
  - ¥300,000 cash handout program for households suffering sharp drops in income due to the COVID-19 pandemic → ¥100,000 handout program for all citizens (total scale of 117.1 trillion JPY from the initial 108.2 trillion)
- The government announced an additional economic stimulus package as the second supplementary budget of FY 2020 (5/27, total scale of 117.1 trillion JPY)
  - Expanded support for medical treatment structures, increased support for SMEs and sole proprietors, introduced local property tax reductions or exemptions, etc.

(*Continued*)

Country	Monetary Policy	Fiscal Policy

		• Announced measures to inject capital into regional lenders (6/12)
		  • Expanded to 15 trillion yen from 12 trillion JPY a pool of funds for ailing banks
		  • Extended by four years a deadline for lenders to apply for a bail-out from March 2022 to March 2026
		• The government announced an additional economic stimulus package as the third supplementary budget of FY 2020 (12/8, total scale of 73.6 trillion JPY).

Korea	• Decided to increase the ceiling on the Bank Intermediated Lending Support Facility by 5 trillion KRW from 25 trillion KRW to 35 trillion KRW (5 trillion KRW on 2/27, 5/14 respectively)
	• Decided to broaden the eligible collateral (securities) that banks could provide when receiving loans from the Bank of Korea (3/12, 3/26, 4/9)
	  • Along with existing government bonds, monetary stabilization bonds, and government–guaranteed bonds; 1) debentures issued by three special banks (the Korea Development Bank, the Industrial Bank of Korea, and the Export-Import Bank of Korea); 2) MBSs issued by the Korea Housing Finance Corporation; 3) bonds issued by public organizations and banks; and 4) bonds issued by the Korea Deposit Insurance Corporation, newly recognized as eligible collateral for lending facilities.
		• Announced a support package of over 16 trillion KRW to respond to the COVID-19 outbreak aimed at stabilizing the livelihoods of the public (2/28)
		  • About 4 trillion KRW, including government reserve funds and policy financing to support disease prevention, local governments, imports of manufacturing supplies, and small merchants
		  • Provided about 7 trillion won in financial and tax support for affected families and businesses (2.8), including 50 percent income tax cuts given to landlords for rent reductions (1.7), lending for small businesses, and supply of P-CBO (2.5) for car purchases, and individual consumption tax cuts to boost consumption
		  • About 9 trillion won of loans, guarantees, and investment through financial institutions and public institutions, including BOK's fund (5.0), collateral expansion (0.5), and support from the financial industry (3.2)

- Announced 100 trillion KRW economic relief package
  - First phase (3/19): supported SMEs, small businesses, and sole proprietors; mitigated financial burden on low-income households, and stabilized financial market
  - Second phase (3/24): expanded loans to small and medium-sized companies to (29.1 trillion KRW), and set up a corporate bond stabilization fund (20 trillion KRW)
- Announced "emergency disaster relief funds" worth 9.1 trillion KRW to support the livelihood of the public, especially low-income households, which includes easing the burden of paying social insurance fees for low-income households and stimulating consumption (3/30)
- Announced another relief package worth 17.7 trillion KRW, including tax benefits for pre-payments and advance purchases, and support for export and start-up companies (4/17)
- President Moon proposed 'New Deal' for jobs as stabilization measures for the private sector and employment (4/22)
  - A package for stabilizing employment (10.1 trillion KRW) will expand subsidies for maintaining employment (0.9), increase job security (1.9), create jobs (3.6), aid unemployment benefits (3.7), etc.
  - Supported private sector stabilization (more than 75 trillion KRW) by expanding financial support to small business owners (10); purchased corporate bonds, CPs, and short-term bonds including low credit ratings (20);[13] supplied additional P-CBO in response to the COVID-19 damages (5); and established a fund to support key industries (more than 40 trillion), etc.

- Base Rate cuts
  - Lowered the base rate from 1.25% → 0.50% (0.50%p, 0.25%p cuts respectively on 3/16 and 5/28)
  - Lowered the rate for Bank Intermediated Lending Support Facility by 25 bps ranging between 0.50% and 0.75% and increased the ceiling from 25 trillion KRW to 35 trillion KRW
  - Broadened securities eligible for open market operations (RP transactions), including bonds issued by banks
- Liquidity injection
  - Implemented purchases of RP systems for securities firms RP (1 trillion and 2.5 trillion KRW on 3/19 and 3/24, respectively)
  - Purchased government bonds (1.5 trillion KRW each on 3/20, 4/10, 7/2, 8/31 and 2 trillion KRW on 9/24)
  - Raised the ceilings on the FX derivatives positions of banks by 25% (3/19)
    - Domestic banks 40% → 50%
    - Foreign bank branches 200% → 250%

Country	Monetary Policy	Fiscal Policy
	• Established a temporary bilateral currency swap arrangement (swap line) for the provision of USD liquidity up to 60 billion USD (3/19) • Extended to expire on March 31, 2021, from September 30, 2020 (7/30) • Decided to ease the FX market stability rules for financial institutions (3/26) • Temporarily lifted levy on financial institutions' non-deposit FX liabilities for three months (from April to June) • Expanded installment payment plans for payments due this year • Implemented Financial Stability Measures including the adoption of Unlimited Liquidity Support Facility (3/26, effective from 4/1) • Supplied an unlimited amount of liquidity at set interest rates based on market demand by buying bonds in repo auction once every week (until June 2020) • Expanded the scope of non-banking RP dealers from the initial five to 16 by adding 11 securities companies (until July 2020)	• Expanded bond market stabilization fund and eligible securities for P-CBO purchasing (5/19)[14] • Announced aims to create 1.56 million jobs mainly in the public sector (5/14, 5/20) • Pushed forward previous job-creating projects and new projects in "untact" (no-face-to-face contact) functions, created jobs for members from low-income households • Prepared measure to support industries hit hard by the COVID-19 pandemic, such as auto parts and textile manufacturers, shippers, and airlines (5/28) • Supplementary budget plans • 2020 Supplementary budget passed with new spending revised up to a total of 11.7 trillion KRW (3/17): Disease prevention and treatment; loans and guarantees for businesses affected; support for affected households; support for local economies affected, etc. • 2nd Supplementary budget passed a total of 12.2 trillion KRW (4/30): financed the household emergency relief program of up to 1 million KRW for each household • 3rd Supplementary budget passed, a total of 35.1 trillion KRW (7/3): included financial support for SMEs and support for job security and Korean New Deal[15] • 4th Supplementary budget proposal, a total of 7.8 trillion KRW (9/22): support for small businesses and SME, emergency employment support, low-income family support, emergency daycare support, and others

- Broadened eligible securities for RP transaction by adding eight public enterprises including Korea Electric Power Corp., Korea Gas Corp., Korea Land & Housing Corp., Korea Railroad Corp, Korea Rail Network Authority, Korea Water Resources Corp., and Korea SMEs and Startup Agency
- Broadened eligible collateral, including eight types of bonds issued by public organizations and bank debentures (until May 2021)

- Expanded financial institutions' collateral capacity (4/2)
  - Lowered the ratio of collateral for guaranteeing net settlements by 20 percentage points (from 70% to 50%) effective April 10, 2020
  - Broadened the eligible collateral for guaranteeing net settlements by including bonds issued by nine public institutions and bank debentures (effective in May)

(Continued)

Country	Monetary Policy	Fiscal Policy

	• Broadened the range of securities eligible for open market operation transactions (4/9) (effective from 4/14)
	  • Along with existing government bonds and government-guaranteed bonds, debentures issued by three specialized banks and MBSs issued by the Korea Housing Finance Corporation made eligible securities for outright transactions
	  • Broadened securities eligible for RP transactions and eligible collateral to include bonds issued by the Korea Deposit Insurance Corporation
	• Launched a new lending scheme, the Corporate Bond–Backed Lending Facility (CBBLF) (4/16, effective from 5/4)
	  • Provided loans to banks and non-bank financial institutions, including securities companies and insurance companies, with high-quality corporate bonds (rated at least AA–) as collateral for up to six months
	  • Shall be operated with a ceiling of 10 trillion won and a term of three months but to be decided later whether or not to expand those figures
	  • Extended expiration from August 3, 2020, to November 3, 2020 (7/30)	

- Decided to increase senior loans for the CBBLF[12] to the total scale of 8 trillion KRW (7/17)
  - Temporary purchasing of low-quality corporate bonds and CP (for six months)

China

- PBOC cut benchmark lending rates
  - Medium-term lending facility (MLF) by 30 bps (2/17, 4/15)
  - One-year loan prime rate (LPR) by 30 bps (2/20, 4/20)
  - 7-day reverse repo rate by 30 bps (2/3, 3/3)
  - 14-day reverse repo rate by 30 bps (2/3, 6/18)
  - Interest rate for excess reserves deposit by 37 bps (4/7)
  - Targeted medium-term lending facility (TMLF) by 20 bps (4/24)
  - Rural-support reloads, and small business report reloads by from 25 bps to 50 bps (7/1)
- Until December 18, the 7-day and 14-day reverse repo rates, MLF rate, and LPR remained unchanged
- Cut the targeted required reserve ratio (RRR)
  - Additional cut for qualified joint-stock banks (large 12.5%, small and medium 10.5%) by 0.5%p–1.0%p (3/16)
  - Cut RRR for small banks for agricultural services by 1.0%p (4/15, 5/15)

- Reduced or exempted corporate social insurance premiums (pension, unemployment, and work injury insurance) for enterprises (2/18)
- Reduced utility charges
  - 5% reduction in industrial electricity charges (2/22)
  - 15% reduction in average internet usage 15% (4/21)

- Announced tax cuts and measures to stimulate consumption (2/25)
  - Tax deductions for disease control companies, value-added tax cuts (3% → 1%, small taxpayers in Hubei province exempted), and deferral of loan repayment deadline
  - Subsidies for automobile purchases, extension of periods for renewable energy vehicles, issuance of regional consumption coupons, etc.
  - Accelerated issuance and use of regional government bonds
  - Expanded early issuance: 1.5 trillion RMB in 1Q20 (30.2% increase YoY)

(Continued)

Country	Monetary Policy	Fiscal Policy
	• Liquidity supply • 5.84 trillion RMB between February and June: Reverse RP (5.08), MLF (0.7), TMLF (0.06) • 1.17 trillion RMB in July: Reverse RP (0.77), MLF (0.4) • 2.7 trillion RMB in August: MLF (0.7), Reverse RP (2.0) • 3.07 trillion RMB in September: MLF (0.6), Reverse RP (2.47) • 1.43 trillion RMB in October: MLF (0.5), Reverse RP (0.93) • 3.96 trillion RMB between November 2 and December 18: MLF (1.95), Reverse RP (2.01) • Expanded re-lending and rediscounting facilities by 1.8 trillion to support micro-, small-, and medium-sized companies affected by the COVID-19 outbreak • Expansion by 440 billion RMB of funds to regional banks to provide new loans and rollover manufacturing loans to small businesses (6/2)	• Proposed policy measures to facilitate investment (3/4) • Early enforcement of infrastructure projects, such as installing 5G base stations • Rent waiver for micro and small firms who are tenants of state-owned properties (4/21) • NPC announced policy measures (5/22) • One trillion yuan of government bonds to be issued for COVID-19 control • The deficit-to-GDP ratio this year to be projected at more than 3.6% from 2.8% in 2019 • Increase in issuance of special bonds by local governments: 2.15 trillion RMB in 2019 → more than 3.75 trillion RMB in 2020 • Further tax and fee cuts of about 2.5 trillion RMB, including reductions of VAT rates and share of employees' basic old-age insurance paid by enterprises

- VAT exemptions (7/28)
  - Applying to public transportation, catering, accommodation, and tourism sectors until the end of the year

Singapore

- Provided USD Funding
  - Established a USD 60 billion swap facility with the US Fed in March 2020, first to September 30, 2020, then extended to expire on March 31, 2021 (3/19, 7/30)
  - The eligible collateral pool at the new facility is expanded to a wider range of cash and debt securities, including investment grade securities in SGD and major currencies (9/28)

- Jobs Support Scheme (JSS)
  - Offset 8% of wages of 1.9m local employees, amounting to S$1.3b (2/18)
  - Increase subsidy rate to 25%, with higher levels for food services, aviation and tourism sectors; extended JSS for another two quarters; total of S$15.1b (3/26)
  - Self-Employed Person Training Support Scheme: extended to Dec 2020, amounting to S$48m; Self-Employed Person Income Relief Scheme (SIRS), amounting to S$1.2b (3/26)
  - 75% of monthly wages for all firms (4/6)
  - JSS at 75% until Aug for firms unable to resume operations after circuit breaker; cost of S$2.9b (5/26)
  - Extended JSS for up to 7 more months to Mar 2021; most businesses will receive wage support ranging from 10% to 75% for 17 months (8/17)

- Wage Credit Scheme (WCS)
  - Enhanced to support wage increases, amounting to S$1.1b benefiting 700,000 employees (2/18)
  - S$16.2b to businesses by Oct 2020; additional S$500m under enhanced WCS, from Sep to end-June 2021 (3/26)
  - Enhanced Workfare Special Payment for lower-income workers; $3,000 each, in cash (26/3)

- Eased monetary policy stance
  - The S$NEER policy band centred at the lower than prevailing level; rate of appreciation of policy band reduced to 0%; and width of policy band maintained at end March 2020 (3/30)
  - Accommodative stance maintained in October 2020 with no change to the width and slope of the policy band and the level at which it was centered (10/14)

(*Continued*)

Country	Monetary Policy	Fiscal Policy

	• Alongside declines in US$ LIBOR, domestic interest rates fell
	  • 3-month S$ SIBOR fell from 1.8% to 1.0% between October 2019 and end March 2020 (3/30)
	  • 3-month S$ SIBOR fell from 1.0% at to 0.4% between end March and October (10/14)
	• Established new SGD Facility to lower cost of loans to SMEs
	  • Low-cost funding (0.1% p.a. for a 2-year tenor) for banks and finance companies to grant loans under Enterprise Singapore's Enterprise Financing Scheme – SME Working Capital Loan and Temporary Bridging Loan Program, until September 30, 2021 (3/31, 10/5)
	• Worked with financial industry to help individuals reduce debt obligations, such as through reduced installment plans for property loans and deferment of residential property loans by individuals (3/31, 4/30, 10/5)
	• Adjusted regulatory and supervisory programs to focus financial institutions on coronavirus priorities.
		• Income Tax Rebate
		  • 25% of tax payable, at a cost of about S$400m; deferring GST hike (2/18)
		  • 3-month automatic deferment of income tax payments for companies and self-employed persons; qualifying commercial properties will pay no property tax for 2020; other affected non-residential properties will enjoy 30% tax rebate for 2020 (3/26)
		• Greater flexibility on rentals, fees, and loans
		  • Rental waiver for industrial, office, and agricultural tenants of government agencies (2/18, 4/6, 5/26)
		  • Freezing of all government fees and charges from April 2020 to March 2021; suspension of all loan repayment and interest charges of student loans for 1 year, ending 31 May 2021 (3/26)
		  • Cash grant to offset the rental costs of SME tenants; cost about S$2b (5/26)
		• Sector-Specific Assistance
		  • 30% property tax rebate for licensed hotels, serviced apartments, and MICE venues; 15% property tax rebate for Changi Airport; 1 month rental waiver to stallholders of hawker centers and markets; half-month rental wavier to commercial tenants of Other Government Agencies such as HDB (2/18)

- As a pre-emptive measure to strengthen the capital positions of locally incorporated banks and finance companies, these are urged to cap their total dividends per share for FY2020 at 60% of the FY2019 level and provide shareholders the option of receiving the dividends in scrip in lieu of cash (4/7, 7/29, 8/7)
- Built financial sector long-term capabilities
- MAS offered a S$125 million support package to financial institutions and Fintech firms to enhance long-term skills and build capabilities. Beyond supporting employee training and manpower cost, included a digital acceleration grant for the adoption of digital solutions by smaller financial institutions and Fintech firms, and supported Fintech firms' access to digital tools (4/8)
- A S$35 million productivity solutions grant co-funded the adoption of digital solutions by smaller financial institutions for regulatory reporting (11/9)

- Transformation and Growth
  - S$8.3b over next three years transforming enterprises and developing people via tertiary education and various SkillsFuture programs for upskilling (2/18)
  - SGUnited 8,000 Traineeships & 10,000 Jobs (3/26)

- Use of Past Reserves
  - President's in-principle support to draw up to S$17b from past reserves (3/26)
  - In Resilience and Solidarity Budgets, the President gave approval to draw up to S$21 billion from past reserves; Fortitude Budget will be funded out of past reserves, with in-principle support from the President, for a further draw of S$31 billion (5/26)

(*Continued*)

Country	Monetary Policy	Fiscal Policy
	• Established a new SGD Term Facility (9/28) • Offering SGD funds in 1-month and 3-month tenors • Expanded collateral pool includes cash and investment-grade (BBB– and above) debt securities issued by governments, central banks, public sector entities, and non-financial corporations, denominated in SGD and G10 currencies • Residential property loans are accepted as collateral for domestic systemically important banks • Asset encumbrance limit imposed on locally incorporated banks raised from 4% to 10%	**Building Economic Resilience (3/26)** • SG Together Enhancing Enterprise Resilience (STEER) program • Enhanced digitalization and productivity programs for SMEs and subsidy for skills upgrading • Extended Enhanced Training Support Package for another 6 months, until 30 June 2021, in view of a gradual economic recovery (10/5) **Support for the unemployed (3/26)** • More flexibility when considering applications for ComCare assistance and other assistances, all amounting to S$145m **Enhanced Care and Support Package (CSP)** • Increased cash payouts to adult Singaporeans ranging from S$300 to S$900, with extra payouts to parents with young children, and the needy; doubled grant of S$20m over 2 years for Self-Help Groups and increased grant of S$75m for Community Development Councils (26/3) • Increased Solidarity Payment of S$600, to be paid starting middle of April (4/6) • Additional S$800 million for the COVID-19 Support Grant; doubled U-Save rebates for eligible households; established one-off S$100 Solidarity Utilities Credit to eligible households (5/26)

- Digital Transformation (26/5)
  - Allocated more than $500 million to support businesses in their digital transformations
- SGUnited Jobs and Skills Package (26/5)
  - Expanded job opportunities to more than 40,000
  - Created about 25,000 traineeship positions this year

1. A new Municipal Liquidity Facility that will offer up to $500 billion in lending to states and municipalities.
2. The Main Street Lending Program (including support for the Main Street New Loan Facility and Main Street Expanded Loan Facility up to 600 billion USD) supports lending to small and medium-sized for-profit businesses and nonprofit organizations that were in sound financial condition before the onset of the COVID-19 pandemic.
3. Main Street Priority Loan Facility: For highly indebted companies, eligible lenders will retain 15%, instead of 5% like in other Main Street Facilities, of each eligible loan.
4. Targeted Longer-Term Refinancing Operations (TLTROs) are Eurosystem operations that provide financing to credit institutions. Offering banks long-term funding with attractive terms strengthens the transmission of monetary policy by further incentivizing bank lending to the real economy.
5. Longer-Term Refinancing Operations (LTRO) is a type of open market operations used by the ECB to control the liquidity in the European banking system via repurchase agreements.
6. The ECB's Pandemic Emergency Purchase Programme (PEPP) is a non-standard monetary policy measure to counter the serious risks to the monetary policy transmission mechanism and the outlook for the euro area in the face of the coronavirus (COVID-19) outbreak.
7. Additional Credit Claims (ACC): The ACC framework provides the possibility to National Central Banks to enlarge the scope of eligible credit claims for counterparties in their jurisdictions. This includes the possibility to accept loans with lower credit quality, loans to other types of debtors, loans not accepted in the ECB's general framework, and foreign-currency loans.
8. Pandemic Emergency Longer-Term Refinancing Operations (PELTRO) will provide liquidity support to the euro area financial system and contribute to preserving the smooth functioning of money markets by providing an effective backstop after the expiry of the bridge longer-term refinancing operations (LTROs) that have been conducted since March 2020 (from May 2020 to September 2021)
9. Temporary Support to Mitigate Unemployment Risks in an Emergency (SURE) provides financial assistance in the form of loans from the EU to affected Member States to address sudden increases in public expenditure to preserve employment.
10. Asset Purchase Facility: The Bank has operated, since January 2009, an APF to buy "high-quality assets financed by the issue of Treasury bills and the DMO's cash management operations" and thereby improve liquidity in the credit markets. It has also provided a mechanism by which the Bank's policy of quantitative easing (QE) is achieved, under the auspices of the MPC.
11. Contingent Term Repo Facility: a flexible liquidity insurance tool that allows participants to borrow central bank reserves (cash) in exchange for other, less liquid assets (collateral).
12. The purchase fund will be created with the Korea Development Bank investment of one trillion KRW, subordinated loans of one trillion KRW, and BOK's senior loans of 8 trillion KRW, including low-credit corporate bonds (AA–BB ratings), CP, and short-term bonds (5/20)
13. The fund includes in the purchase list bonds (fallen angels) downgraded to A+ (which were previously AA– or higher) as of the effective date of April 1 and expands eligible bonds to A+ or higher corporate bonds of specialized credit finance companies. P-CBO newly includes corporate bonds of specialized credit finance companies (limited to A– rating or higher) in the eligible bonds, starting from the end of June.
14. Announced the Korea New Deal, including the Digital New Deal, Green New Deal, and strengthening employment and the social safety nets (which some refer to as the "human" pillar) (160 trillion KRW within a five-year period) (7/14)
15. The purchase fund will be created with the Korea Development Bank investment of one trillion KRW, subordinated loans of one trillion KRW, and BOK's senior loans of 8 trillion KRW, including low-credit corporate bonds (AA–BB grades), CP, and short-term bonds (5/20)

Index

Note: Page numbers with *italic* and **bold** indicating figures and table respectively.

Printed in the United States
by Baker & Taylor Publisher Services